WHAT READERS ARE SAYING ABOUT
LIVING ON THE EMPTY STAGE

"This stuff isn't taught in schools. People of all generations can benefit with the knowledge of how to recreate themselves. This book will help people not only in their personal lives but in their business lives as well. It is fascinating and very well written, with a lot of new information that needs thinking about. I'm definitely drawn to taking the classes."

~ Anne Johnson, tax accountant, NYC, New York

"I consider this book a pr er in the process of learning how to express our abilities in all aspects of life. It provides a foundation for the ongoing practice of living a more complete life. Especially while reading the scenarios, I saw the work I could be doing to transform several of my tragic traits to the comic side. I would unequivocally suggest this book to anyone interested in improving the quality of their life and relationships with others. Sondra has done a great service to humanity through this expression of her work."

~ Ron Williams, stock and commodities trader, Dallas, TX.

"This book spoke to me. I like the way it was set up with metaphors to describe life and the many characters we play – easy to follow and the scripted areas help to put it all in context."

~ Olga Singer, Designer at Simply Two, San Diego, CA.

"The writing is brilliant - this teaching is amazing!!! It's helping me with all my interactions with family and business, etc. There is so much information, it must be equivalent to a number of years in therapy, which I've never done but can imagine."

~ Anna Bogdanovich, entertainer, writer and producer, Los Angeles, CA.

"The process in this book can bring the generations together as well as diverse groups of people."

~ Mary Jo Healy, Feldenkrais Practitioner, Ojai, CA.

"This is a brilliant practice for working on yourself that anyone can relate to in a playful way."

~ Bette Hadler, speech pathologist, Boulder, CO.

Living

on the

Empty Stage

Living on the Empty Stage

Performing Daily Life in the Light of Self-Awareness

Sondra Bennett

NEW INSIGHTS PRESS

Published by New Insights Press, Los Angeles, CA

Editorial Direction: Rick Benzel
Editing: Rick Benzel
Cover Design: Ciara Staggs
Book Design: Jose Pepito Jr

Printed in the United States of America
ISBN: 978-0-9995801-6-5 (print)
ISBN: 978-0-9995801-7-2 (eBook)

Library of Congress Control Number: 2018961127

CONTENTS

Throughout this book, you will see some words with an asterisk * after them.
This indicates you can look up the word in the Glossary at the end of the book.

DEDICATION

Because humanity has yet to establish ways to act in life that promote goodwill, security and well-being, the practice of altruism is needed. As extreme as that may sound, it is needed to counteract the extreme self-serving actions that have led to the hatred, insecurity, violence, and affliction that people are experiencing across the globe.

If we love life, recognizing the unhappy results our flawed character traits bring will help us aspire to perform daily at our best. Maintaining good character is practical. It brings the individual "life actor" greater success in everyday endeavors and deepens personal fulfillment. This book offers Life Performance Practices to help all of us attain this exceptional goal.

As a person whose faults are many, I dedicate this book to my highly esteemed teachers whose virtues and intent have set the example and given me the strength to pursue a life of greater meaning and concern for all. In addition, I offer this book to those who are not daunted by the challenge of learning healthier, wiser ways of acting that can seriously improve one's own life, and also support and enrich the lives of others on the world stage.

Sincerely,
Sondra Bennett
Founding Director of Life Performance Practices

P R O L O G U E

And as imagination bodies forth the forms of things
unknown, the poet's pen turns them to shapes, and gives
to airy nothing a local habitation and a name.

~ Midsummer Night's Dream

Why on earth would anyone want to *live* on an empty stage? There's nothing there…or is there?

Actually, something is there – it's just not visible. The empty stage represents the open space that holds our creative potential – everything imaginable is there waiting to take form. It is the prequel to whatever happens next.

In theatre, the empty stage exists before the set is created, the actors appear, and the audience arrives. In life, the empty stage represents the spacious clarity of your mind, the inner platform from which you see, feel, imagine and make active choices every day.

Living on the Empty Stage is then a natural metaphor for living clearly, creatively and sanely throughout your life. It is based on the notion that theatre is drawn from life and life can often be quite theatrical. As a "life actor,"* your empty stage awareness is your discerning eye for making the best character* and performance choices every day.

The focal point of the book is the Empty Stage Awareness (ESA).* As a practice, the ESA centers you in the conscious act of living while being spiritually rooted in ancient wisdom.

While mastering the ESA, you also learn "Life Performance Practices" (LPP) – a new way to think about yourself. It helps you see if the way you are acting in life brings the results you want and if not, you learn new ways of acting to attain your goals. LPP is a performance-based process designed to give you creative choices

1

and greater command over the internal characters that form your outer identity. The Practices teach you how to attain Genuine Presence* and character awareness. You will gain the ability to quickly change your emotional character as needed to accomplish your intentions.*

LPP is valuable because most of us don't notice how our daily performance and emotional character habits affect the outcome of situations in our lives. Without such character awareness, we don't realize that we create our own fortune – or misfortunate – through the actions we take and the attitudes we display every day. We are not trained and practiced enough in life performance to know how to make perceptive character choices that produce the best outcome.

Unaware of our potential performance power, each of us goes out into the world using only a limited set of performance skills and a small cast of characters* that we have come to rely on to define who we are in the world. Our routine characters sometimes help us succeed, but other times they actually get in the way and cause creative blocks* to our happiness and success.

As you will learn, by living on the empty stage of your mind, you can become more aware of your Performance Style,* the roles you play, the character choices you make and the actions you take. You will also become aware of other people's character and instinctively know how to best co-play a life scenario with them. Most importantly, you will learn how to turn your creative blocks* into creative skills* and open up to unfamiliar parts of yourself to improve the results you get out of life.

The Life Performance Practices in this book do not train you to be an actor so you can "pretend" to be someone you are not. They are not aimed at teaching you to be false or disingenuous towards others. In fact, living on the empty stage is all about developing awareness, genuine presence, and an honest, unaffected daily performance. You will become more resourceful and effective at whatever you do in the truest way possible.

WE ARE ALL ACTORS IN LIFE

> *All the world's a stage, And all the men and women*
> *merely players, They have their exits and their entrances,*
> *And one man in his time plays many parts...*
>
> ~ *As You Like It*

You may not feel that you are an "actor" in life, or that you need "acting skills." But, as Shakespeare wisely sought to teach us, all the world is a stage and we are indeed players on it. Our lives progress in a series of comedies and tragedies, divided into acts and scenes. Our conversations with others are like impromptu dialogues.

We all act every day. Throughout human history, we have performed for one another in an effort to win love, attention, power, prestige, and success.

We act cheerful around those we want to impress, polite to those whose feelings we don't want to hurt, and cool toward those who have hurt or rejected us. We have all assumed a pretense at some time, in one way or another, when we felt deception was necessary. For instance, we might play up to our boss in order to get a raise or just to keep our job.

Yet, how you act is the big question. Bad acting happens when we act out of confusion – when we are just *marking it**, going through the motions, not fully engaged in what we are doing. It's a bit like sleepwalking – you have no self-command. Instead, you might say or do foolish things that create problems and don't get the results you wanted. You may later kick yourself because you're ashamed of how you were acting.

Then there is great acting, which happens when you have good motivation* and you are aware of what you are doing. You are present in the moment, self-reflective, able to perform at your best without fear or doubt. Your skills in using your body, voice, emotions, intellect, and your senses come naturally. You can act with self-command and your daily performance gets the results you want.

So, are you a good actor or a bad one? Does the way you act in life fully serve your needs? Has it helped you achieve what you hoped for in your personal and professional life? How do you rate your life performance?

If you are like most people, you will probably say your life performance is good, but not stellar. You might admit you wouldn't win an Academy Award and could possibly use some lessons. This book is meant to help.

The Empty Stage and Life Performance

The time of life is short! To spend that
shortness basely were too long.

~ Henry IV

Though acting is the one art all human beings have in common, most of us have not studied the art of acting to improve how we live our lives. Life performance is not a required subject in elementary school, so we grow in childhood learning manners and etiquette that follow conditioned behaviors according to our respective culture, education, religion, family imprints, traditions, and belief systems.

High school curriculums rarely offer courses in life performance skills to help us recognize the rewards or consequences of our actions before we commit them. We may go to college to learn to be a good teacher, lawyer, doctor, firefighter and so on, yet we are not trained in how to excel at being human. Then, as we get older and go through the school of hard knocks, we develop Character Sclerosis* by hardening our character either in reaction to or in obedience of our upbringing. In short, we either limit or exaggerate our sense of self.

As Life Actors, most of us never get the opportunity to be in a laboratory, classroom, or on a stage to experiment with how we can improve our performance in real-life situations. We seldom learn how to use our range of vocal powers, or our body, our senses, our emotional expression and creative thinking to be excellent life performers. Instead, we continue to play just one or two "Defining Roles," limiting our options for greater enjoyment and success.

What most of us are missing is a process for performing confidently in everyday situations so that we can truly create the life we choose. The Life Performance Practices presented in this book are designed exactly to that end. They give you a whole new way of seeing yourself as a life actor. Rather than identifying with limited talents and fixed character traits* that you habitually call "Me," the Empty Stage teaches you to identify with "Awareness" as "the real me."

4

Your "empty mindstage"* is not dull or stupid but is free of junk thinking. This gives you the creative independence to choose who you need to be in any given moment. Instead of a limited self-image, you can learn how to use your fuller emotional range* and talents within you. Your ability to accomplish things and enjoy life is not diminished by preconceptions and predictable character traits. You can change the way you act to better support your needs and that of others, ultimately attaining new heights.

Is LPP a Form of Psychology or Therapy?

Some licensed therapists use a method called "role-play." This therapeutic term was first introduced in 1934 by Dr. Jacob Levy Moreno, a psychiatrist who coined the phrase in conjunction with Psychodrama, which he pioneered. Moreno used role-play to help his patients work through their personal problems probing into personal history.

The Life Performance Practices are different from this and other psychological processes. Though you might experience a sense of healing from The Practices, that is not their prime purpose. In contrast to various therapies, role-play, and life coaching, LPP is an educational process that teaches you the things you need to know about acting imaginatively and lucidly in everyday life scenarios.

LPP offers a unique, performance-based process that helps you make creative character choices* to perform at your daily best. Using theatrical terminology and daily performance insights, you learn how to self-correct and be in self-command. You also learn to ground yourself in presence.

LPP may also bring you some physical benefits. Through testing the Character Study Practices for this book, I healed my chronic back pain by discovering the character in me that "needed" the pain. The performance process that followed allowed me to free up many immobilizing and hardened character stances and I am now creatively active like never before. And I might add, I am not alone. Many of my clients have seen these kinds of physical changes too.

How To Use This Book

Continuing the theme that our life performance is our personal theatre, *Living on the Empty Stage* lays out a sequence for using the Empty Stage Awareness and the Life Performance Practices as the foundation for developing your natural abilities—your talents. As in a Shakespearean play, the book is divided into 5 Acts. Each Act is composed of many scenes, some narrative to illuminate an idea and some instructive with practices* for you to do. The following is an overview of the 5 Acts:

- **Act I: Using the Empty Stage Awareness to Develop Genuine Presence**
  This Act defines the nature of the Empty Stage Awareness and explains its basic use as the core practice in LPP, opening you into expanded awareness and genuine presence. The ESA is the pivotal footing for all of the Life Performance Practices in the remainder of the book. Genuine Presence gives you steadiness of mind, so you can perform your daily activities with versatility in action.

- **Act II: Understanding Your Five Performance Styles**
  This Act is about your Human Instrument* and how important it is to develop all five parts of yourself. The main portion of Act II is devoted to describing 5 Performance Styles (PS)* that we all have within us. The PS define our ways of acting in life. We are usually dominant in one or two styles but, as life actors, we can broaden our experience to use all five. Each style has four ranges of character traits: tragic, extreme tragic, comic, and supreme comic. By reading about these and taking your own PS Profile, you will discover your dominant Performance Styles and begin to understand the PS of people around you.

- **Act III: Learning How Your Tragic Side Causes Creative Blocks**
  This Act goes deeper into the 5 Performance Styles, specifically the tragic, negative side of each that holds you back from the success you desire in life. Whenever you choose to play a tragic character trait of any Performance Style, you are effectively throwing a "creative block" in your own way. We will walk through each Performance Style and point out the common tragic

characters that many of us play in life. Through characteristic scenarios, you will see how someone playing their routine tragic character can make a quick change and choose a comic character to play the same scene.

- **Act IV: Learning to Use Your Comic Side for Creative Skills**
  This act focuses on rehearsing the positive emotional characters that stem from the comedic side of each of the 5 Performance Styles. Rehearsal* helps you learn how to "set" a few specific positive characters that you can choose to play whenever you are in challenging situations, rather than resorting to your routine tragic traits such as anger, resistance, anxiety, confusion, fear and more. In rehearsing, you will expand your comic character repertoire such as joy, contentment, humor, open-heartedness, to have more options.

- **Act V: Using the Empty Stage to Become a Quick Change Artist (QCA)**
  This culminating Act delves into LPP's ultimate goal – showing you what it means to be a *Quick Change Artist,* someone whose awareness is expansive and whose daily performance is flexible and fluid. As a Quick Change Artist, you become a well-rounded life actor and world player, capable of interacting with diverse people whose Performance Style differs from your own. You develop a readiness to act and make turnarounds with versatility. As a QCA, the ESA becomes your means for transitioning freely in and out of Performance Styles, roles and character whenever the situation calls for Change-Ability*.

***

I strongly suggest you read through the entire book first to see the complete scope of what is possible for you and then begin to practice the process. Even if you feel a section doesn't apply to you personally, it may apply to others you know and help in your interactions with them. Like any study, you can learn the LPP process one step at a time, and/or reference it for specific issues going on in your life.

We are complicated individuals, who create complicated lives. *Living on the Empty Stage* separates our complexities into parts so that we can understand the whole of ourselves. Each Act of the book may bring up different thoughts, memories, and feelings for you. So, work slowly and thoughtfully as you read. Since each of us has different objectives in using The Practices, I suggest, you use **Logging your Practice** found in the back of the book to accompany your reading and progress. If you don't understand a word or phrase, you can find its meaning in the **Glossary of Terms** also in the back.

In order to become a QCA and well-rounded life actor, practicing the ESAwareness and becoming skilled in the Five Performance Styles is the necessary goal. Each of us has our own learning style, so once you've read it through, go about the practices at your own pace. From my POV,* life is an "on-growing" work of art. If you read this book as your lodestar for cultivating a healthier, saner life, for evolving stronger relationships, and for excelling in your work, you will see every circumstance you encounter, whether comic or tragic, as an opportunity for improving your own work of art – You.

With few exceptions, all quotes in this book are from William Shakespeare. His eloquent words remain quite relevant to our lives today.

ORIGINS OF LIFE PERFORMANCE PRACTICES

People often ask me how I came to develop the Practices. Actually, they started formulating when I was very young. Since childhood, I loved to entertain. I always saw the world as my stage and was fearless in my love for performing…both on stage and off. At 21, I left the safe confines of my family in Dallas, Texas, where I had become a bit of a local celebrity and went to New York City to try out my talents on Broadway. However, in The Big Apple, I became just one of thousands of hopefuls. Even though I thought I was a talented actor/singer – and had numerous hometown newspaper reviews to prove it – in New York City I was surrounded by many equally talented actors, who also had their hometown reviews. Suddenly I was dealing with lots of competition and, despite some acceptance, I was experiencing more rejection than I was used to.

I began noticing, after a year or so on my own, that my everyday "life performance" lacked the brilliance I felt when I was on stage. In fact, the dramatic highs and lows of my off-stage performance were tarnishing the confidence that I needed to shine professionally. In secret moments with myself, I could see that the way I was acting in my real life was affecting the outcome of many personal situations. Deep down, I knew I was playing at life, impersonating who I wanted to be, thought I should be, wished I could be, or tried to be according to what someone else thought I should be. Trying to find the Real Me became very convoluted.

As professional actors* are naturally very expressive, I thought my issues were just an occupational hazard. Then I began noticing similar issues existing among friends and relatives in their professions. As life actors, all of us can be brilliant in certain roles we play, yet unable to translate that brilliance into the total experience of living. As we all clamor for success, love, recognition, and the fulfillment of our desires, we induce highs and lows.

Slowly it began to dawn on me that this problem was not exclusive to the trained actor but was part of the human dilemma. I saw that regardless of a person's position in life, each of us, in our own way, creates all kinds of unnatural characters and stressful life scenarios while trying to look important and acceptable to others. It seemed as if everyone was auditioning* with great hopes of landing the starring role in a life with a happy ending.

PUTTING PRESENCE BEHIND LIFE PERFORMANCE

Years later, in Los Angeles, California, following a forsaken theatrical career and a divorce, I found myself unexpectedly in a spiritual crisis. I felt confused, groundless and without direction. "Surely," I thought, "there must be some meaning to life...but what? Where do I find it?"

It was the era of the Beatles, rock 'n roll, tie-dye shirts, drugs, and lucky for me...Eastern Philosophy. For the first time in history, due to the Chinese invasion of Tibet, Gurus (teachers who, through spiritual practice, are freed from human ignorance) were coming to the United States from India and Tibet offering their spiritual wisdom to Western students. While some women of that period became Rock 'n Roll Groupies, I became a "Gurupie," shifting about from one Eastern guru to another, trying to find the "Genuine One" whose wisdom could free my doubts and confusions about God, explain my place in the universe, and settle my wild young mind. This was much harder than pursuing romance with a rock star.

In the mid-1970s, I moved to Ojai, California, where I was fortunate to meet and spend time with the East Indian philosopher, J. Krishnamurti as well as several scientists who were trying to bridge the gap between science and spirituality.

Among them was the revered Dr. David Bohm, theoretical physicist and philosopher, whose work ranged from his Super Quantum Theory to his investigation into the nature of thought. David and his wife Saral would come to the Ojai Valley every spring to visit and sit in dialogue with Krishnamurti and a few of us who were interested in exploring universal concepts, thought, and meditation.

On one of those late April afternoons, Krishnamurti, David, Saral, a few friends, and I were out for a sunset walk. Deep in discussion, David and I fell behind the others. "You know," he said, "you and I have something in common." I reacted with high-spirited surprise, "We do?" "Yes," he gently replied. "Did you know that the words 'theory' and 'theatre' come from the same Greek root – which means to put something up for viewing, to make a spectacle of, to look at?"

I was amazed that he had found a common ground in our dissimilar work.

"I do that with my theories," he continued. "I put them up for viewing so that my colleagues in the scientific community can discuss my work and either prove or disprove my theories."

He paused and looked at me to see if I was following him. I nodded affirmatively. "You do that with theatre too, you see. You put the human condition up for viewing so we can observe ourselves more clearly and make personal adjustments in order to better our lives and our world."

That walk was one of those life-changing moments for me. Never had I viewed my work as an actor and writer as a way to help people better their lives and the world. That day, my life took a left turn. Dr. Bohm inspired me to rethink how I wanted to use myself as an artist. His viewpoint encouraged me to explore anew. I began creating an everyday performance process for mastering the unpredictable act of living by cultivating the everyday art of acting.

A few years later, while developing the foundations of Life Performance Practices (LPP), I met the one who would become my long-term spiritual teacher, the Venerable Gyatrul Rinpoche, a humble Tibetan Lama. His sense of humor and subtle (and sometimes not so subtle) ways of pointing out my faults and introducing methods to steady the mind, has held my attention, respect, and appreciation of Vajrayana Buddhism ever since.

Though I was proud, resistant and to this day not a good practitioner, I have received many teachings and learned much about the Buddhist path to spiritual awakening over the past 40 years. Just being around so many great teachers has filled me with many blessings and given me a greater understanding of how to live with the uncertainty that exists for us as human beings.

Owing to the non-sectarian and expansive view of the Buddhist path, I personally developed an affection and respect for all spiritual and religious paths. Despite their various differences, at their core, all paths seek to know God, or some greater presence, and the meaning of life in a way that resonates with one's upbringing and personal affinities.

I do not bring the Buddhist path into the LPP process itself, yet this book reflects the richness of a collective spiritual foundation that I feel has been missing in our daily life performance. It develops genuine presence and promotes our innate human goodness, which makes our ever-changing life dramas easier to understand and work within.

Each of us, in our own way, seeks to be in control of our own life, to live in harmony with others, to enjoy peace of mind, financial security, good health, love and happiness. So, over time, I created these Life Performance Practices as a discipline that not only gives people practical tools for acting in daily life, but also aims to help achieve those shared basic human desires. I feel that each of us can achieve greater well-being by paying closer attention to how we are acting, and by taking serious note of the results we are getting from our cumulative daily performance.

FURTHER EVOLUTION OF LPP

I have been teaching and evolving LPP since the 1980's. Among my first clients, was a speech therapist, Bette Hadler. She worked at a Los Angeles hospital for stroke and head-injury patients. Most of her patients had aphasia – the inability to retrieve words and correctly identify objects. Many of them had lost hope and were living on the "tragic side" of life. Bette wanted me to help them find new performance skills and rediscover their "comic side." To that end, we received a grant from MGM Studios to produce a play for the general public entitled, *I Can't...I Can!*

We paired professional actors and stroke and head-injury actors together on stage. The pro-actors liked having a script to follow while the aphasic actors had difficulty remembering lines and preferred to improvise. Using my LPPractices and Bette's speech therapy techniques, we resolved this dilemma by developing a system of communication for the aphasic actors that they eventually transferred into their daily life scenarios.

I then went on to teach LPP to cancer patients who found the idea of choosing and changing character a useful way of dealing with the highs and lows of their disease.

These two experiences gave me proof that LPP was effective. I became convinced that anyone was capable of quickly changing from a negative character to a positive one, providing they had a clear process for recognizing, choosing, and changing their character. Using these performance practices, I felt that any life actor could have creative choice in playing out life situations in more productive ways.

If the professional actor, who is first an actor in life, has the internal mechanism to make on-the-spot emotional transitions at choice, then we as life actors can learn to do the same. We all have *Change-Ability* within us. It's simply a matter of learning to use it with care, honesty and responsibility to the personal and global picture.

I have since taught LPP to executives at numerous corporations, to men and women looking for career change or seeking to reenter the job market after taking time off or who had been laid off due to company downsizing. I have worked with lawyers, doctors, sales managers, writers, actors, accountants, entertainment professionals, professors and university students – people in all walks of life. Whatever you do, you will find The Practices life empowering.

In particular, business people appreciated the focus on developing teamwork and positive business relations that increase creative interactions and innovative thinking. With greater understanding of their Performance Styles and character, executives and employees alike can better interact with each other and discover how to take their personal performance to new heights. They find greater ease and honesty in communication while learning to make quick changes when necessary.

Today my production company, called Quick Change Studio, teaches Life Performance Practices as a valuable performance-based process applicable to all areas of living. When people ask if LPP would work for their particular business, organization or group, I simply ask, *Are they human beings?* LPP can be oriented toward any specific topic. Whether in the workplace, or in personal life, you can become a Quick Change Artist,* capable of making responsible changes to meet the needs of almost any given situation.

Through this book, you can gain new creative skills, including:

- Developing a present, alert mind, open to potential and able to preempt many problems
- The ability to clarify confusing thoughts and balance feelings
- Awareness of your primary *Performance Style* and how to maximize it
- Greater self-command over your inner cast of characters
- The ability to change your *tragic character traits** that sabotage your goals, relationships, and career
- An expansion of your inner *comic character traits** to help you succeed with goals, relationships, and career
- Versatility in making quick character changes to create better outcomes in ordinary and challenging situations
- The ability to be with people whose Performance Style differs from yours

Whatever career you are in, or none at all, LPP is a unique process designed to help you develop genuine presence in life performance skills that strengthen and expand your inborn human talents. In developing these skills, you slowly begin to avoid real-life performance blunders.

We are transient beings,
transiting through space.

Act 1

The Empty Stage Awareness – Developing Genuine Presence

SCENE 1 THE EMPTY STAGE AWARENESS (ESA)

We are such stuff as dreams are made on,
And our little life is rounded with a sleep.

~ *The Tempest*

Imagine yourself in an empty space anywhere, anytime. You could be out in the open air beneath the stars, walking in a field, even in a parking lot, or just experiencing the space in a room. You feel alive. The openness gives you a sense of freedom. You can breathe easily, dream out loud, be honest and real. The empty space gives you permission to move and create. Things seems possible.

Everyone needs empty space. We are transient beings, always changing, always performing under the light of the sun, the moon and the stars. Empty space is how we transition from one scene to another on the revolving stage* of life. We use this space to change our mind, to have a change of heart, and to make a change in plans. It is our natural instinct to use and enjoy empty space. Yet, are we aware of it?

Carl Sagan, cosmologist and host of the 1978 TV series, *Cosmos*, was quoted as saying, "Our planet, our society, and we ourselves are built of star stuff."

What does that have to do with our daily lives? Well, just about everything. When we look out into space, we see blue skies by day and the twinkling stars at night– yet we don't think of that space as the womb of our existence. If we actually come from star stuff, we are more related to empty space than you may think.

Space holds everything imaginable – all the archives, knowledge, and legends of our past, present, and future. Although it appears empty, the space around us contains vast energies filled with the potential to manifest in a bazillion different ways. Perhaps this is why scientists equate space with potential; the information is out there if we can only tap into it.

From the perspective of simple everyday living, our relationship to space – this goldmine of all potential powers and information, goes practically unnoticed. Space is an element in our lives that many of us have yet to explore for our personal use. Humans have explored outer space, but we are fundamentally unaware and uninformed about the power of empty space within and around us.

By ignoring our relationship to empty space, we fail to connect with its vast possibilities. Unaware of how to constructively use it, we *zone out*, feel blocked, and stay stuck in safe places. We disconnect with space by filling it with activities – watching TV, listening to our iPods, watching videos and reading social media on our smartphones. Even when we try to be quiet, after a short time we start longing for something to happen. We clutter our mind space with constant self-talk and chatter every minute of every day – the proverbial "black box theatre" playing brain babble* in our head.

Our inexperience in perceptively connecting with the clear, intangible space of our mind causes us to lose touch with our creative potential. Our thoughts and desires turn outward and take on personal attitudes and priorities, often acting against our best interest.

You may not realize it, but when you are confused and waiting for answers or inspiration to hit, you are actually waiting for your mind to clear. You are waiting for that moment when space can intervene and open you to your natural receptivity. Sometimes it seems as if answers or ideas come from nowhere – like out of the blue. In truth, you have simply opened your mind and downloaded the available information from space.

Just as we learned to use earth, air, wind, water and fire to our advantage, we can learn to use space. So how can we personally connect with space when we can't see, feel, hear or touch this mysterious creative potential?

SCENE 2 THE EMPTY STAGE AWARENESS (ESA) PRACTICE

The Empty Stage Awareness (ESA) is the key practice. It is the spacious, internal environment within you. Learning to live in the ESA gives you greater access to clear thinking and practical judgment. Awareness becomes your true identity. Given our dualistic struggle between feelings of comedy* or tragedy,* the ESA is a third place for the mind to go. It is not a vulnerable state of dullness, but a keen and balanced mental state. With ESAwareness to guide you, you can easily connect with the potential space has to offer.

In LPP, "Living on the Empty Stage" means developing unbroken awareness. From the empty stage – the observation platform of your mind – you have a panoramic view of life and can accurately see all that is going on, without self-induced boundaries. You have the capability to release wandering, confusing thought themes into immediate awareness – like clouds suddenly clearing to reveal a limitless blue sky. The Empty Stage Practice highlights self-awareness.

When you go to the ESA, you are not caught up in your own dramas. You know how to explore the questions and can make clearer decisions. As a creative resource, the ESA opens your mind for receiving new ideas. Whenever you struggle with conflicting thoughts and feelings, it acts as neutral ground for gaining your equilibrium. Through the ESA practice, you begin to recognize whether your thoughts and actions are working for or against you.

The ESA practice helps you develop your relationship with space and deepens your ability to be genuinely present. Gradually, you will cultivate a connection with the greater presence of space and your own personal presence. If you fall into dullness, think of it as a cue* to awaken from your stupor.

The more familiar you become with the clarity and potential that exists within your empty mindstage*, the more you will be able to accomplish in life. You will feel comfortable, able to listen, and participate with people and what's going on around you. It feels like your whole being is sinking into pure reality as never before. To gain Genuine Presence, sincere and daily practice of ESA is necessary as consistent awareness is not our habit.

THE EMPTY STAGE AWARENESS (ESA) PRACTICE

The Empty Stage Practice is the pivotal, transitional tool in Life Performance Practices. It is the foundational practice for developing awareness, presence, and creative freedom. It is also the pivotal practice for everything you will do in Life Performance Practices. Do the following practice three or more times until you feel genuinely present.

Directions

Sit comfortably relaxed; erect enough so that your breath can flow freely through your body. Keeping your eyes half-open, allow your gaze to fall gently on the space in front of you. Do not focus on objects. Relax your eyes into a sense of steadiness, like a cued-up camera resting on a tripod.

With your mouth closed, take in a slow, deep breath through your nostrils. In the same way a strong wind blows the smog out of a valley, let the air blow through your brain, clearing out all thoughts, concepts, attitudes, judgments, and attachments. Stay alert and sense the freedom.

On the out-breath, release the air in a steady, even stream through your mouth. As you do, turn your attention in to your body. Feel all points of contact...your feet on the ground...your buttocks on the chair, etc. Keeping your eyes half-open and steady as you expand your peripheral vision. Sense your surrounding environment. Do not think about it. Stabilize your sensory awareness into the present moment.

Now rest in Genuine Presence.

Remember:
- **IN-BREATH – Clear your mind of all thoughts, images, attitudes and judgments.**
- **OUT-BREATH – Ground your body, expand your peripheral vision, and open your sensory awareness.**
- **REST IN Genuine Presence**

PURPOSE & GOALS

The ESA practice has many applications that you will discover the more you practice it. The spacious state of mind in the Empty Stage Awareness allows you to see with an unbiased view. Most importantly, it is an inner free space to gain clarity on the effectiveness of your daily performance. It provides the mental and emotional spaciousness to make changes in your character and actions. The internal goal is to feel *Genuine Presence* supported by awareness. The external goal is to perform with *Creative Presence* and versatility in your daily interactions. The ultimate goal is to hold the ESA as the backdrop for all your activities.

When doing the ESA practice, if you become bored or your thoughts begin to wander, it is usually because of your inexperience in maintaining a perceptive, clear mind. Most of us don't know what to do with presence of mind so we fall into our habitual speedy, dull, or sleepy mind. You may even feel stupid or anxious. All these sensations are normal in the beginning stages of practice.

Yet, you might practice filtering out the layers of thought, images and brain babble as if you are a miner, sifting through the muddy waters to find the gold. Become sensitive to the little insights that arise and fall away. Allow ease to stream into your body. It takes practice to develop awareness. Be patient and don't give up. The rewards far outweigh the learning curve.

USING THE ESA PRACTICE

You will find many times during the course of a day that the ESA practice can be applied. Use it when you want to:

- Establish Genuine Presence (confidence) in a presentation, meeting or personal situation.
- Clear brain babble to check your motivation and intention in a situation.
- Clarify a confusing issue and see your options.
- Diminish stage fright* (self-doubt).
- Relax your body and energize your mind.
- Clear a creative block (tragic character trait) that obstructs a desired effect.
- Make better creative choices in your life performance. Identify who in you is interacting with others. Is it the happy, angry, or hurt one?
- Increase intuition – sense the underlying nature of a situation.
- Be confident in your decision-making.

- Change your Performance Style to fit the needs of a situation.

When your mind is in the ESAwareness, put any challenging life scenario up on your mindstage and review it with objectivity. You will become much more aware of your character choices and see new ways to achieve the goals you have had difficulty with in the past.

Keep in mind you are not trying to stop thoughts all together as thinking is a function of the brain. However, the ESA practice can lessen the compulsive, agitated thinking and brighten your brain between thoughts. Given that the brain is our most complex organ, practicing the ESA saves undue wear and tear on its functioning power and other body parts that our brain influences.

If you practice the ESA in quiet, private moments, yet still experience difficulty releasing babble and junk thinking,* you are probably dealing with tragic characters of frustration, confusion, or resistance. These are likely habitual characters that exist in many of your other efforts as well. If so, you will find a practice called *Allowing #1* in Act 3 that will help you release character traits causing creative blocks. Becoming familiar with your habitual traits through the ESA Practice is the start of the life actor's education.

Is The Empty Stage Awareness Practice a Meditation?

Many people ask me if the ESA Practice isn't just another form of meditation. It is and it isn't, depending on what you mean by meditation. Some meditations give you visualizations to focus your mind on the positive, while certain religious or spiritual meditations are a form of prayer. There are also healing meditations and still other deeper meditations that take you far beyond mind.

The Empty Stage Awareness practice is not specifically meant as any of the above, though it can be applied in similar ways. If you use it before prayer, it helps you to pray in presence. In that way, it resembles some meditation practices. In addition, the ESA helps you relax and rejuvenate the brain.

But the main purpose of the Empty Stage Practice is to develop genuine presence as an on-growing daily practice. In time, a moment to moment awareness of your conduct arises allowing you to make informed character choices. From the perspective of our life performance, it is a meditation on character.

Awareness as Your Real "Me"

When we refer to our self as "I" or "me," we are thinking of self as a whole person. However, given the many characters we reactively break into, we tend to identify with each character part* we are playing as fixed. In doing so, we believe that part of us, good or bad, is the real and only Me. However, awareness is flexible and fluid, and so too are all our characters.

If you set Awareness as the real me, you don't have to identify with being happy or sad, smart or stupid just because you are feeling it. You have the option to draw on any needed part of yourself to accomplish whatever is necessary at any given time. Your Awareness recognizes it as an emotional energy that has taken a character form yet is changeable.

Awareness becomes your sense of wholeness and your true identity. It is the knowingness in you; it is not confused or uncertain. Then, if you identify with and set any one character, it becomes an artistic and creative choice.

SCENE 3 LIVING LIFE AS ART

Whether you realize it or not, living life as art* is essential to your happiness, health, and success. Most dictionaries define art as *"The production of something beautiful or thought-provoking."* In daily life, art is not only expressed by those in an artistic career, but art is the natural expression of beauty that lies within us all. Without Art in our lives, we would be left with ugliness and thoughtlessness.

Art has the power to make us feel better. Why else would you bring a beautiful bouquet of flowers to someone who is ill? Why would you offer an "artfelt*" gift to someone you love? Art can also be exciting and provocative, having the power to attract. Otherwise, why would you stand in front of the mirror trying to make yourself look attractive if you weren't interested in attracting attention, position, or love?

Art plays a role in helping to heal illness and inspire healthy living. Working together on an artistic project can rekindle a broken friendship or business relation. We've also seen how the creative arts have given ghetto gang members opportunities to become talented, valuable citizens.

Yet, many of us live in an artistic void and don't realize it. Stifled and unable to express love and beauty, we feel frustrated and unfulfilled by this lack. Some have lost any sense of aesthetics and feel their life is entrenched in a dreary day-to-day grind. Our own tragic performance overwhelms our ability to function artistically and enjoy life. We may begin to act in opposition to art, carrying a kind of toxicity that threatens our self and those around us.

One of the biggest challenges we all face on today's world stage is how to live artfully despite the stressful context of our everyday lives. Just watching the nightly news informing us of violent events and ugly people doing vile things can play into our own anxieties, causing us to act with fear and resistance to the world. At work, demanding pressures to produce above and beyond your limits can create a neurotic, aggressively competitive workplace, with little sense of art.

This tenseness may cause you to overlook the beauty and connection that exists in ordinary moments and familiar interactions.

However, when acting from the artfelt part of ourselves, there is the potential for art in all we do. If designed well, our work environments could inspire beauty in natural, unforced artistic ways. Employees and executives alike would feel happier, safer, and more energetic. If we can live and work in a profit-making culture that honestly cares about each other's welfare, we can get creative. Products can be produced not out of greed, fear, or the need to sensationalize, but out of the wisdom for what's important, beautifying and sustaining to life. Using technology as its partner, art can boost the economy in stable, more reliable ways.

Most importantly, in these times, art can counteract violence. By acting on our obsession with aggression, we are simply training ourselves in tragedy.

Whatever happens in the world, a commitment to live an artfelt existence peaceably with goodwill needn't be beyond our imagination.

Imagination arises from our innate desire and ability to create. We all have it. The art is in knowing how you are using it and when. Most of us do not realize that when we pretend to like someone or something, we are using our imagination. Yet every day, we mindlessly use our imagination to create negative or positive characterizations.

If we clutter our mindstage with negative attitudes, our positive attitudes are blocked. There is no opening for the favorable rewards around us to get through. When we use imagination meaningfully to create our character, we can get the results we want and feel good about who we are. Imagine: What if, through your own everyday performance practices, you could create a life so radiant, so superior – so astonishingly extraordinary that the tragedies you consistently perform now would become a forgotten dream?

As a performing artist in life, you can express and experience art in many ways – from the way you respond to your boss's irritability, to how you collaborate with colleagues, to how you interact with friends and neighbors. You can apply artfelt routines to your daily performance at work, with family, or even in your alone time. LPP shows how multifaceted we are in character and presents a framework for using the many facets of our persona more successfully. To counteract your fears and tragic tendencies, imagine art and beauty in your life.

The Peril of Misinterpreting Life as Art

Living your life as a work of art is important, but there are perils. I am referring especially to the art of pleasure-seeking, an unquenchable pursuit for many. It keeps us in constant flight from one desire to the next, never happy with what is. You may not wake up every morning saying, *"Today I will pleasure seek!"* But it is what you and I do when we go on a shopping spree, go out to dinner, or head to a bar to meet friends. Whatever we do, we want to have a great experience. And why not? Who wants to go out pain seeking?

There is a difference, however, between immersing yourself in the beauty of life and being caught up in constant pleasure seeking. In the latter, we tend to get involved with things that distract us from the boredom, fear, and dissatisfaction of our lives. Our mindstage is lit up in the glitzy, glittering lights of a lifestyle that keeps us afloat on a cloud of "everything's okay."

For some, this kind of entertaining entrapment eventually forces a desire for something deeper. The futility of the chase for more riches, more power, more love, and more sensational experiences becomes boring and tiresome. And so, some turn their focus from grasping at the outer world for inner satisfaction to realizing that everything we really need can be created artfully from within.

Fair warning: *Life is short; art is long*, as Hippocrates observed. As a doctor, he realized that to discover results in the healing arts often took longer than a lifespan. In our personal discoveries, some may feel, *"You only live once – so live it up."* But even if that were true, why not take advantage of your short time on earth to create as beautiful and meaningful a life as you can?

SCENE 4 WHAT TO DO WITH THE FEELING OF EMPTINESS?

It harrows me with fear and wonder.

~ Hamlet

Even if one has an inner or spiritual path, for many of us, the unsettling discomfort that envelops when we feel empty inside is due to our inexperience in being alone with an expansive mind. We can fall into fright not knowing how to interact with spaciousness and mistake that empty feeling as fear, flight, or despair.

But, you have a choice – either to let your mindstage go dark or turn on the lights and get creative! Use the ESAwareness and re-vision your fear into something productive.

How can you redirect your empty feeling? First, change the set that's staged on your mind. In a theatre, the backdrop on the stage sets the environment, creating an ambience and mood for the actors to express the play's theme. In life, many of us walk around with a mental backdrop of hidden fears, which creates an internal ambiance of confusion and periodic self-doubt.

But when we practice The ESAwareness, we develop spaciousness and clarity as the backdrop on our mindstage. Sanity becomes our internal setting, and that ambiance gives us the creative freedom to perform whatever character choice we see as appropriate to the scene.

SCENE 5 DEVELOPING GENUINE PRESENCE

All things be ready, if our minds be so.
~ Henry V

There is a lot of talk today about mindfulness or *being present*. And yet, being truly present is not just the result of a simple self-command to accomplish. It does take some effort. Though some people are more naturally present, most of us have not explored what it takes to really be present.

You might say there are two levels of "Genuine Presence." The first is based on "attentiveness," such as being alert during a business meeting or personal interaction. In that moment, you are actively listening and prepared to act as needed. We are all familiar with this the kind of presence, though many of us could use some help in developing it to a greater degree.

But there is another level of genuine presence based on "existence." In this state, we are not just attentive, but we are "being awareness." For most of us, this state of just existing in the moment – maintaining awareness as a living act – is much harder. Like a bee darts from flower to flower, we flit from one thought to another, unable to settle. The idea of calming our racing brain might be perceived as boring or unproductive.

Perhaps we are afraid that nothing is there. But that is, in fact, the point. When you are genuinely present, there is no one there – just presence acting from awareness. There's no arrogance, stubbornness or aggression ready to jump out. There's no such thing as "my opinion." Learning to maintain Genuine Presence while playing the best character in a particular situation is the supreme art of life performance.

Through this deep contemplative practice in "just being", you release many layers of thought themes and opinions that have kept you static and unable to be totally present to life as it exists. Of course, we all need to think about things as we participate in everyday activities. Yet, those who can attain this deeper level of presence can maintain a steadiness and clarity of mind, even as ideas, feelings, people, and events come and go. Being present is like watching different movies on the same screen. The integrity and wisdom of unattached awareness on your mindstage is never lost, regardless of what is happening or what you are doing.

When you are performing daily tasks, Genuine Presence becomes creative, giving you presence in action.

Most of us, including myself, try all kinds of short cuts thinking we are present in situations when in actuality, we have a million thoughts racing in our head. So, don't kid yourself. Just as you need to sacrifice eating that loaded double cheese-burger and go to the gym instead, you have to sacrifice dullness and self-centered attitudes, and instead practice Genuine Presence – every day.

Being present helps you:
- Learn more
- Avoid accidents
- Have better timing
- Intuit the needs of your clients and colleagues, friends and relatives
- Develop patience
- Make necessary character and performance changes as needed

Keep in mind, none of your characters are solid or unchangeable. They are simply energies taking form when your inner stage manager gives them the cue. Though they are all available, being attached to any one way of acting creates rigidity and leaves you with less character choice for solving an issue. Just remember that the ESA is your transitional tool.

Try adopting the ESA as your main identity and see what happens. Sense yourself as expansive and aware. Notice if the discomfort of aversions and the grasping at fulfillment eases. It may take the pressure off the longings, the must-haves, and the feelings of hate, fear, and disappointment. Experience yourself as a creative instrument, able to work imaginatively with challenges. True freedom comes when we free ourselves of our own hardened views.

SCENE 6 WHY IS THE ESA IMPORTANT TODAY?

Wouldst thou…live a coward in thine own esteem,
Letting "I dare not" wait upon "I would…"

~ Macbeth

Most of us haven't given enough importance to the built-in attribute of awareness living within us. Why should we? We have managed to live reasonably happy lives without being steadily aware. So why now?

Well, for one thing, when your awareness can distinguish which thoughts are useful and healthy versus which are not, you can cut the overload. Presence can develop. Living on the Empty Stage of your mind allows you to put clear space between your thoughts and your actions. Your body, voice and mind become more coordinated…you aren't saying one thing and meaning or doing another. Your life performance choices are more accurate, effective, and rewarding.

You can also stop taking yourself too seriously. If you have no attachment to how gorgeous you look or how brilliant you are, then there is no problem. You won't embarrass so easily. Spinach in your teeth will be a new form of "green art." A bad hair day becomes your unique form of branding. Things won't upset you so much and you will be able to have fun with Mis-Takes.* Living on your comic side will take hold. If you fall and break your leg, you will sing the pain instead of screaming it. Creativity will take new avenues.

If your mind isn't so cluttered with ka-ka-poo-poo, you can look for the humor in a situation and be inventive, even daring. You can be lighter with things that happen instead of getting irritated or insisting it be your way. Also, when we look for actuality in each situation, we can see how and why someone's character and actions bring about success or failure. We gain the value of lessons learned instead of wallowing in disappointment or pain.

A HEALTHY PRESENCE

The ESA is a lifetime practice and usually matures in stages as you practice it. The beauty of it is that you can practice it anywhere – at a tense business meeting, a stressful interaction, or a joyful wedding. It can relieve the ordinary pressures of daily living and help you do things that you might otherwise complicate with overthinking. With this level of mental freedom, you can act with more enjoyment and self-trust.

ESA is the hardest and most important thing a person can achieve. It gives you a sense of wholeness to act from – though not a solid wholeness, because it does not fix your view as things change. When you maintain a firm self-image, egotism comes into play and you act to complement your self-image. ESA can level the deflated or exaggerated ego and give you the ability to adapt into whatever is needed.

I must emphasize here that without the ability to access a steady, free space within, we will always be wandering, searching, and caught up in the quagmire of emotional and mental gymnastics. We will always be subject to outside influences without much choice. Confusion will prevail with only periods of clarity and enjoyment. Being grounded in spacious awareness keeps us awake and genuine throughout our life.

In summary, here are 3 reasons to develop the ESA within you.

1. Genuine Presence

This the "being" aspect of the ESA. To gain Genuine Presence, sincere and daily practice of ESA is necessary. With that you are able to perform your daily activities using Creative Presence. You feel steady-minded, active and comfortable, able to listen and participate in what's going on around you. Your whole person will sink into "being present" as never before.

2. *Creative Choice*

The ESA is your creative resource for making choices. Most of the time, our choices are either routine or reactionary, and we may suffer the consequences or reap the rewards. The ESA is the only place where we can make perceptive, unbiased, creative choices in our daily life. To your personal advantage, Creative Choice can pull you out of a funk or help you relate to someone you care about in a more valuable way. Practices for making creative choices will be found in Act IV.

3. *Change-Ability*

Having gained composure in Genuine Presence, you can direct yourself through open space with self-command. That is the power of Change-Ability. It requires that you maintain openness, versatility and flexibility. It is your inner tool for transitioning fluidly in and out of Performance Styles, roles,* and characters whenever the situation calls for Change-Ability.

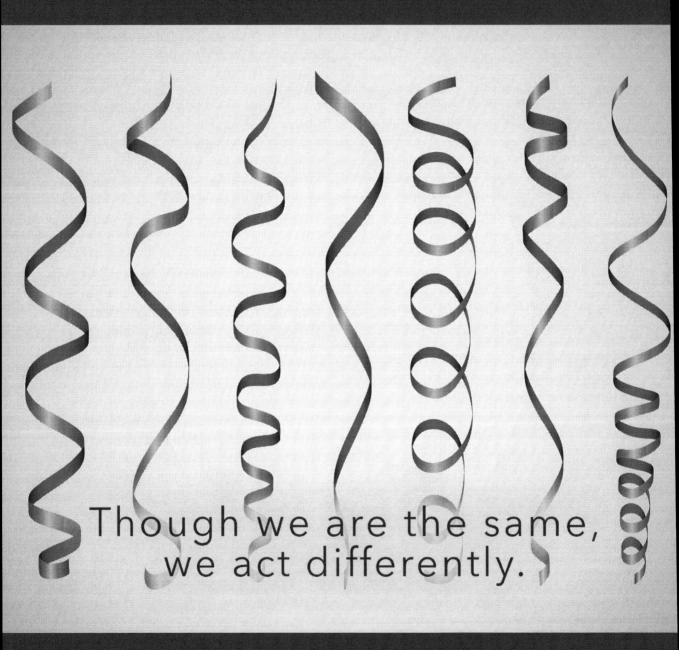

Though we are the same,
we act differently.

Act II

Our Five Performance Styles

SCENE 1 LIFE PERFORMANCE...
WHAT WE CAN LEARN FROM THE ACTOR'S CRAFT

...The purpose of playing, whose end both at first, and now,
was and is, to hold as 'twere a mirror up to nature...

~ *Hamlet*

Since early Greek theatre, actors have been there to show us things we might never see or experience otherwise. Their art is as much to inspire, provoke, and educate as it is to entertain. They effect change in us by mirroring who we are, who we can be, and who we don't want to be. The professional actor has always been a servant for humanity's window into itself.

The well-trained actor takes on a fictitious role and, in order to play it realistically, he or she must know the emotional, physical, and mental tendencies of the role and be able to transition fluidly from one character trait into another. It requires in-depth study of the Human Instrument*, extensive discipline, and total self-command to use the actor's talents effectively.

As life actors, we are not so different. We, too, need effective performance abilities. However, the difference is that professional actors, unless typecast,* deliberately assume a character dissimilar from their own. Whereas we, as life actors, most always typecast ourselves. Day after day, we unknowingly rehearse the same emotional character traits and manners – some to our advantage and some not.

The art for us as life actors is to learn to play our everyday roles using the best possible character choices – to gain awareness of the effect our daily performance has on us, our personal relations and on society. And most of all, we need to develop the power to change when necessary. Learning to transition fluidly from one scene or role into another is a very useful skill in daily life.

The glitch as life actors, is we are usually unskilled in the art of performance and in choosing our character. In fact, most people insist they are not actors and resist the idea of performance training. When I ask people what they think acting is about, the usual response is that it involves pretense; to them, acting is to be phony. This is often said with a strong implication that they never see themselves as phony nor conjure pretense in themselves.

If you have ever felt this way, ask yourself: Have I never put on a bit of an air around someone I wanted to impress? Have I never pretended to be nice to someone I couldn't stand? Do I act sexy or flirtatious when I want to attract someone? Have I never found myself "faking it" on a particular occasion?

The point is, whether we admit it or not, we all pretend...and we all lie occasionally. We may justify our pretense, saying things like, *"I didn't want to hurt her feelings,"* or, *"I could lose my job if I told him what I really thought!"* But whatever your rationale, this is *acting with pretense*. In daily life, we don't have a script – we are improv actors. So why not get good at it? Why not learn to act using your creative skills and enjoy greater success and effectiveness in your life?

In life performance, the art is in mastering the wisdom of self-awareness (which you do through the ESA) and the craft is in developing performance skills. That's what Act 2 is all about – learning the art of acting to elevate the act of living.

Many actors today teach acting to the layperson using time-honored techniques developed by famous masters whose names you might know: Constantin Stanislavski, Lee Strasberg, Stella Adler, and Stanley Meisner. This is great training for anyone adventurous enough to get up on a stage and challenge his or her inhibitions and talents.

LPPractices, however, are specifically designed for the Life Actor to use during daily social, family, spiritual, and business interactions. It is a performance-based process designed to help people make relevant character choices in how they perform their lives. The Practices train you to identify and access the part of you needed in a given situation. You learn how best to meet your own needs and be creatively flexible with changing situations and diverse people. By expanding your daily talents and developing better interactive skills, you become more resourceful and honest. And as a side effect, being versatile makes you more interesting to others.

For all of us, acting is a lifetime vocation, so it's curious that for the most part, we have not been given mandatory schooling in learning the art and craft of life performance as we have with math or language. We learn how to act through the school of hard knocks. As a result, most of us have been routinely rehearsing bad performance habits all our lives. We just accept them as part of who we are. We have refined and set our tragic performance traits on automatic – repeatedly performing the same routine, even when we know we are annoying others or harming ourselves.

Think of the time it has taken you to get to be the person you are? Think of the constant rehearsals you've performed to establish your character traits – some good but some awful. Like me, I'm sure you have traits you would like to change. But for most of us, there is a defensive attachment to our tragic traits that makes it hard to recognize our mis-takes, much less change them. Like a horse, we bolt when someone calls us on a character flaw. We've never learned creative critiquing.

Here is where learning a craft is indispensable. Having a process specifically designed to develop your skills and break through your creative blocks helps you realize how to live freely within a given structure. LPP offers a craft – your own set of performance skills that you can use and cultivate for the rest of your life. Of course, like any craft, the learning curve requires your patience, interest, effort, and time. Just think of your life as your on-growing personal work of art.

THE LIFE ACTOR'S HUMAN INSTRUMENT

As the piano is a pianist's instrument, the entire person is the professional actor's instrument. An actor's training develops and fine tunes the *infinite faculties* of their human instrument. They learn how to use their mind to make the right choices and their body to create admirable action and movement. They develop their vocal power, study the senses, and stretch their emotional range for greater expression. Their practice is to develop all parts of their human instrument so that they can masterfully communicate the dialogue, actions, and purpose of their role to an audience. In short, the genius of an actor is dependent on how skillfully and creatively they use their instrument.

As Life Actors, we too must use our Human Instrument every day to play out scenarios within our own personal theatre at our work, our home, and wherever we go. How we portray our roles in each situation can affect our health, relationships, creativity, and productivity. Your performance can alter the outcome of any given situation.

The LPPractices will develop all parts of your instrument so that you can interact enjoyably and effectively with family, friends, business associates and even strangers. To cultivate the performance genius within you, you too must learn how to use the five innate faculties of your instrument:

1) Our **brain** gives us thought and reasoning.
2) Our **emotions** give expression to our feelings.

3) Our **body** gives us mobility for action.
4) Our **senses** allow us to see, hear, touch, smell, taste and perceive life.
5) Our **voice** projects our personal power.

Mastering these faculties provide us with infinite possibilities for fulfilling our life goals. Yet, like Hamlet, understanding *this quintessence of dust* (see Scene 2 quote) and how to use it well remains a mystery for most of us. The LPP process is designed to help clarify that mystery and teach you to use your human instrument to its peak capacity.

▬▬▬ SCENE 2 ▬▬▬ YOUR FIVE PERFORMANCE STYLES (PS)

What a piece of work is man. How noble in reason, how infinite
in faculties, in form and moving, how express and admirable
in action…yet to me, what is this quintessence of dust?

~ Hamlet

Using our human instrument begins with learning how the five Performance Styles align with our five main powers and talents:

- **The Mental PS (MPS)** is the power of the intellect. Our talent is logic, structural thinking, and innovative ideas.
- **The Emotional PS (EPS)** is the power of feeling. Our talent is communication, expression, entertaining, and relationship.
- **The Physical PS (PPS)** is the power of the body. Our talent is healing, high function, action, and task completion.
- **The Dynamic PS (DPS)** is the power of charisma. Our talent is our voice, magnetism, and leadership.
- **The Spiritual PS (SPS)** is the power of intuition. Our talent lies in the 5 senses and our keen overall sense perception.

We all possess these five Performance Styles to different degrees, though we might be prone to act from one or two of them more often than the others. In fact, we usually identify with our strongest PS. As a Mental PS, for instance, you may be good at math, so you become a valued accountant. As an Emotional PS who's good at communication, you may become a successful entertainer, chef, or counselor. These are examples of good self-casting, where you have managed to match your career with your primary PS.

But there is also bad self-casting. You might be a Physical PS who loves action but falls into a boring desk job that you hate. Or you are a Spiritual PS who is given the job of office manager and can't handle the pressure. You might be a Dynamic PS who is forced to work under someone whose poor leadership skills annoy you. These are cases of being miscast.*

It is important to know your PS and how it fits the role(s) you play in your life. If your PS can't accomplish the task necessary for each role you are playing, you will need to change your PS…or the role. The overall objective, though, is to learn to use all 5 PS freely so you can match your PS to suit the needs of each situation. You may have no choice but to perform a job in which you feel miscast but learning to make it work is possible through this study. By utilizing all 5 PSs, you can avoid getting stuck or "caught up shit's creek without a paddle." Your paddle is versatility.

Your Comic vs. Tragic Character Traits

Each of the five Performance Styles has a comic and a tragic side. The Ancient Greeks were the first to recognize that human character is a duality, portraying us with comic and tragic masks. Though the scenery and costumes have changed, today centuries later, our divided self is still universally true. Comedy and tragedy are the timeworn dueling sides of the human heart.

We all have a comic side that's expansive, light-hearted, and constructive. We also have a tragic side that's restrictive, heavy-hearted, and destructive. In general, our comic side has positive tendencies and is poised to bring about a fortunate outcome, while our tragic side has negative tendencies and provokes unfortunate consequences. This classic duality keeps us floating between good and evil, happiness and sadness, and in effect, dictates how we see our world. Daily, if not moment-to-moment, we act from one side or the other. We take on various comic or tragic emotions to give character to our actions and are often unaware which side of our character we are acting from.

The tragic side of human character expresses the negative side of our nature. It is the side of us that is fearful, insecure, unhappy and immoral. We know tragedy as it relates to painful trials and tribulations that we must overcome individually. Sometimes our troubles seem insurmountable and we try to avoid them by ignoring their presence, only worsening their outcome. But as much as we try to keep tragedy out of our lives, it repeatedly overshadows our potential power. We get caught in its trap and let it consume us. We act and react in self-serving ways that cause harm and bring misfortune. Fearing the worst parts of ourselves, and not knowing how to access our best, we over-react or underplay, becoming moody, irritable, or artificial in order to stuff the ugliness back inside. We actually detest our tragic side and suppress it in ourselves and avoid it in others.

On the flip side is our comic ability, viewed as something good. It is the side of us that is confident, secure, happy and moral. Comedy offers us a break from the harsh, sharp edges of day-to-day living. Medical science has proven laughter is healing, and a brighter attitude in life can open us to the love we seek and encourage happier endings. In LPP, comedy brings us to our positive side. Our comedic side acts and reacts in ways that create joy, love, and strength of character. Our brighter side also has a full range of colors and shades to play with, from calm to exuberant. When we play our comic characters with good intent, we offer encouragement and pleasure to an otherwise unhappy heart. Though real life is not a series of constant mirth and happy endings, we can always endeavor to produce the best finales possible.

Understanding your comic vs. tragic character traits allows you to make emotional choices and play your roles in more productive ways when you realize that your current choice is not working. If you routinely act from the tragic side of your primary PS, your emotional character choices often cause creative blocks that make you feel bad. But if you make more suitable choices, you can use your creative skills to feel good.

Unfortunately, most of us play out a rather limited and unchanging cast of inner characters based on our primary Performance Style and habitually act out of one side of the comic/tragic duality. Our routine character choices give us a sense of safety and comfort, though we run the risk of becoming uninteresting and predictable, losing our creative spark.

Also, our habitual PS and character traits can at times conflict with those around us. Unaware of how we are acting, we can find ourselves embattled with friends, co-workers, or family members without realizing all we need to do is change our PS or character to turn a bad situation into a successful one.

Comedy and Tragedy are a fact of life. Understanding how and when to aptly use a comic or tragic character is the art. Sometimes fear or anger can be useful, sometimes courage or kindness. Which side of your character can bring you the best results in each situation? For instance, you may habitually play tragedy as your norm, running dark, knee-jerk reactions to everything. You might not stop to observe a better character choice in that moment.

Life Scenario: Example of the Tragic Side Taking Over

Julie often goes to the local bar to meet her friends for Happy Hour after work. It's Friday and she's had a stressful week and just wants to have some fun! She and her friends find a table in the middle of the action, order drinks, and start talking about…people at work, life partners or lack thereof, all the latest …and on and on. After a couple of drinks, they try to tackle the problems of the world. Julie has now had a few drinks more than usual on the belief her stress warrants it and she can finally get a good night's sleep.

After a few hours, she says her goodbyes and stumbles out to her car. She gets in, *"I'm cool…in controool…"* she thinks reassuring herself as she pulls out of her parking space…then CRUNCH! *"Ooopps…"* she says with a slight giggle. She carefully gets out of her car…" *Oh it's just a fender bender…But I'm sure the A-hole who belongs to this car will make a big deal out it…Damn, this could cost me a fortune,"* she imagines in her stupor.

She stares at both cars as she holds on tightly to her door. *"Should I just leave?"* she asks herself. *"Most people would!"* she thinks convincingly. *"If I fess-up, I could get a ticket for drunk driving…even though I'm not really drunk…Hmm…it really wasn't my fault – his car is sticking out – isn't it? I better get outta here and fast!"* And she leaves.

***

Three sheets to the wind, Julie has chosen to act out her tragic traits: 1) Drinking too much – indulgence; 2) Trying to drive knowing she was drunk – stupid; 3) Wrongly accusing another – lying; and 4) Leaving the scene of an accident – felony. Is this her character habit? Though she doesn't have fender benders every day, are there other situations where she over indulges, blames others, defends her own wrong actions and avoids reality? Probably.

***

Becoming aware of what desires and motivations drive your character choices is crucial in making more effective performance and character changes. For example: If you feel angry, you instinctively act angry and are seen by others as an angry character. Is "anger" your character choice? Would "assertive" be better? LPP therefore puts a lot of emphasis on personal character study to help you see how the comic and tragic character choices you make impact the outcome of situations in your life. Using the LPPractices, you will gain the awareness to effectively and honestly change character when necessary and expand your range of choices.

STUDYING THE FIVE PERFORMANCE STYLES

The remainder of this Act is devoted to learning about each Performance Style, including the comic and tragic traits in each. This self-knowledge will help you understand your specific life performance habits and how they impact the outcome of your daily performance. You will get to know the parts of yourself in an accurate way, so you can begin to recognize when to enhance or change them. With this clarity, you can start to make better choices and utilize more of yourself. You will also recognize why you are attracted to one person and repelled by another.

As you come to know all five Performance Styles, you will see that you can be brilliant on the comic side in one PS and a total screw-up on the tragic side in another. For example:

- You can be a great business leader in your comic Dynamic, but sexually abusive on the tragic side of your Physical PS.
- You can be a wonderful teacher on the comic side of your Mental PS, but completely absent-minded when it comes to finances on your tragic Spiritual PS.
- You can be all about saving the earth's environment on your comic Physical side and tragically blocked when it comes to communicating with your partner on your comic Emotional side.

We are all complex characters in the way we act, but if you learn all five Performance Styles, you will have a better chance at unraveling the mystery of your many selves. You can become aware of your own creative blocks and skills and develop more compassion for others and yourself. Why limit your Human Instrument when you can expand your playing field and function from all Five PSs within you?

For example, if you are primarily a Mental PS, and you notice how you tend to have tragic character traits in your Physical PS, like aggression, you can rehearse some of the PPS comic traits, such as being productive or responsive, to help counteract your tragic ones. Learning the five PSs helps you turn your character flaws into character flairs.

In addition, when you familiarize yourself with each PS, you won't feel intimidated by or react critically toward those who have a different style from your own. You will be able to recognize their comic and tragic character traits and interact with them in more confident, enjoyable ways.

There are also times when you might adopt a new PS to impress someone, then discover that since it is not your normal style, it is difficult to "keep up the act." Or you might choose a partner whose comic PS traits attract you, only to later discover that he or she has tragic traits you didn't sign up for. After a while, since you initially acted in ways that were not natural to your PS, you discover that you are living their life rather than the one you want for yourself given your talents.

These things happen because we are unfamiliar with our five Performance Styles and haven't learned to recognize them in ourselves, much less in others. Instead, we live our lives subject to the whims of external conditions without awareness of what PS best suits the situation.

When the Empty Stage Awareness becomes your true identity and you are not attached to a fixed self-image, you can access your versatility with greater ease. The ultimate goal is to know your Human Instrument well enough to make effective on-the-spot changes when necessary.

SCENE 3 YOUR PERFORMANCE STYLE PROFILE

Happy is Your Grace that can translate the stubbornness
of fortune into so quiet and so sweet a style.

~ As You Like It

Before we review each of the 5 Performance Styles, it is useful and fun to evaluate yourself with this Performance Style Profile. This will help you determine the degree to which you use and possess each Performance Style. Use pencil or make copies because you might want to take this profile again after learning about and rehearsing your undeveloped Performance Styles. Retaking the profile at a later date might also provide insight into how you have changed and what you might like to practice next.

Just as knowing the mix of chemical compounds in a bottle helps you determine its potency, knowing the varying mix of each PS within you helps you determine the potency of your talents. When you know which of the Performance Styles you activate most often in your daily activities – e.g., which are your primary, secondary, and successive styles – you can understand why you make certain career choices in your work, the way in which you relate to family and friends, and even your choice of personal interests. You can also use this Performance Style Profile to assess (from your own point of view) the Performance Styles of your family, friends, and business relations. This could help you understand them and relate to them better.

PERFORMANCE STYLE PROFILE

Evaluation Point Scale

1 – *I do this most of the time.*

1/2 – *Sometimes, depending upon the situation.*

0 – *I seldom, if ever, act this way.*

Part 1

This indicates the way you view yourself performing in your daily life. Use the evaluation point scale as shown on the prior page to assess the level of identification you have with the following descriptives.

Are you?

1) _____ a hard worker		14) _____ a loner
2) _____ witty		15) _____ influential
3) _____ dramatic		16) _____ competitive
4) _____ free spirited		17) _____ serious/intense
5) _____ powerful		18) _____ indulgent
6) _____ athletic		19) _____ idealistic
7) _____ insightful		20) _____ romantic
8) _____ empathetic		21) _____ practical
9) _____ altruistic (unselfish)		22) _____ thoughtful
10) _____ high-risk activities		23) _____ conversational
11) _____ routine oriented		24) _____ perceptive
12) _____ a worrier		25) _____ enterprising
13) _____ optimistic		

Now, transfer your evaluation points from the above descriptives into its matching number below, and then add up each column for your results:

A 1	B 1	C 1	D 1	E 1
1) ____	2) ____	3) ____	4) ____	5) ____
+ 6) ____	+ 7) ____	+ 8) ____	+ 9) ____	+10) ____
+11) ____	+12) ____	+13) ____	+14) ____	+15) ____
+16) ____	+17) ____	+18) ____	+19) ____	+20) ____
+21) ____	+22) ____	+23) ____	+24) ____	+25) ____
= ____	= ____	= ____	= ____	= ____

Part 2

This indicates the things you are attracted to, but do not necessarily act out yourself. Use the same system of assigning points:

Evaluation Point Scale
1 – *I watch this genre frequently.*
1/2 – *I watch this genre sometimes, depending upon the situation.*
0 – *I seldom, if ever, watch this genre.*

Assuming you are watching a great production in each genre below, rate how you gravitate toward each category.

1)	slap-stick comedy		14)	avant garde (off-beat)
2)	smart humor		15)	heroic epics
3)	situation comedy		16)	war films (conflict)
4)	fairy tales/fantasy		17)	mystery (who done it?)
5)	political programs		18)	romantic/musical comedy
6)	action/adventure		19)	sci-fi, futuristic
7)	news shows		20)	historical drama
8)	food shows		21)	risqué, or bathroom humor
9)	religious/bible stories		22)	classical (cultured arts)
10)	intrigue/danger		23)	dramatic TV series
11)	sports programs (football...)		24)	supernatural or horror
12)	satire, parody		25)	business programs
13)	talk shows			

Now transfer your evaluation points from above numbers into its matching number below. Then add up each column for results:

A 2	B 2	C 2	D 2	E 2
1)	2)	3)	4)	5)
+ 6)	+ 7)	+ 8)	+ 9)	+10)
+11)	+12)	+13)	+14)	+15)
+16)	+17)	+18)	+19)	+20)
+21)	+22)	+23)	+24)	+25)
=	=	=	=	=

Part 3: Take a Guess at Your PS

Before you add up your LPP Profile results, rank the following according to how you view yourself in the Performance Style you use most regularly to the least.

Choose from: **MENTAL PS, EMOTIONAL PS, PHYSICAL PS, DYNAMIC PS, SPIRITUAL PS**

1. _____

2. _____

3. _____

4. _____

5. _____

Part 4: Scoring Your Performance Style Profile Results

To learn the degrees to which you possess each Performance Style, add together the numerical result of column A in both Parts 1 & 2 and put the final number into the A space below. Do the same with the remaining columns B, C, D, and E.

_____ **A = PHYSICAL PS – THE POWER OF THE BODY**

_____ **B = MENTAL PS – THE POWER OF THE INTELLECT**

_____ **C = EMOTIONAL PS – THE POWER OF EXPRESSION**

_____ **D = SPIRITUAL PS – THE POWER OF INTUITION**

_____ **E = DYNAMIC PS – THE POWER OF CHARISMA**

HOW TO USE THE PROFILE

1. To determine your most dominant PS, which score is your highest? Which is your second highest? Third? Etc.

2. Compare "Your Guess" results with what the Performance Style Profile showed.

3. Go back and look at Part 1 again. Think about how you scored each characteristic.

   - If you gave yourself a "0," note what that characteristic brings up for you, if anything. Is there dislike or other feelings toward it?

   - If you scored more than a "0" on any of them, examine why and how. For example, if you said you are a "hard worker," what makes you say this? Do you enjoy physical labor and exercise? Do you labor at a desk? How does hard work make you feel? Or, in the case of "dramatic," do you use drama because you need attention or because you need to get a point across? Do you need to reexamine or change anything? Do your answers comply with your present self-image? What might you change?

4. Now notice in Part 2 if there are any genres that correlate well with your PSs.

   - Do your entertainment choices stimulate your tragic or comic traits?

   - Do your choices reflect parts you would like to play in life but don't?

   - Would you like to explore new genres? Which and why?

5. The practice here is to notice your reactions and motivation for all your profile answers and think about how you use them. If you changed your answer, would you be better off? What PS do you want or need to practice and why? Honest creative critiquing leads to improved performance.

6. Now read the rest of Act II. Then revisit this page.

Appreciation of Your Human Instrument

Not all of us have full use of our human instrument. Some of us have physical, mental and emotional disabilities, yet function with a greater spirit than many of us. In truth, we all operate in life at a disadvantage because we have disabled parts of our self that could help us function to a fuller degree.

Understanding the following 5 Performance Styles gives you a deeper appreciation of the life you have been given. It keeps us from self-pity because we learn to utilize the missing parts we never knew we had. So, regardless of your particular instrument's condition, valuing what you have and how you treat yourself helps you gain respect for the limitations and talents in us all.

SCENE 4 THE MENTAL PERFORMANCE STYLE (MPS) – THE POWER OF THE INTELLECT

There is nothing either good or bad but thinking makes it so.

~ Hamlet

GENERAL ORIENTATION

Likes structure, elegance, classical art, complexity, details, perfection, beliefs, tradition, theory, order, ideas, concepts, systems, technology

OBJECTIVES

To think things out, be right, gain acknowledgment, show intelligence, learn new information, have mental control

TALENTS

Teaching, writing, composing, mathematics, finance, electronics, science, law, strategy, research, debate, investigation

ENJOYMENTS

Music, chess, board games, golf, reading, languages, studying, puzzles, mystery, interesting discussions, religion

COMIC CHARACTER TRAITS (CREATIVE SKILLS)

Logic, focused, clear-thinking, precise, analytical, patient, attentive, kind, inquisitive, thoughtful, considerate, open-minded

TRAGIC CHARACTER TRAITS (CREATIVE BLOCKS)

Resentful, worry, anger, judgmental, argumentative, cynical, intense, prejudice, intolerant, suspicious, close-minded

THE COMIC MPS

When acting from our comic traits, we display mental alertness, intelligence, good comprehension, listening skills, and thoughtfulness. We are knowledgeable, upright, and operate from a sense of moral conscience. We have a strong ability to focus and can stay involved for hours at a time. The comic MPS is also a diligent note-taker and list-maker. Structure and strategy make us feel secure.

With single-pointedness, we can project our thoughts without saying a word. That talent is great when we want to convey a creative idea. We think on our feet and are quick to come up with ideas and solutions to things that require reasoning and clear judgment.

We have a sophisticated sense of humor and are quick with a witty remark. Aside from intelligence, wit is one of our most sociable qualities, which can make us popular at parties. We are also very effective in the education and culture of others, as we love to teach and are good teachers. We are the inventors, the creative and progressive thinkers, the scholars, the mathematicians and scientists. We love electronics, smart gadgetry, and must have the latest devices. We are the techies and the statistic experts of the world.

Because we like to examine all sides of a situation, we are good at business management. We are the best when it comes to problem solving, logically and lucidly figuring it out. If we don't know the answer to something, we will spend hours, days and months trying to figure it out and ultimately make it successful. Steve Jobs of Apple fame was one of those tenacious MPSs. Like him, many of us wear eyeglasses, as much of the time we are in our heads thinking and processing so having an extra set of lenses assists us in seeing the outside world with clarity and sharpness.

The comic MPS likes an orderly desk as well as a clean office and home. We can't think if things are too messy. We can be quite sharp and meticulous, noticing the details of most everything. Others find us either interesting for this trait or infuriating. We enjoy perfection and, with a discerning eye, strive for excellence in most everything we do.

The pure MPS is naturally elegant. Our clean, lean and intelligent approach to design comes across in our chic understated, but sophisticated style in clothes, cars, and in our work and living environments. We often like the modern look, but if we enjoy other styles, it is usually attributed to its value in antiquity or class.

Mentally alert, we watch the news to keep up on world affairs and have no qualms in telling others our beliefs about each news item. Yet, we are also interested in others, in their ideas and opinions. We love stimulating conversation. We are kind and patient with those who are not as smart as us. We have a wonderful way of collaborating, as any great idea is an idea to build on. Even if it is not our concept, we give credit where credit is due and help develop it.

We like to read and research. We have fun being the first to tell you about the latest discovery, high-tech invention, or news item. Having gathered all the information, we take delight in sharing our opinion about things…after all, *opinions are us*. Some of us use our comic wit on the theatrical stage to present our clever views about the state of the world, politics, or the human dilemma, even if it does stir controversy. In these ways, we use humor to make people think about important issues. The funny thing is we are usually spot on.

THE SUPREME COMIC MPS

As supreme comic MPSs, we are the Nobel Prize winners in science and literature. We invent and discover new ways to make life better and write about things that stimulate innovative thinking. At our absolute best, we use our minds, as Albert Einstein said, *"To raise new questions, new possibilities, to regard old problems from a new angle…"* With conscientious purpose, we use our brainpower to encourage intelligent thinking and progressive discoveries. It may at times seem that we condescendingly challenge people and their ideas. However, by using thought-provoking methods, we make people push their own mental boundaries.

We research medicines that will advance medical science. We write music that soothes and sweetens the heart or stirs emotion. We write books, articles and film scripts that raise important questions and rouse stimulating ideas and feelings in others. We design informative programs and invent technology that will advance work and living conditions. As an example, inspired by his wife and mother's interest in education, Microsoft's Bill Gates has, at this time in his life, focused his intellectual expertise on worldwide educational issues.

As supreme comic MPSs, we are the ones who think up ingenious strategies that will constructively change the way the world operates. It was Apple's Steve Jobs who said, *"The ones who are crazy enough to think that they can change the world, are the ones who do."* Yes, we Mental Performance Styles, are the geniuses, each in our own way.

THE TRAGIC MPS

When an MPS is acting from the tragic side, we can be very "judge-mental," holding resentment and contempt toward someone longer than any other PS. We can be quite unforgiving in that way. We take satisfaction in our prejudices, as this intolerance seems to feed our need to be right. We have a hard time taking advice and become snobbishly arrogant if you dare to contradict us.

We can't be told anything because we already know it. If a colleague tells us they had a great new idea, we let them know we've already had it. If we don't like their idea, we tell them it won't work and why! We have all the answers…and everyone else is wrong or stupid. If you call us stupid, we will snub you for all time! Unfortunately, our snobbery and critical attitude could alienate good friends. *"But then,"* we say, *"my brain is my best friend, so who needs friends?"*

We are always on time and HATE it when others are late. We think, *"Time is MY precious commodity."* Others must conform to our way of seeing things. If someone opposes our view, our comic wit tragically counters with cutting, but amusing, tart humor. If that someone pisses us off – we have been known to lose our cool. Unable to deal with the self-image of being wrong, we use sarcasm to insult and prove our mental supremacy. Some of us are traditionalists. Holding to what is tried and true, we find it hard to break out of our established concepts.

Interestingly, we are hardest on ourselves. Our expectations are great – after all, we are brilliant! We don't make mistakes! However, when we don't live up to our perfection, we begin to feel disappointment, as if we have failed. This self-image can become a growing worry that causes constant dissatisfaction with almost every situation in life. To regain personal authority, we begin projecting the judgment we feel about ourselves onto others, so that others are the wrong and stupid ones. In our self-judgment, we begin thinking others are judging us…and eventually they do. This makes us angry and bitter.

Another tragic performance issue we have is that we think too much. We are always absorbed in our own thoughts. We categorize and try to nail things down that are by nature unsubstantial. We must have answers! Needing to convince and be accurate, we harden our ideas, leaving little room to be flexible or open. Locked in our mind's little black box theatre and sure of being right, we continue thinking in very controlled ways. This self-imposed stress squeezes our brain and creates psychological tension. We can lose our sense of color and movement, as everything in our world becomes intense, linear, angular, and black or white. Our life takes on hard edges and, in our rigidity, we can't see the options in the tiny cracks between thoughts.

We can also be cold and unsympathetic to the needs of others. In fact, we live in our heads and often don't even notice others. If anyone argues with us, we become sharp-tongued and short-tempered, spewing out clever remarks intended to hurt. For us, it is hard to hear criticism; unable to admit we're hurt, we react by attacking the person with accusations about them. We can quickly "go-off" on someone for seemingly no good reason, surprising an unsuspecting loved one or colleague. Resentful if no one acknowledges our intelligence, we cut communications with them. Giving the nod to someone else's intelligence is very hard – so forget collaboration.

The Extreme Tragic MPS

The extreme tragic MPS can be verbally abusive and downright mean and spiteful. If wronged, our defiant character is anger. Our brilliance can design shrewd schemes of malice toward others. Our intelligent and elegant way with language is used to lie, cheat, and mastermind fraudulent strategies, such as wealth manager Bernie Madoff, who stole millions from his clients. Whether it is about politics, religion, or lifestyle, our belief systems are so strong that we disdainfully separate ourselves from those who do not believe as we do. Our bright mind becomes tarnished with intolerant beliefs about others, building into hatred and eating away at our clarity of mind. All this can make us highly suspicious of others, when in truth we are the ones to suspect.

Living on the extreme tragic side of our mental power, we control people by projecting penetrating thoughts of disapproval and anger at them. Though our subject may not be aware of how deeply our thoughts have penetrated them, they may nonetheless feel weak, inferior, and walk on eggshells when in our company. Even when our targeted person is out of physical proximity, our judgmental projections linger and veil their sense of well-being. Our nastiness is felt without verbal exchange and people may do our bidding to avoid our wrath. That is how powerful our thoughts can be. We commit tele-cerebral blackmail.

Carried to extremes, we can get fixated on a person or issue and focus on it to the point of ruin. We can become phobic and mentally deranged with fits of madness, laughter, or violent verbal outbursts. We might display unreasonable emotions and talk of crazy ideas. We may not be able to restrain ourselves from saying and doing things that alarm others. Like a mad scientist, we enjoy the sense of being the superior expert, but are unaware of our irrationality. Our behavior can become uncontrollable and cause friends and family to call for the police or a psychiatrist to bring over a strait jacket! In the eyes of those around us, we have gone mad.

But if we are not a hateful-type mad person, we may be an intelligent MPS who has strange idiosyncrasies that make us appear "mad as a hatter," but still lovable and forgivable due to our genius, or our social and political status. This is said of such people as Winston Churchill, British Prime Minister during WWII, who reportedly enjoyed parading around nude in his office. There are many of us who have odd notions – like sleeping with our shoes on, or weird and neurotic tendencies. If not designed to hurt anyone, all these peculiarities reflect the strange concepts we ascribe to our thinking.

HOW DO YOU CAST YOURSELF?

Creative Blocks

[ ] You can be so focused on your ideas and projects that you ignore everything & everyone.

[ ] Do you anger easily and say unkind things?

Creative Skills

[ ] You can focus on your projects and ideas, and still attend to the world around you.

[ ] You recognize anger as a recurring habit when challenged. You practice kindness.

SCENE 5 THE EMOTIONAL PERFORMANCE STYLE (EPS) – THE POWER OF FEELING

O, throw away the worser part of it, and
live the purer with the other half.

~ Hamlet

GENERAL ORIENTATION

Likes entertainment, beauty, art, self-expression, relationships, communication, community, family, children, animals

OBJECTIVES

To touch, connect, have an effect on others, love and be loved, enjoy life and friends, be noticed

TALENTS

Collaboration, sociability, decorating, entertaining, psychology, counseling, visual & performing arts, design, imagination

ENJOYMENTS

Movies, theatre, cooking, dining out, friendships, theatrics, shopping, intimacy & heart connections

COMIC CHARACTER TRAITS (CREATIVE SKILLS)

Happy, warm, enthusiastic, supportive, loving, empathic, expressive, affectionate, creative, artistic

TRAGIC CHARACTER TRAITS (CREATIVE BLOCKS)

Scattered, needy, dramatic, talkative, gossipy, insecure, defensive, shamed, easily hurt, negative

THE COMIC EPS

The EPS is the aspect of our instrument that has an honest need for love. When an EPS lives on the comic side, we work hard to make relationships work. We learn to give and take, disagree and find a common ground. When it comes to intimacy, we don't just want sex but are looking for something deeper and long lasting. We want and need someone to share our life experiences, and we are very giving to our loved ones. For some, raising children and caring for animals seem to complete our enjoyment of life. Love makes us feel safe. We enjoy family, being around lots of people, togetherness, and creating fun-loving activities that are bonding. We like creative and artistic careers.

We are all about happy endings. As a comic EPS, we have *joie de vivre*, a natural joy for life itself and it is a joy to be around us. It gives us great pleasure to make people happy. As part of that, we are great communicators. The EPS is a sympathetic friend with an understanding ear for listening to problems. We have an ability to connect and collaborate with others. Because we choose to love, we are forgiving and accepting of everyone's character flaws.

Most EPS people have an eye for attractive things and we use our imagination in artistic ways. We love to make life beautiful. We decorate our homes to display our sense of beauty and offer a warm and welcoming atmosphere. We love to entertain, feed the masses (or oneself) and throw parties. We like bringing people together so they can make loving and useful connections. We are warm hearted and supportive of one another's lives, loves and work.

The EPS make good psychologists, human resource managers, realtors, artists, chefs, professional actors and entertainers. We are good with any work requiring social interaction, creativity, and artistry. As a comic EPS, we are easy to work with and are good colleagues. We develop our power by stretching and learning to use our feelings in sincere and responsive ways.

THE SUPREME COMIC EPS

We have an enormous well-spring of love within us and because we can be expressive, others feel it when in our presence. We add color, feeling, and texture to otherwise bland situations and issues. We radiate enthusiasm and happiness, which makes people want to join in our experience. We are powerful expressions of love and joy.

Because of our ability to express, we are the lighthearted comedy writers, beauty-oriented artists, designers, entertainers, directors, and creators who contribute to cultural advancement. If we are not artist ourselves, we might be an involved enthusiast or supporter of the arts and humanities. We want our children to grow up not only with an academic education, but also with creative abilities. We may offer tutelage to others by joining or forming organizations and institutions that promote the arts and entertainment. We "absolutely get" the value of art in daily life.

If we are an entertainer, we might win a Golden Globe or other award for creative projects. Yet many of us are not solely interested in entertainment. The supreme comic EPS is interested in advancing human relations – personally, locally and internationally. As exceptional communicators, we use various media to expose the human indignities existing all over the world. Because we know happiness within ourselves, we want others to feel happy as well.

Because we consider the human factor in most all situations, we are motivated to raise public awareness about horrific real-life situations in the hopes that we can create positive change in humankind. We feel deeply for people who have been marginalized, abused, or are sick and hungry, so we try to create opportunities for them. We also like to bring encouraging stories of different cultures to light and present their artists who might otherwise not be seen. Our work is designed to bring joy, beauty, love and understanding to the human heart. To this end our efforts win us personal rewards and public awards for contributions in the Arts and Humanities.

THE TRAGIC EPS

Since we feel things more keenly than others, the tragic EPS will often take things and people too personally. Due to our insecurity, we are easily hurt and offended. We are extremely susceptible to Emotional Osmosis*. Almost like a sponge, we take on other people's moods and feelings. In fact, it can be confusing and agonizing if we haven't established awareness of whose feelings are whose.

Love is the end-all for us and we can spend a lifetime searching for our "soul mate." Curiously, if we haven't learned self-love, we may find ourselves moving in and out of ill-chosen relationships and marriages. As tragic emotionals, we can become flirtatious and grasp at whoever is glancing our way. We can smother admirers with our need for love, get attached to those who show us affection, and have a very hard time with separation.

If we have loved and been hurt, when love does come our way, we might dismiss it with self-defeating reactions. We either don't feel worthy of love, or we fear it and all the things it implies to us – inevitable loss, vulnerability, intimacy and sacrifice. Our quest for true love becomes an ongoing theme fueling our attachment to emotional drama. We don't know we are searching for self-love – the inner love light within us all.

Our emotionality can throw us off balance and make us feel needy, scattered, and overwhelmed, blocking our ability to relate to others as well as we would like. We might be perceived as too zealous, overly dramatic and/or obsessively involved with other people's lives. We excite quickly, cry easily, and react impulsively, which can increase our delusion. When overreacting to the moment, we might later say, *I'm sorry, I wasn't feeling well that day.* We learn to make excuses for our tragic characters.

Though we are exceptionally good at entertaining, we can get overly elaborate and overplay the necessary preparations for a party or work project. We get so emotionally invested in what we are doing that we become overwhelmed with angst, even illness, for fear things won't go well. Though our comic side's motivation is to make things wonderful for others, if we are honest, we will see that our unloved tragic character needs applause. That unappreciated part of us needs approval and compliments to feel good.

Emotional tragedians will engage others in endless, mindless chatter empty of substance. We need to fill our mindstage because silence makes us uncomfortable. We have an attraction to excitability – it's the love of drama syndrome. This incites rambling thoughts, so we get scattered in our responsibilities and activities. As EPS tragics, curbing our appetite for exaggeration can save us from our embellished expectations and the daunting downslide.

We can also shoulder feelings of guilt and shame. Because we feel bad about ourselves, we are frequently unhappy and project our misery onto everyone and everything. In an effort to feel more acceptable, we gossip about other people's unacceptable traits. In order to not take responsibility for our own actions, we "guilt-sling," laying blame on some other terrible, horrible, shameful person. Unaware of our motives, we want others to look as bad as we feel.

Our insecurity can cause us to hide our faults and limitations, fearing intimidation by people we believe to be important. Thus, we try to impress them with our contrived performance. Our insecurity can also cause us to misread the slightest gesture or words from another. Nursing our emotional wounds, we communicate our hurt by performing over-the-top dramas and are not aware of how our performance looks, much less how we might be affecting others.

If creatively unfulfilled, we like to validate our self-worth by retelling compliments we've received or reviewing wonderful deeds we have done so that others will know how wonderful we are. Great is the EPS tragedian's desperate need for love, attention, and sympathy.

Others of us are emotionally repressed and find it hard to express what we are really feeling. Sensitive to hurt, we may not want to hurt someone else's feelings by speaking out. Deep down we might know how much we are holding in and may not trust ourselves to express our true feelings. We fear what would happen if we let it out, or be embarrassed about how we really feel – so we stuff it.

Another issue we have is that if someone criticizes us, rather than taking it as a grateful cue for character development, we become defensive. We make up stories supporting our actions and dismiss suggestions from others. We tell everyone every little feeling we have as our way of being honest. We don't know how to be honest with ourselves, which is vital to a balanced emotional life.

More than any other PS, the tragic EPS can run the gamut of emotions from feeling unbelievably fantastic to feeling like the dirt on a dungeon floor. Innately we have a big heart, though we must guard against times when it blubbers too much. These characteristics and more can cause creative blocks within us, obstructing our joy for life and weakening our relations with others.

The Extreme Tragic EPS

The Emotional Extremist can react with unpredictable behavior, producing many kinds of precarious situations. Our erratic feelings cause erratic actions that trigger everything from small mishaps to fatal accidents. Given our susceptibility to Emotional Osmosis, in our extreme EPS display, our volatile emotionality can affect others adversely. We frequently create disastrous and painful situations due to emotional unevenness. These extremes often turn into self-loathing and we can become non-functional.

Though at heart we are givers, living on the extremely tragic side, we wish for more than our hearts are capable of giving. We can sink so deeply into negativity that we become paranoid. Somewhere along the line, for whatever reasons, we developed feelings of worthlessness and not being good enough in the eyes of others and never will be. As a result, we are never satisfied with ourselves. Feeling powerless, we unconsciously rehearse "the good-for-nothing loser" or "the walking wounded," relying on others for our wellbeing. We become needy and burdensome. Unable to help ourselves, we exist in this pathetic, hopeless state until something happens, one way or the other.

The result is that we may act out in desperate attention-getting ways. We do things to distract others from what they are doing and scream to be noticed. We pull all sorts of antics, from dressing up in flamboyant ways to considering suicide. Feeling only our own unhappiness, our craving for love and acceptance will make us do anything to satisfy our needs.

The awful part about it is that even when we are having a good time, we never get enough. Because deep down, we feel so hollow, our need for attention and gratification is insatiable. Without an approach for reaching a sense of "equipoise," we are prone to extremes, excessive euphoria and high drama, or we fall into the depths of despair when things don't work out to our liking. Whether suffering from unrequited love or unfulfilled creativity, this emotional roller coaster steals our power to express our beauty.

How do you cast yourself?

Creative Blocks
- [ ] You are creatively unsatisfied; feel disappointed if things do not go your way.
- [ ] You complain and gossip about the faults of others or misinterpret facts.
- [ ] You get defensive when someone suggests you are wrong or ill-mannered.
- [ ] Your pride may not let you try things. You may not be good enough; it's paralyzing.

Creative Skills
- [ ] You have an artistic flair and express yourself without expectation. Creativity flows.

Creative Skills (cont'd)

[ ] You approve of yourself. You see the talent in others and applaud their triumphs.

[ ] You appreciate that others have corrected you and thank them for their observations.

[ ] You are not afraid to try new things, you take pride and interest in expanding your life.

SCENE 6 THE PHYSICAL PERFORMANCE STYLE (PPS) – THE POWER OF THE BODY

O, it is excellent to have a giant's strength, but
it is tyrannous to use it like a giant.

~ Measure for Measure

GENERAL ORIENTATION

Likes action, competition, hard work, a plan of action, tasks, organization, practicality, fitness

OBJECTIVES

To be the strongest, accomplish things, to win, play hard, get the job done, live a healthy lifestyle

TALENTS

Healing bodywork, massage, surgeon, fixing things, mechanics, combat, rescue work, construction, sports

ENJOYMENTS

Baseball, football, gardening, TV, helping others, sex, exercise, dance, alcohol, playing hard, travel, motorcycles, motorhomes

COMIC CHARACTER TRAITS (CREATIVE SKILLS)

Disciplined, reliable, loyal, brave, assertive, protective, body strong, organizational, helpful

TRAGIC CHARACTER TRAITS (CREATIVE BLOCKS)

Tough, dense, stubborn, vulgar, tactless, aggressive, jealous, anxious, gullible, promiscuous, resistant

THE COMIC PPS

Our talent is our body. We use it to accomplish practical and sometimes heroic activities. We have the grace of a dancer and/or the physique of an athlete. Physically strong, we take action quickly and are flexible in movement. Being disciplined, we are "The Doers" who like to fix what's broken, organize and build things. Some of us have lean athletic bodies while others of us are muscular and full-bodied.

Our resolve is to maintain a healthy body and to function at our optimum. Our motto is, "You can do this!" and "Do it! Do it now!" With our focus on the body, most of us are into physical fitness – working out at the gym, biking, running, and other types of exercise. Those of us who have a more warrior-like disposition might join the military, go to a shooting range, or take up disciplines like boxing or a martial art that also offers us a spiritual view. Some of us find dance and yoga to be our physical activity.

For many of us, our mission is to dutifully serve others and get the job done. We like ground rules to help us tangibly complete and accomplish things in the world. Life is simple that way and working on behalf of others makes us feel good.

However, we have little patience with those who aren't physically active. We are action-driven and need to experience solid, tangible results – otherwise we have no value! We are good organizers and like performing whatever job presents itself. When someone has done something admirable, we yell out, "Good job!!!" Action-oriented and high on adrenaline, we make "things" happen! And don't worry – we've got your back!

Discipline is one of our main characters. It keeps us going and helps us reach our goals. We know that training in anything requires self-discipline. Akin to rehearsal, once training is complete, the doing becomes easy. Yet, our comic side has also learned to guard against becoming too regimented. Experience tells us that routines can make things boring. We know that certain jobs can become dangerous when we go on autopilot. So, we add carefulness to our list of disciplines.

Love relationships must be sexual, as a physical connection is of the utmost importance. For us, great sex heightens and accelerates our love. We also demonstrate our love by physically doing things for one another. Taking care of people in our lives is one of our duties – as caretakers we feel useful and honorable. Because we have great regard for the body, we eat healthy and are great healers. The Comic

Physical demonstrates the part of the human instrument that is grounded and functional. We respect the environment and do whatever we can to take care of the planet. We are salt of the earth people and embody fundamental earthly goodness.

We have street smarts, play team sports like baseball and football; some of us like to drive hard, ride motorcycles, drive RV's, and trucks. Some of us sport tattoos. We don't mind working in the trenches, planting the land, or doing construction. We love animals and care for them as our close friends. Though sometimes raunchy or slapstick goofy, we have a fun-loving sense of humor and like to play practical jokes on people. Even when people don't think we're very funny, we'll laugh at our own jokes – we get a kick out of ourselves! We are out for fun, just plain ole fun!

THE SUPREME COMIC PPS

We are the Olympic Medal Winners, the ones who transport the human body beyond ordinary actions to extraordinary feats. Our energy is like a bolt of lightning when we run, dance, and move. We are the valiant soldiers and civilians who win the Medal of Honor for our bravery. We are fighters! We will fight for our countries, and loyal in duty, readily go to war to ensure the safety of our families and community. We are the heroes and heroines who use our bodies to help and defend others. As nurses, acupuncturists, surgeons, and other kinds of body healers, we save lives. We work tirelessly, even putting our own life at risk to save another's.

We inspire people with our eagerness to accomplish our goals, do a good job, to protect and make the world a safer, healthier place. Endurance is our middle name. Taking the "never give up" stance, we see physical hardship as a challenge. We are the ones to call when you have a flat on the freeway at 3 a.m. We will come to the rescue! We will run into a burning building to save the lives of those trapped within. We will jump into a fight provoked by thugs to defend the one being attacked. We are the good men and women.

THE TRAGIC PPS

On the tragic side, the PPS is the part of us that will pick a fight and be abusive to others. Or we can be abusive to ourselves playing addictive roles like the Excessive Eater, whose self-abuse is gluttony, or the Drug Addict who blots out his clear mind, or the Drunk who self-destroys her liver and slowly weakens body function.

Self-abuse can also be subtle – from the nail biter to the one who is lazy and lets their body go, to the over-achiever who can't stop competing with himself. Even the stubborn refusal to make healthy character choices is a form of careless self-abuse. Whatever our choice of abuse, the overall effect restricts our health and relationships.

As a tragic Physical, our worst addiction is to violence. If we are not instigating it, then we like to watch it on TV, at the movies, or on the street corner. For entertainment, we rush to see the latest violent action-adventure movies and regularly watch TV shows that parade murder and crime before our eyes. We might even enjoy hearing about or being a bystander to a fight between friends, relatives, or business partners. Violence excites our adrenaline, providing a vicarious release of our own antagonism.

The tragic PPS is hooked on violence, although our comic side may paradoxically wonder why there is so much fear in the world. So, one part of us can abuse our body while our healthier side suffers it. In the end, if the addiction side wins out, we allow every part in us to identify with the addicted part. We see that as the only ME! Without the knowledge that we have other character choices for the roles we play, we lose sight of other parts of us that could be our saving grace. "Addiction" becomes the starring role in our personal theatre.

For some tragic PPS people, physical appearance becomes the obsession. Dissatisfied with what Mother Nature gave us, we go for elective cosmetic surgery. And there are those who work out obsessively at the gym, not for health and fitness, but with the intent of body building in Hulk-like proportions. Some justify this fixation on the body as a form of self-expression, a way to be creative. Others say it is simply the result of self-dissatisfaction – a fear of appearing ugly, weak, or old. Still some might do it to impress others, or to boost self-esteem. Whatever our motives, body altering has become an accepted societal practice. Recognizing your character's motivation for needing to change your appearance helps you make the healthiest decisions.

On the softer tragic side, the PPS can simply be a couch potato, slovenly lying around as others do all the work. We can start a project with great gusto and halfway through it, lose steam with a multitude of excuses for not finishing it. We can be undisciplined, uncouth, clumsy, and tactless. We can be so set in our familiar routines that when asked to do something even the slightest bit different, we look up with that "Duh?" expression on our face. This is not a male or female thing – it's about your comic or tragic choices in your Physical Performance Style. We all have this *Duh???* character in us.

THE EXTREME TRAGIC PPS

When acting from the extreme tragic side, the PPS can be downright thugs – hit men and women, killers, or even terrorists! This extreme part of our human instrument has the constitution and instinct to actually do "the kill" face to face. If not a killer, the extreme tragic PPSs are the thieves and rapists. Envy or aggression are our motivations to destroy. Our power is brainless – based on sheer physical force. We want the good life but haven't practiced our comic side enough to get it in positive ways.

Without thought of consequences, some of us can provoke a drunken brawl just because we don't like somebody or believe they insulted us. Because it loosens the body, alcohol is the drug of choice for Physical Extremes. We love our guns; whether our motive is protection against our fears, or to deliberately kill, we feel powerful and safe behind a gun. In our sadistic moments, our jokester takes pleasure in turning a so-called practical joke into a nasty experience – like offering someone a chair and pulling it out from under them when they sit down. When it comes to having sex, we need a conquest and can get brutishly kinky or commit perverted erotic acts. Tragically, we can be sexually stupid, selfish, and abusive.

As natural as caring and healing is to our Physical comedic side, abuse and violence can be automatic on our extreme tragic side – it's our "killer instinct." This killer in us is probably the most dimwitted part of human character. We don't know what we are doing, even if our act of killing is premeditated. We don't have the depth of wisdom to know what it means to kill – even those little insects that *bug* the hell out of us. The Physical Tragedian's extremism is profound ignorance, even though we may believe we have a multitude of good reasons to justify our killing. Killer instinct is in all of us. The extent to which we rehearse our "Killer" character displays our level of self-ignorance.

Because the thought themes in our Physical PS are regulated by simple instinct and our emotional range is limited to basic needs, this ignorance can bleed into stupidity and cause much harm in other aspects of our life performance, like relationships and work. Interest in learning and rehearsing our comic physical traits is essential for the extreme tragic Physical.

Whether you chose to play the good guy, or the bad girl really depends on your level of fear and ignorance. It also depends on your love of life. If you have no love or regard for your own life, you demonstrate it by thoughtless self-abuse and/or harming the lives of others. Ignorant of our real power, we go into our destroyer mode, to feel powerful. Pigheadedly we proclaim, *"Don't mess with me dude. I'm stronger than you!"* But what we don't get is that the extreme terror we project onto others is evidence of our cowardice – our unconscious fear of being weakened by love and defeated by life itself.

How do you cast yourself?

Creative Blocks

[ ] You are competitive; must win at all cost; to be the best; to accomplish, to prove your worth.

[ ] You get tough; unconsciously act without thinking of consequences.

Creative Skills

[ ] You have team spirit. You take loss with good nature and strife for win-win situations.

[ ] You see what's needed. Your basic instinct is to do good. You are dependable.

SCENE 7 THE DYNAMIC PERFORMANCE STYLE (DPS) – THE POWER OF CHARISMA

The abuse of greatness is when it disjoints remorse from power.
~ Julius Caesar

GENERAL ORIENTATION

Likes power, taking risks, ownership, passion, magnetism, glamor, adventure, ambition, success

OBJECTIVES

To be great, influential, have self-command, to prosper, be respected, be a leader, have privilege

TALENTS

The voice, motivational speaking, confidence, leadership, enterprise, politics, gambling, honor

ENJOYMENTS

Likes luxury, racecars, boating, airplanes, romance, seduction, travel, hunting, the exotic, grandeur

COMIC CHARACTER TRAITS (CREATIVE SKILLS)

Magnetism, inspirational, charm, empowering, devoted, courageous, diplomatic, respectful

TRAGIC CHARACTER TRAITS (CREATIVE BLOCKS)

Greedy, narcissistic, dishonest, possessive, tyrannical, cruel, intimidating, demanding, disrespectful

THE COMIC DPS

Each PS has its own form of power, and for the DPS, it's the power of magnetism – a charismatic presence which attracts people on a grand scale. As a comic

DPS, we captivate others through our voice and powerful presence. We have the kind of power that can excite the masses to war or elevate them to peace. We are also the passionate lovers of the world with irresistible romantic charm.

Acting from our comic side, we are established in our power and there is little need to prove our dominance over anyone. We are self-motivated and have an adventurous attitude toward life that gives us power to proceed without doubt. Content with life, we are devoted and generous to our loved ones and maintain a strong commitment to their welfare. In business, we are a valuable and stimulating asset to our colleagues and company because we are trustworthy. Whatever our own field of endeavor, we pursue our interests with passion and respect for others and our self.

Our greatest talent is our voice. Confident when we speak, our speech has both meaning and resonance for others. The comic DPS has stage-like presence; people notice when we walk into a room. It might be our impressive style or our natural sense of confidence. When we speak publicly, everyone in the audience feels we are talking to them personally. In conversation, we look directly into someone's eyes and they know we are interested in what they have to say.

Others see us as their role models and either want to rival or imitate us. If we intimidate others, it is not because we are physically threatening, but rather because of our self-command. A skillful comic DPS can withstand the bullets of character assassination from competitors while retaining respect toward them, and grateful for the praise of supporters. Maintaining integrity, we know our worth – not through a display of self-importance but from our natural confidence.

THE SUPREME COMIC DPS

We are the most prominent luminaries – the ethical politicians, bosses, entrepreneurs, and great leaders of the world. We are the magnanimous dignitaries and celebrities in any profession. We give what we can to charities, hospitals, and educational institutions because we want to give back, and, in turn, we become the recipients of charitable awards. The supreme comic DPS has the courage to take bold risks because we are not motivated by greed, but by generosity. We have no fear of loss as we have faith in our ability to manifest.

The comic DPS voice is awe-inspiring to hear; it is unique and fascinating in its tone and cadence. We are capable of rallying people around us to serve good causes and manifest great things. There is an allure in the sound of our voice that lets others know we are in command. We feel self-empowered and want to enable others by leading alliances for equal rights and supporting the underdog in finding their own voice. Our motivation is to empower others.

We are the diplomats in politics, religion, law, and business – and some of us even have the diplomacy of royalty. Our interest is in changing ineffectual and destructive global issues and making community a better place to live. Because of our charisma, we are the great negotiators and peacemakers. We have the personal command to mediate the best possible deal between opposing parties. We also know how to avoid and settle confused and conflicted interactions. We are very clear with ourselves about what and how we discuss the issues on the table.

As leaders ourselves, we like to nurture new leaders. Our main commitment is to inspire others to succeed in whatever promising ventures they choose. We know that sharing the limelight and facilitating the rich talents of others makes the world a happier and healthier place. We understand the process of *"you win some and you lose some,"* and hold no grudges. We just keep moving forward with dignity.

The supreme comic DPS excels at spearheading projects with certainty, as we are natural promoters. We are excellent at gathering the right people around us to do the right job. We know it takes collaboration to get something off the ground, so we are always appreciative of those with whom we work. Our aim is to build a better world and invest in talented people who are motivated to do the same.

We have a natural gravitation to the grand, the worldly, and some of us magnetize and enjoy abundant wealth. We have the talents to achieve fame and fortune. But not all of us need or want the limelight. Most of us who are Supreme Comic Dynamics are gratified to guide and motivate those around us, whether it is our children, clients, friends and family, or coworkers and local community.

THE TRAGIC DPS

But beware; the tragic DPS can charm you into buying a totally unneeded product or get you to do something that is against your better judgment. Our big display of personal power makes us feel and look important, which can easily convince an innocent follower or gullible co-worker to buy into our game.

Desire, bling, and romance fill the atmosphere around us, so we can be very seductive with our amorous moves. Even if we are in a committed relationship, we love to magnetize a new lover. But once the sweet perfume of passion dissipates, like a bee, we move on to the next sweet flower. Being a romantic, we are searching for the special, the extraordinary love, yet no one can live up to our own mirror's image. It's hard for us to love another deeply because when it comes to love, it's "all about ME."

We can be possessive and demanding in a relationship, causing friction and lack of freedom for our professed partner. This overbearing attitude causes confusion because when we shift to our comic side, we are lovingly generous. Which side should others believe? Should they believe the part of us trying to buy our love by "acting loving" or, the part who is truly giving from the heart? Generally, believe the side we display the most.

Though we may have a strong voice, for the tragic DPS, it can be loud and irritating and turn people off. Though we want to be important, our tragic character traits may weaken our power to follow through. In such a case, though we are attracted to fame and fortune, we can't always manifest it for ourselves. Instead, we put people on a pedestal and hang out with those we think are important and famous. The love of title, money, and prestige is what we value.

Being risk takers, we are passionate gamblers. Our unreliable impulses get us involved in shaky deals that promise huge gains. We like to play the stock market, the lottery, and other games with high stakes. The tragic DPS likes to live big but doesn't have the self-assurance and composure that belongs to our comic side. Instead, we gamble on slim odds in hopes of a quick, big success.

Tragic Dynamics can be ostentatious, flaunting money and possessions around to make a good impression. We play "important" giving off an air of "Assumed Nobility," yet underneath it all is the fear of being insignificant. We love to be respected for our greatness while discounting good people we see as beneath us.

As a tragic DPS, we have the same magnetizing talents as our comedic side, but we use them for our own selfish gain. We demand respect but show no respect for others. Because we are surrounded with an aura of power, we can attract the naïve into our business deals with promises of making them lots of money. We are capable of seducing clients and colleagues into our world, using their talents and discarding them as crudely as one would spit into the street gutter. We know how to steal another's power to empower ourselves, leaving our victim wasted and disempowered. We are motivated by greed and self-importance.

Egomania is the tragic DPS's biggest challenge. Mirror-gazing is one of our favorite pastimes. Unaware of how we *really* look, we can often be seen checking our façade in the rearview mirror of our car. We can get very wrapped up in self-adoration and spend hours trying to find the best face to wear that day. The Dynamic Tragedian's motto is – *What's in it for ME?*

THE EXTREME TRAGIC DPS

At the extreme, we are the dictators and tyrants of the world. Of course, who could forget Marlon Brando's famous line from The Godfather, *"I'm gonna make him an offer he can't refuse."* And in reality, think of the Mafia's John Gotti ordering his lackeys to knock off those who couldn't return his favors. And there's WWII's dictator, Adolf Hitler, who ordered the extermination of six million Jews, or China's Mao Tse Tung who was accountable for the death of millions of Tibetans and Chinese during his so-called Cultural Revolution.

If you think the extreme tragic DPS is just a male thing, remember Biljana Plavsic of the Serb Republic, who led Bosnia-Herzegovina into the Serbian genocides. She claimed ethnic cleansing was "a natural thing" and six million Serbs needed to die.

Presently there are plenty of modern world leaders ordering the deaths of nationals simply because they want to globally brand their power and seize control of people and land that is not theirs. We are the infamous examples of extremely tragic DPSs. We don't commit the murders ourselves, but attract and activate others to perform the kill. We are particularly vile individuals because we are not just responsible for the deaths and selfish deeds we decree, but we are also accountable for the crimes of the poor fools who do our dirty work. In the finale, we are to be pitied because we create our own toothless demise due to our extreme fear of being overpowered by others. Leaving a trail of death and suffering behind us, our fall is inevitable, and we create our own hell.

Throughout history, the fate of the world has been unfortunately dependent on the power-hungry desires of many tragic DPS leaders. Not all of us are as murderous as the tyrants described above, yet still, we are demanding, callous, and greedy for ruling power. We can be corporate CEOs, presidents, or government and political leaders. We can be family heads, religious and spiritual leaders, persuasive sales people, celebrities, business owners and shop proprietors – just about anyone, male or female, who exercises egomaniacal power over others.

The incredulous thing about us is that we have the audacity to presume we can live a life of corruption without suffering any consequences. We are shameless, overconfident, tactless and, in the end, impotent. If someone challenges or differs with us, we will discredit them through character assassination. We can lie, steal, cheat, or bribe with such charm and self-assurance that others believe us to be trustworthy. We are extraordinary con-actors. Unaware of ourselves, our life performance displays the depths to which we are disempowered.

We can be brash loudmouths flaunting our power and wealth (if we have it) around with flashy display. We love compliments and so we give them freely without much genuineness to those who are taken in by our dazzle. If we have our act down, people who work for us and naively believe in our VIP status, usually reinforce our sense of self-importance. This is how we boost our ego.

In children and teens, it's known as bullying and it extends into adulthood. As adult Dynamic Tragedians, we trick others with our deceptive acts of charisma. Even if we believe our own press, our need to be important is motivated by our fear of being common. To quote another Brando line from the classic film, *On the Waterfront*, "I coulda had class, I coulda been a contender. I coulda been somebody... instead of a bum...which is what I am."

We have the ability to hide our own fear through the Cover Character* of *Assumed Nobility*. Regardless of our physique, we act powerful to put others in their place – the groveling position. Our powerful display of self-importance is threatening to others. They mis-take it for their own fear and either follow to pacify us, or they "get the hell outta Dodge." But bravely standing up to this level of extreme fear-inducing power is usually postponed until it gets so out of control that our tragic Dynamic power is hard to defeat.

How do you cast yourself?

Creative Blocks

[ ] You can be power hungry, magnetizing and usurping other's talent without accrediting them.

[ ] You use your voice to commit character assassination. Publicly ridicule others to feel more powerful.

[ ] You are domineering and demanding. Your big voice gets people to do your bidding.

Creative Skills

[ ] Secure in your own power, you empower others by acknowledging and developing their talent

[ ] With self-confidence, you speak to support others while stating your case with magnetism and grace.

[ ] Your integrity and cooperation draw people to you naturally.

SCENE 8 THE SPIRITUAL PERFORMANCE STYLE (SPS) – THE POWER OF INTUITION

> *Glendower: I can call spirits from the vastly deep.*
> *Hotspur: Why so can I, or so can any man;*
> *But will they come when you call for them?*
>
> *~ Henry IV, Part 1*

ORIENTATION

Space, spirit, symbolism, dreams, visions, magic, contemplation, theology, the unknown

OBJECTIVES

To have freedom and independence, be unique, realize our human potential, gain wisdom

TALENTS

Intuition, sense-ability, foresight, astrology, astronomy, philosophy, space industry, architect

ENJOYMENTS

Introspection, nature, hiking, swimming, solitude, sci-fi, mystical, mythology, mind-altering drugs

COMIC CHARACTER TRAITS (CREATIVE SKILLS)

Patience, perceptive, spacious, gentle, free-spirited, curious, whimsical, sensitive, compassionate

TRAGIC CHARACTER TRAITS (CREATIVE BLOCKS)

Indifferent, procrastinator, spacey, secretive, can't take pressure, insensitive, weird, elusive

Being a Spiritual PS does not necessarily mean you are a religious person, as there is a difference between the two. Most religions are rooted in venerable texts such as the Western Bible, Eastern and Middle Eastern scriptures, as well as revelations from religious prophets in more recent times. If one belongs to a religion it generally means these texts are used as a foundation for one's views of God, prophets, and divine guidance. Based on what these ancient texts tell us, we form our beliefs and live our lives according to what our specific religious leaders and Holy Scriptures have taught us. In many ways, the religious belong to the Mental PS as our various belief systems in God or The Divine are founded in time-honored thought forms.

When I speak of the Spiritual Performance Style, I am not talking about a religious person as described above. The SPS seeks to learn through self-discovery. We have an intuitive sense that there is something much greater than an individual's power yet has no encoded beliefs about the divine. Though many religious people sense a greater power, you might say a SPS represents a way of being and acting in life which allows us to understand the divine through the practice of awareness.

Since everyone possesses all five PSs, a religious person who is rooted in specific beliefs will definitely have some SPS traits such as I will describe but may not act them out as a SPS would. If one's religious principles contradict the SPS's manner of acting in life, you may, from time to time, feel a strange inner conflict between what you have been taught and what you experience. Some have found a way to comfortably blend the two.

THE COMIC SPS

If we are predominantly a Spiritual PS, we have the talent of sensory perception. That means some of us can sense things in almost uncanny ways. We have the gift of intuition and are extremely good at seeing the big picture. We can walk into a room and immediately tune into people and what is happening. This is done not by intellectual scrutiny, but through direct sense-ability.

The comedic SPS enjoys alone time and doesn't seem to get lonely. We appreciate quiet and peaceful surroundings and are most comfortable in spacious, clear environments whether at home or at the office. In fact, on a dark, warm night we love sleeping outside under the vastness of the sky with the twinkling stars as our blanket. We can merge our mind with a grain of sand on the beach or with a blade of grass while lying on a hilltop. We like to hike in the forest, bathe in a river, and for hours we can rest under a tree while reading, writing, or just contemplating our navel. Nature and open space are our natural habitat.

We are the dreamers, the unconventional sorts, and the visionaries of the future. Though sometimes we may feel like a social outcast, we like being different and coming up with things no one else would ever imagine. We love costuming – not just as a fashionista but for playfulness. We enjoy sacred stories, fairy tales, futuristic and ancient mythological stories, fantasy of any kind, and can live in a whimsical Peter Pan world of our own. If we could fly, we would! Some of us are light and graceful on our feet, some gentle and soft-spoken in appearance.

The comic SPS has a sense of wonder for life. We ponder the big questions: *Who am I? Where did I come from? When did the universe begin?* We want to explore the unknown, *"to boldly go where no man has gone before."* Yes, we like Star Trek, Star Wars, and other space odysseys. We have a blue-sky imagination and are not only the ones who read and watch science fiction, but we write it. We are experimental and love to discover new art forms, invent and play with futuristic gadgetry. In short – we are out there!

Having a bright and optimistic outlook, we can live on the edge. We can be idealistic, which can make us appear naïve or high-minded. Yet even if our view is unrealistic to others, these altruistic ideals are evident to us. We are unassuming in attitude and are unselfish and self-sacrificing when it comes to putting the needs of others before our own. As a comic SPS, we more naturally live on the Empty Stage than any other Performance Style.

The Supreme Comic SPS

Those who act with sensitivity toward the whole of humanity are supreme comic Spirituals. People like Mother Teresa and Nelson Mandela worked magic for the benefit of others. With sincere compassion, their life performance was all about the welfare of others.

Different from an everyday hunch, many supreme Spirituals have a stronger intuition, enabling sense perceptions normally hidden to easily be revealed. If we can stay grounded in open mindedness, more and more will reveal itself. But if we are also prone to the Emotional PS's excitement, or if we have the Mental PS's need for immediate explanation, we will lose the truth of incoming revelations and start making up things about the information that has shown itself.

It is also important to state here that as a supreme comic Spiritual with deep sense-abilities, we are not performing some weird, macabre black magic, nor are we the "channel" for religious miracles. In the same way the MPS is open to gathering intellectual information, and the PPS is open to receiving signals from the body, we are open to receiving information and signals from spatial surroundings.

Mysterious as this may seem, this heightened sense-ability happens because at least for that moment of spatial receptivity, our brain is not muddled with countless levels of thought themes. Our mind is free to receive phenomena that are not audible to ordinary hearing or obvious to the naked eye. It's really fairly ordinary reality when the mind is subtle and uncluttered.

We are very sensitive to the world around us that others regard as non-existent. Most people are like Hamlet's mother, who, when she witnessed him speaking to his father's ghost, asked, *"Alas, how is't with you, that you do bend your eye on vacancy, and with th' incorporeal air do hold discourse?"*

Though most supreme Spirituals do not talk to ghosts or even identify our talent in this way, our sensitivity may seem weird to others and cause us to withdraw or appear aloof. Conversely, our gift is the ability to help others see beyond the obvious and appreciate what is not apparent but nonetheless present. This can range from clearly seeing another's personal obstacles to sensing future events.

On our deepest level, a supreme Spiritual is a seeker of truth. We sense the suffering and fear we all feel inside and want to alleviate it. Knowing that our deepest fear is the great unknown, we resolutely examine our own fears and confusion. We work hard to uproot negative attitudes and actions that have blocked our freedom to love and feel safe.

We are the peacemakers. As John Lennon put it in song so innocently, *imagine all the people living life in peace.* We wonder what life would be like if we could view the world and all within it without the blinders of our prejudices, divisive belief systems, and hostilities? Imagine what truths would be revealed to us if we could see with the eyes of pure vision? What if we could move beyond the barriers of our cluttered mind and mirror love instead of hate? Unrealistic as it seems to most, as supreme Spirituals, we altruistically have that resolve of spirit.

Unlike the extreme tragic SPS, whose fear senses infinite space as horrific darkness, our comic side finds compassionate joy and creative potential in space. With abandonment and enterprise, we reach the *"final frontier."* There we gain timeless wisdom and learn to function with a stable, yet radiant, spacious mind. Such is the undaunted pursuit of truth for the supreme comic SPS.

THE TRAGIC SPS

In our unique way, we have a bit of the rebel in us and don't like to conform to rules that would make us like everyone else. For those who do live by rules and regulations, our reluctance to go along can be quite irritating. We like going at our own pace, which is usually a lot slower than others. In the eyes of those trying to live or work with us, we can seem unbearably vague and absent. Not always functional, we are in our own world and often appear to be on another planet.

To us, the physical world is brutal, gross, and unsafe. We can have trouble staying earthbound, as there is a fear of landing in safety. We are flighty, transitioning quickly from one topic to another, unable to maintain focus and attention. We don't like structure or being held to deadlines, so office jobs can be difficult. Making decisions isn't always quick or easy either, and others get impatient waiting for us to complete a job. Eventually we will get it done...when the pressure is off. If pressured, we simply turn off or give up.

Challenges, arguments, and fighting are not our thing. We don't care if we lose – we never entered the contest. We don't like confrontation and will fly away if anyone tries to pin us down – after all we are spirit. Subtly though, we can be passive-aggressive. Consequently, if you ask us to do something we don't want to do, we will avoid or postpone a response – which can aggravate the hell out of the one doing the asking. We don't always want to engage in chitchat or deal with mundane needs. However, we also don't want to hurt or offend you, so instead, we avoid you.

In fact, we will neglect our own needs. We are not good with handling money, domestic life, business details, or even taking care of our own health, so there is an avoidance of it all. We are not very good communicators. We don't always return calls or communicate what we are thinking and feeling. Instead of responding, we leave people guessing. We have an unrealistic belief that things will take care of themselves; sometimes they do but most of the time people and things need our attention.

Life is just too burdensome. We know the bills need to get paid and can see the faucet is leaking, but our motto is, *"Whatever..."* As procrastinators, we can look at our dirty, messy house and not lift a finger to clean it. This is not because we can be lazy and sloppy like the tragic Physical, but because the material world just doesn't matter – our heads are in the clouds. This of course drives a grounded *"Do it! Do it now,"* Comic Physical crazy. But…tarry we will.

Too much stimuli from people and external sources can not only disturb us, but also make us physically ill. If we do not know how to recognize sensory overload and avert it, we might easily be overwhelmed by crowds, traffic, and busy environments. We become defenseless and frightened. These experiences can cause us to be disoriented from reality. Our head is our imagination studio and whatever is going on in there becomes our reality.

Basically, we are loners and at times, we can seem unfriendly or secretive. For us commitment is too confining and therefore we don't make the best of partners in love or in business – unless we choose another SPS who is like us. But then, your lives might be like two people living in an opium den playing out pipedreams. We need a Physical PS to help ground us, if they can put up with us. Moreover, the Spiritual Tragedian doesn't want to grow up and take on the business of responsibility. We make fantasy our world, using it as distractions to keep us from living in the cold, hard concrete world.

Not all of us are this disengaged; yet even inklings of these character traits can annoy friends, coworkers, and family. The thing to remember when living and working with a SPS is that as intuitive and sensitive as we can be on our lighter side, we can be as equally spaced out and insensitive on our darker side.

The Extreme Tragic SPS

Space is our domain and as an extreme tragic, we identify it with loneliness and fear. We can become incredibly bewildered and unable to function in the real world. Afraid of anything unknown, we experience darkness as horrifying and frightful. There is no bottom or reasoning to our fear – it's existential. Because we are not grounded in our existing life, ongoing fear feeds our need to remain dysfunctional and keeps us bound to the dread of life.

Our sense-abilities become desensitized – and we shut down in terror. The spirit and spatial orientation is still there, but has now become dispirited and disoriented. The unknown fear factor makes us uncertain. Instead of creatively choosing to explore the unknown potential of our inner space, we imagine the cold depths of dark, deep space as if sucked into a black hole. We experience this void as paralyzing. Many of us isolate ourselves and fall into deep depression, so much so that we don't see a way out and may even develop suicidal tendencies. We are literally lost in space.

This misguided take on inner space can also lead us into the sinister "spirit world" of black magic. Choosing to dabble in scary, supernatural magic gives us a sense of control over our fears of the dark. We mistakenly use our imagination to create visions of ghosts, ghouls, and vampires, taking chilling delight in tales of terror. Somehow, we like to play with the titillation of fright, either with the idea that we will master our fear or discover some unworldly secrets. But, the tragic Spiritual Extremists are very prone to sensational spirituality and are intuitively naïve. We must be careful not to take our nightmarish imaginings too seriously. Belief in these things might only heighten our everyday fears and deepen insecurity. We can develop all kinds of phobias and anxieties about doing simple, ordinary things.

Our inexperience with being grounded in space makes us fantasize in strange ways. Especially in the night when deep space is felt all around us, boogey-man visions appear to folks of all ages. Fears of all kinds dance in the dark. Some of us like to tell ourselves stories with happy endings to brighten the dark. Others keep the brain running at full speed to avoid experiencing nocturnal uncertainties. But fear not, as a spiritual tragedian, practice the ESAwareness and rest in the grace of space.

How do you cast yourself?

Creative Blocks
[ ] You let your imagination envision things that are negative or not actual.
[ ] You put things off. Space out. Get involved in other things that please you.

Creative Skills
[ ] You use your sense-ability to see the reality of situations.
[ ] You take care of the necessities, valuing things and sensing the needs of others.

REVIEW YOUR PERFORMANCE STYLE PROFILE

Now that you have read about each of the Five Performance Styles and their comic, supreme comic, tragic, and extreme tragic sides, take time to go back and review your Performance Style Profile. Ask yourself these questions:

1. Do you feel it accurately reflects your most dominant Performance Style(s)?
2. Do you feel that you can learn to enhance those Performance Styles that you are not strong in?
3. Identify people you know who have each of the Performance Styles and try to indicate whether each person acts from their comic, supreme comic, tragic, or extreme tragic side.

We all have a comic and
a tragic side to our character.

Act III

Character Study –
Identifying Your Tragic Characters

As you learned in Act II, each Performance Style has its particular comic and tragic character traits. Act III is devoted to working with those tragic character traits, whatever your Performance Style. Any time you fall into acting from your tragic side, you run the risk of encountering any number of creative blocks that will interfere with successfully directing the situation you are in. By learning to recognize when you may be acting from your tragic side and how to counteract those tendencies, you can turn these potential creative blocks into creative skills.

SCENE 1 DISPELLING UNIVERSAL PERFORMANCE TRAPS

> *Sometimes we are devils to ourselves*
> *When we will tempt the frailty of our powers,*
> *Presuming on their changeful potency.*
>
> *~ Troilus and Cressida*

Rarely do we recognize how to use our powers and their changeability. Therefore, before we delve into the study of each PS's tragic traits, it is helpful to first discuss 7 types of bothersome Performance Traps that most of us experience from time to time in our daily activities. These traps are behaviors and habits that cause us to act in unproductive, even destructive ways. They are "universal," in that they affect us all, regardless of our Performance Style.

See if you can identify times when you fall into these traps. Use the practices provided for each to learn how to halt yourself from succumbing to these performance traps.

1. OBSTACLE CHARACTERS*

> *There is some soul of goodness in things evil,*
> *would men observingly distill it out.*
>
> *~ Henry V*

Even the best of us face personal obstacles. For eons, we have been accustomed to taking a pill, a drink or a vitamin to feel better. Maybe we blame someone else for our misery or use distraction therapy to keep us from coming face to face with the undesirable in us. Rarely do we stop to take a look in the mirror.

So, as you begin The Practices, be prepared to engage with your Tragic Characters who cause obstacles – creative blocks that can be felt as dominance, resistance, hatred, irritation, anxiety, or other undesirable feelings. However, you experience them, they have a story to tell and other parts of you need to listen. Don't deny or push them away. Otherwise they will sabotage your progress and block your opportunities.

When obstacle characters cause havoc, let them speak out loud. Otherwise they roam around in your head like a jailed prisoner waiting for a chance to make a break. Like anyone who is having a hard time, these characters in us will complain, lay blame, and act out until they are heard. When they take center stage, they can fester as an illness, become an inner character conflict,* or make you act badly towards others. At that point, all other characters in you are forced off-stage. Your whole being is left to feel only what your Obstacle Character feels – misery! So, it is crucial to let each Obstacle Character have its say.

For example, there may be a character in you who feels defiant, yet every time it tries to act out, your conscience character censors it – *"No, now be a good little boy (girl)."* But, Defiance has a monologue that other parts of you need to hear. As painful as it might be to listen, it is the only way to understand why that part of you needs to be defiant.

Some tragic characters are so hardened, so routine and so resilient that they are tough to get off your mindstage. They claim squatter's rights. Hearing them out is crucial. Like a neglected child throwing a temper tantrum, these parts of us need to be heard and respected. They hold valuable information that can help in bringing your whole cast of characters to a more functional resolution. Not all parts of you want to be in pain. So, listen to your unhappy characters as though you are comforting a friend in trouble who needs your help. Access your empathetic character who is interested in learning why that part of you has been so difficult and unhappy.

Soon thereafter, you will find other characters in you who can come to the rescue. You can bring out those characters who have been waiting in the wings* but have been held back by your Obstacle Characters. The only reason you remain attached to your tragic characters is because you believe them to be solid and take them too seriously. Always remember that what you have hardened as your reality is a changeable energy.

The following practice will help you deal with your Obstacle Characters.

Practice – Character Allowing #1: Speaking Your Character's Truth

Since pre-Freudian days, the idea of talking to yourself meant that you were crazy. That conventional concept still holds today. It's based on the notion, if you have to talk to yourself, you must not be a very stable person. However, in practicing what I call *"Character Allowing,"* speaking your mind with introspective awareness is not just mumbling in some stupefied state or even letting off steam. It's a deliberate effort to clearly verbalize the problematic storylines causing Obstacle Characters in your life.

It is helpful to video or audio record your *Allowing* monologue so that when each character speaks, your full attention is on being *"in character"* rather than trying to listen to yourself. Later, you can play it back to take notes and learn more. But, don't let anything or anyone stop the flow of your character's stream of consciousness.

Directions Part 1

Find the right time and place to "Allow" your unhappy characters to speak. Make sure it is a place where you feel uninhibited.

1. First, go to the mirror and take note of how you look.
2. Turn on recorder. State the date and time, so you can keep a record of this character speaking to you in case you need to come back to it again.
3. Now let the most pained or needy character start talking. Whatever comes up, allow your character to talk freely, un-interrupted until he/she is finished.
4. Do not censor! Speak in the 1st person ("I"). Stay in character.
5. If at some point, you need to walk, sit, run or lie down – let this character do what he/she needs to do. Your character actions are a clue as to its needs.

6. If it is a loud or angry character, be sure you are in a place where you feel safe to let him or her act out.

7. If your character becomes repetitive then it may be trying to emphasize a point or is just winding down.

8. Before stopping, ask your character if there is anything else it has to say? If not, go to the mirror and note any change in your appearance. After completion, name the role you were playing. Example: Tommy Troll, Wanda Witch, Willie Wimp, Jack Jock, Stella Star.

Directions Part 2

Playback the recording and listen as if you are a friend to the character speaking. Listen with awareness, affection, and interest in that part of you who wants to be heard.

1. Take notes if you like.

2. Who in you is listening? Are you angry? Saddened? Empathetic? Compassionate?

3. What new information is the recorded character giving?

4. What are your recorded character's concerns? List them.

5. What is he/she feeling & doing? List them.

6. What is motivating your character? (What desires, fears?)

7. What is his/her intention? (Plan of action?)

8. As your character's friend, what have you learned from the recording?

9. How does the friend in you choose to complete the interaction with your recorded obstacle character?

10. If this was the same character you recorded once before, notice if anything has changed. Is he/she repeating the same concern months later? Is it a new issue? Do you need to call out a different character to listen to him/her this time? The Disciplinary? The Adventurer? Who?

Directions Part 3

1. If you are dealing with Character Conflict* (see #4 below), repeat above steps. Allow your opposing Obstacle Character to speak out loud to the other character in you.

2. What have you learned about each character in you?

3. What changes can you make in your daily life to improve this inner conflict?

Note: Remember, the purpose here is to spotlight any Obstacle Character issues and listen without judgment to the needs, motivation and intent of each. To ensure support and safety, get professional supervision if you know your character can be dangerous.

Character vs. Role, Motivation, Intention and Objective

To work better with your inner characters, let's clarify some LPP terms used in Act III, our tragic side, and Act IV, our comic side.

- **Character vs. Role.** A role is task oriented. When you tell someone that you are a manicurist, a father, or a salesperson, they know what job you perform. The character that you give to that role is emotionally-based, like a *caring* doctor or a *nasty* boss. So, the role you play lets people know what you do, and the character you display lets people know how you feel in that role.

  Recognizing your role in a particular life scene is important. For instance, you may leave the house in the morning as a dad, hugging your kids good-bye. When you reach your workplace, you become an executive, teacher, computer programmer, or other. Even at work you may assume various roles within your title. When you stop off at the grocery on your way home from work, you become a customer. When you reach your home, you get out of your car and your neighbor wants to sell you a ticket to her church raffle – you take on the role of the neighbor. Back in the house, you are the husband and father again. And so, with every scene change, your role and character changes on the revolving stage of life.

  When you're aware of your role and character, instead of just blindly walking into a situation, your awareness can choose to play the most effective character possible in that role. In doing that, here are three other terms that LPP borrows from theatrical performance training which are useful when performing your daily roles and character choices.

- **Motivation** – When an actor studies a new script, he or she will ask the question, "What is my character's motivation in this scene?" Does he want to get the girl? Does she want revenge? It is unlikely that most people ask themselves that question before entering an everyday scenario. But to intentionally ask *"What is my motivation?"* can help explain why you act in a certain way under certain circumstances. Becoming clear about your wants and desires can avoid those *"Why did I say that?"* moments. Motive-awareness gives you the opportunity to adjust your motivation, so you can prepare to say what you need to say in the best possible way.

- **Intention** – Motivation is your desire, but intent refers to the plan of action that helps you fulfill your motivation. If love is motivating you and your girlfriend's father doesn't like you, your intent may be to prove your worth to him. If some guy bullied you and revenge is your motivation, your intent may be to get back at him. It's worth giving a closer look to your unidentified intentions and how they might act unconsciously based on your motivation. Recognizing your motivation allows you to plan your intention.

- **Objective** – In theatrical scripts, an actor's objectives are broken down into scenes and even units within the scenes. The life actor has no script, so having and setting goals day-by-day, or even hour-by-hour, can help you get the job done. Objectives can vitalize your ability to accomplish things and help with time management.

2. Hidden Characters

> *O, what may man within him hide, though angel on the outward side.*
>
> ~ *Measure for Measure*

A scrim* is a see-thru stage curtain that appears as a solid backdrop when a scene is lit in front of it. The audience only sees the main stage action and doesn't see what is hiding behind the scrim. When a scene is lit from behind the scrim, the unseen action becomes visible. Similarly, the scenes we are playing in our daily lives are visible to us, but we are often unaware of the unlit characters hidden behind the scrim of our mindstage. Although when something happens on our main stage that disturbs and awakens our hidden characters, those dark scenarios behind our scrim get spotlighted and start to act up as pain or undesirable actions.

In LPP, we are working with a somewhat unconventional concept of human behaviors. In our character study,* each illness or problem we have takes on a specific character, like irritable, angry or sad, and emotes according to his or her needs. For instance, if you have sexual or intimacy issues, you may act in excessive or fearful ways that provoke dis-eases in your genital or other related areas. If you have unacknowledged sorrow or on-going stress, it may weigh heavily on your heart and you might develop coronary problems. If cancer, there are any number of unidentified issues that might be eating away at you. Like the homing pigeon instinctively knows where to go, our unhappy characters instinctively find their way into the part of our body that corresponds to our condition or grievance.

If the troubled character in you is unable to express the problem, like a tick that burrows deeper into your skin if not removed, your character's ailments burrow into their relevant body lodgings. The longer they hide out, the weightier they become – emotionally, mentally, or physically – eventually requiring medical attention. They steal your power and spirit. They don't want to come out, but other parts of you can't take the pain and pressure. So these unhappy parts of us either fester, or express in harmful ways.

Those clandestine tragic characters each have their particular backstory. Sometimes they are hard to detect and seem unrelated to our dis-ease. However, like any mystery, if we dig deep enough, the clues will lead us to an answer. If Character Allowing #1 is unable to bring out your hidden characters, the following Allowing # 2 practice may help.

Practice – Character Allowing #2: Finding Your Character's Hiding Place

This is a physical body scan meant to find characters that are hiding in your body and allowing them to express. They have been tightly locked away in your body's memory. This practice can help release the storyline.

Directions Part 1

- Sitting in a chair, begin with the Empty Stage Practice.
- Then place your hands close over, but not touching your feet, and allow a sound to emerge that expresses the feeling/sensation in your feet. (One foot at a time if necessary.)
- Don't think about it. Just focus your attention on what you are feeling and allow that feeling/sensation to groan, sigh, cry, tickle, or scream.
- If there is no particular feeling or sensation, then just make a one note hum-like sound.
- Then move your hands up your body – to your ankle, then calf, knee, thigh, groin, stomach, waist, chest, shoulders, neck, face, arms and back.
- As you move your hands up your body, allow sounds to express the feeling that particular part of your body is holding. This helps you connect the sensations in your body with your feelings.
- Go through your body up and down, front and back. When you have finished the scan, go back to the part of your body where you felt the strongest sensation.
- Hold your hands over that part, close your eyes and allow the sound to continue.
- You may find that visual imagery will come up, or words, phrases and sentences characteristically speak out. Whole storylines might begin to emerge. These are parts of us we have imprisoned in our bodies that have a great deal of information.
- This exercise creatively and caringly allows these blocked parts of us to speak out loud – to learn why they are hiding.

Directions Part 2

Once you have heard the storyline, support is now in order. Once the hidden character has come out from behind the scrim, you can name him or her, so you don't continually dismiss the character back to its hiding place, but recognize it. You may need to get more information and repeat the physical scan as many times as necessary. Whatever characters have appeared, connect the dots – the emotional components to the physical pain. Recognizing them will help eliminate creative blocks and assist in expressing your chosen characters. You may want to audio or video your process, so you can review it as needed.

**Note: If you have serious illness that has to do with painful personal history, use these practices with your therapist. LPP is not a replacement for needed therapy. It is meant for those of us who have minor to self-managing ailments and need a practice to help illuminate emotional issues. It can reduce or eliminate aches and pains as it did for me with chronic back pain. Be patient, as it is a process.

3. CHARACTER SCLEROSIS

> *Refrain tonight, And that shall lend a kind of*
> *easiness to the next abstinence; the next more easy;*
> *For use almost can change the stamp of nature.*
>
> ~ *Hamlet*

When we become set in our ways, we develop Character Sclerosis,* hardening of character. That emotional character develops social and personal routines that, even if harmful, feels safe. Performance routine* is difficult to crack because we become attached to it as a normal sense of self. Those traits become our comfort zone – our "default character"* or our "go-to character habit."*

One morning I woke up on "the wrong side of the bed." I was feeling grumpy. While at work, I let my Grumpy Greta act out for a couple of lost hours trying to figure out what was bothering me. Suddenly I realized it was nothing more than my habit of being grumpy. Grumpy Greta's leading character traits of unhappiness and dissatisfaction about my life were the motivators for bad behavior. I routinely played this character ensemble to distract me from moving forward.

It is very easy for any of us to fall into many uncreative habits. We go numb and dumb. Playing your same routine character may feel comfortable and safe but it won't produce new and better results. However, recognizing your unproductive character habits coupled with willingness to let go of them and enthusiasm for change, can rectify it.

The thing is, Character Sclerosis never looks in a mirror. Unless a loved one or friend tells you how annoying your habit is, you seldom see yourself. And a bad habit only becomes worse through unconscious rehearsal. The following practice can help you rehearse a more productive, happier you. If you can't see it, you can't be it.

Practice – Reversing Character Sclerosis

This is a fun practice for trying out and rehearsing emotions that may be new or unfamiliar to you but are useful and productive to counter-act Character Sclerosis. Use the Character Study Chart (pg. 129-130) in the *Emotional Performance Style* section to make new character choices.

Directions

1. Look up the meaning of the emotion that is your set Character Sclerosis. Anger? Lazy? Thoughtless? Know who you are dealing with.
2. Then clear by going to the ESA. In that free space, find a character you want to try, be it "happy," "persistent," "loving" or another. Contemplate its meaning also.
3. Notice people who express this character. Understudy them. Rehearse your character choice often. Experience the feeling and begin to make it your own.
4. Sometimes a particularly obstinate character habit won't leave your mindstage, like angry or greedy. In that case, deliberately exaggerate that character when you feel it. Play it as caricature – make it into parody. It usually cracks the mirror and you won't need to take these characters so seriously.

5.   Then go to the ESA and make a new character choice. It also
     helps to deliberately play out tragic characters to gain better
     understanding of them in yourself and others.

6.   In this way, you will expand your character repertoire* and
     not need to rely on that old Character Sclerosis.

4. CHARACTER CONFLICT

> *Poor Brutus, with himself at war.*
>
> ~ *Julius Caesar*

Often when we feel conflicted we say, "One part of me wants one thing and another part of me wants something else." We have two characters within us who
are front stage center duking it out! We feel two opposing characters, yet we don't
know which ME to identify with.

In LPP, this is called Character Conflict. If it is out and out war, then it could be
affecting your health, relationships, and your work. Inner conflicts float around in
our heads as unidentified, fragmented thoughts. As a result, things in our life get
sabotaged. Decision-making becomes impossible and some activities get put on
hold.

In working with this creative crisis, here is a practice that will help you get
clarification on the conflict.

Practice – Mediation

1.   First identify the two conflicting roles you are playing. Who
     wants what? Identify the emotional character of each role
     and their motive and intent.

2.   Once you have clarified the two parts of you in conflict,
     name the roles for distinction. Ex: Peter Perturbed vs. Arie
     Airhead.

3.   What are the Performance Styles of each role? Are they
     Mental, Physical or another style? What task are they trying
     to accomplish and is that Performance Style capable of ac-
     complishing it? What are their emotional characters?

4. Then your Mediator, a third role, can step in and ask, as in any dispute, each party to present its case – a monologue about their needs, motivation, and plan of action. If possible, record each.

5. Finally, it's time to negotiate – with both of you. With this information, your Mediator can better settle the dispute. Both parts of you can get what they want or it will become clear which part is best for the whole of you and which part must acquiesce.

5. Character Residue

> *Let us not burden our remembrance with a heaviness that's gone.*
>
> ~ *The Tempest*

When a part of you is caught up in something that happened hours or days ago and inappropriately carries it from one life scenario into the next, you are in Character Residue,* living in replay. When you are carrying the emotional residue from the past, it keeps you from being present.

Others will either wonder what's bothering you or may even take it personally. And because your acting character is stuck in replay,* it will take a bit of emotional discipline* to know when to stop. Listening to someone's complaint once or twice is okay, but when you find an inner character getting repetitive or indulgent, then it is time to come into the present...unless you enjoy listening to reruns.

On the lighter side of Character Residue are times when something wonderful has happened and we don't want to let go of the feeling. So, we spin it, pumping up our energy. If aware of your inner pep rally, fine...but beware, a low could follow.

We might say that all states of Character Residue steal our attention. As a result, most of the time we are not playing in the present moment but living in the past or imagining a future. By noticing when you are in Character Residue, you can develop choice over how you feel and spend your time.

Practice – Who's Acting? A Self-Discovery Practice

When Character Residue takes center stage, it is because someone in you has been hurt, offended, or embarrassed by someone or something you did. We replay these scenarios over and over in our mind trying to justify or change what happened and make ourselves feel better. This practice aims to uncover the motive for the repetition and find a resolve for that character stuck in residue.

1. First, name the character: Hurt Hugo, Mortified Morty, Outraged Olga, Embarrassed Emma, etc.
2. Now give the opposing person in your scene a character name. Offensive Octavio, Bitchy Belinda, Andy Asshole, Bitter Betty.
3. Now go to the ESA. Clear, ground and expand your awareness.
4. Once grounded and aware, put the scenario in question on your mindstage for reviewing. Ask who in you is acting? Hurt Hugo? Bitter Betty? Who?
5. Now was the opposing character justified in doing what she/ he did? Were you doing or saying something that could have hurt her? Was she projecting her feelings onto you? Was jealousy involved?
6. What were your feelings in the situation? Insecurity? Anger? Love? Be honest in your inner research.*
7. As a detective would investigate a crime scene, investigate and get to the "feeling" motive of the situation.
8. When you can objectively understand the emotional character of each person in the scene, you can determine if you need to apologize, or if you need to ask for an apology. Is forgiveness needed? Maybe let it go?
9. Just make sure you know who in you is taking a recourse action. Be sure you are sincere and feeling balanced about your choices.
10. Once you have established honesty in the ESA, Character Residue is not necessary.

6. COVER CHARACTERS

To have what we would have, we speak not what we mean.

~ Measure for Measure

There are many times during the course of a day when we reactively use a Cover Character. This happens when we feel the need to defend or hide our true feelings. If it is fear of being found out, we might lie to cover our backs. Sometimes we put on an act, like pretend to know something we really don't know. There are those times when we make a big deal over someone trying to impress them or get them to like you. And then there is playing up to someone because you want something and you *"speak not what you mean."*

There are many motivations for using a Cover Character. Most of the time we do it automatically. Cover Characters can be valuable and normal when used with honest motivation and intent. But if you are doing it for personal gain, you might walk away feeling pleased with your ever-so-clever self or, a little insecure if you didn't like your performance.

Getting to know your Cover Characters and their impulses helps you be more natural. When you become familiar with them you may not need to fabricate them in unnatural ways.

Practice – Cover Character Awareness

1. If you feel uncomfortable around someone, chances are you feel the need for pretense.
2. Notice who in you is pretending. Notice your motivation.
3. In that moment, go to the ESA.
4. Catching your Cover Character in the act helps you assess whether it's necessary. If so, you can consciously play it with greater truth and ease.
5. Or, you might choose to make another character choice that's more natural to the situation. Of course, the best choice is to let the Empty Stage Awareness guide you.

7. EMOTIONAL OSMOSIS

> *Juliet: What satisfaction canst thou have tonight?*
> *Romeo: Th' exchange of thy love's faithful vow for mine.*
>
> *~ Romeo and Juliet*

When it comes to love, exchanging feelings is a good thing. However, we exchange feelings and ideas with other people all the time and don't realize it. Have you ever walked into a room feeling good and walked out feeling like shit? It could be that you have unconsciously taken on the mood of the people or person you've just encountered.

In our daily performance, we reflect each other's feelings through the emotional range within us all. If we are not strong in mental clarity and stability of mind, then we are subject to strong reaction and Emotional Osmosis and unconscious absorption of other people's feelings.

Practice – Clarifying Feelings

1. If you are confused about what you are feeling you may have exchanged feelings with another person.
2. Go to the Empty Stage and release Brain Babble. Open into Awareness.
3. Notice the emotional character of the other person. Is it the same as yours?
4. Clarify who in you is acting. Identify what emotion is taking character and you will know if what you are feeling is emanating from you or another person.
5. If what you are feeling is a character you want to maintain, set and play it.
6. If it is not what you choose to feel or be in that situation, then in the clarity of the ESA, see the emotional realities and make another character choice based on that.
7. Character feelings are easy to change if you…a) recognize your tragic character, b) allow the ESAwareness to clear it, c) make a new character choice, and d) have the skill to play it truthfully.

SCENE 2 RELATING TO YOUR TRAGIC BACKSTORY

Let me embrace thee, sour adversity, for wise
men say it is the wisest course.

~ Henry VI part 3

Many of our tragic character traits are derived from some tragic backstory. Memorizing dialogues and scenes of terrible scenarios from our past, we solidify the tragic characters we played back then by inadvertently rehearsing them daily in our current actions. Even if we see our self as a good person who is just in a bad mood, we may unknowingly use our tragic backstory as justification for acting irritable, sickly, or stressed out. We excuse our hardened bad traits – chalking it up to too much caffeine, being tired or no sleep. Oddly, we feel obligated to that old negative character in us and enjoy milking it as if possessed by our tragic past.

These old characters take on new motivations and intent and we don't recognize them or remember from whence they came. More often than not, we are unaware of who in us has taken character and is acting in a given moment. We say, *"I don't know why I did that!"* We protest – *I just wasn't myself.* But if it wasn't you, then who was it? Your long-lost cousin?

We assume there is a single I or Me, but when we reject disliked parts of our self, we actually demonstrate how fragmented we really are. There are many characters in each of us. So the question isn't "why," but "who" in you said or did something contrary to who you think you are? Basically, you've had an "awareness blackout*" and are not recognizing a self that is just as much your reality as the characters you vividly parade in your mind as "The Real Me".

Though we may say we want to change, we won't be able to if we continue playing the characters who don't want to change. To change any unwanted character trait, whether from our backstory or current storyline, we first have to accept it as a part of us. This is often the hardest part of the process because we don't like to see ourselves in a bad light. But once we discover a way to accept our outcast characters as part of our character repertoire, those undesirable parts can begin interacting with brighter parts of us and learn to take new direction.

102

As you begin your Life Performance studies, having an interest in getting to know your whole human instrument with a willingness to change what needs to change, is key. By understanding how your backstory provokes your destructive characters to act out, you will no longer be embarrassed or afraid of them. You won't need to hide them because you will know who they are, if and when they arise. You will realize that they are like ghost stories – dead and gone.

They are not the only part of you, and don't have to occupy your whole being. In Character Study, you will relate with them and make other character choices. If you don't allow the tragic side of you to express truthfully and safely, you will live in denial and these uninvited parts of you will subversively run your life.

SEEING OURSELVES IN OTHERS

Some may think they don't have a tragic backstory that hinders their present performance. However, while we don't recognize negative behavior in ourselves, we see it in others. We get enraged when we see someone acting in rude or despicable ways. "They" are alien to saintly "ME."

But the truth is, if we really look closely, we are actually seeing ourselves in others. As the saying goes, "it takes one to know one."

Let your criticisms of others be a tip off that you may be hiding your own tragic flaws and come to admit and appreciate your tragic side. During your studies, knowing you are not alone, you can allow your unlikable parts to be seen and heard in constructive ways. Then they can make a transition.

The Practices in this book, give you a process for understanding your tragic parts without wanting to punish, curse, or banish them to the underworld. In LPP, you learn to rehearse and increase your emotional repertoire for greater expression and flexibility.

Our tragic characters often overwhelm our comic life performance. So, it is important to rehearse and set comic emotions, so you can instinctively go to them as automatically as you would your tragic feelings. And never forget, Awareness is your backdrop for any and all your activities.

Thus play I in one person many people, And none contented:
~ Richard II

Now we can explore our specific tragic character traits, the emotional mood-sets natural to each Performance Style and how they affect our health, our relationships and our success in life. If we habitually think, sense, feel and act from our tragic side, it will inevitably cause Creative Blocks (CBs). Over time, these blocks can harden into Character Sclerosis and set character traits like resistance, sadness, aggression and resentment – each character having its story to tell.

When we get stuck playing a tragic character, we feel bad about our self. Urgently wanting to feel better, we resent and resist, trying to push our tragic character off our mindstage. We want to quickly shift from tragedy to comedy and can't. Transitioning from Tragedy into Comedy without a neutral space to clear mental conflict usually triggers characters like Stanley Struggle and Frannie Frustration. We need a bridge, a 3rd place for the mind to go, to unwind and view things clearly. That space is the ESAwareness.

Most all our tragic actions arise from two emotional parts in our self – hurt and fear. In this Act, we learn to recognize our tragic characters and redirect our hurt and fearful habits. Like Ebenezer Scrooge was awakened from his bad dreams by the ghost of Christmas Past, we too can awaken from our bad dreams by acknowledging the ghost of Hurts Past. We needn't drag the heavy chains of old miseries everywhere we go.

Routine replay of old hurt amplifies our fears and we live the present as if the past is our director. But if we were to acknowledge our hurt characters and redirect them to a comfortable backstage area, they would not be standing in the wings on call for instant replay. With character awareness, we can develop creative self-command.

Comedy and tragedy are part of life and being perpetually happy is not the goal. Rather, awareness is. It is about having access to the part of you that can bring the best results. Sometimes it might be necessary to use anger – to yell or express annoyance at someone because they won't hear your constructive message any other way. However, you must be sure of your own motivation and intent. If your motive is for personal dominance, or to feel better by blowing off at someone, then go to the ESAwareness and redirect any egocentric motives.

Sometimes to stand your ground on something, you may use what appears as stubbornness. Just know the difference between pigheadedness and self-confidence. Also, in playing a strong emotional part, don't develop Character Residue*. Transition quickly to a healthier part, always using the ESA as your transitional ground.

Our normal habit is to fight off our negative thoughts and feelings, which only intensifies them. Awareness, on the other hand, can dissolve or change them. By examining your tragic side, you learn to identify your go-to tragic characters in each of the Five Performance Styles and self-correct when necessary.

The rest of Act III describes each of the five Performance Styles and some of their Tragic Character Traits. A short scenario follows each description, so you can see how these Performance Styles and their traits play out in daily life. Each scenario has 6 elements:

- **The Scenario** – This presents a situation using character traits that cause Creative Blocks (CB) or problems between the players.
- **Character Evaluation** – How the character's performance affects health, relations and productivity.
- **Director's Notes** – These are my creative critiques for the main character. Creative Critiquing helps the character make positive changes in the scene's replay.
- **Scenario Replay** – Here you see how the players might reenact the same scene using comic traits that display their creative skills.
- **Reader's Take** – This is a reflection practice for you to consider after reading the scenario
- **Performance Practices** – a list of activities to overcome the blocks.

The scenarios in Act III are composites of research I've done and character studies of myself, people I know, people on the street, stories I've heard or experienced, or those I've created. The scenarios depict the Five Performance Styles (PS) that are common to all people, though everyone uses them to different degrees. They are not specific to race, gender, sexual preference, professional or social status; nor do they describe cultural or religious backgrounds.

Rather, the characters and situations represent performance tendencies of the human race. In addition, as you read, though it is tempting to identify friends and relatives, try to identify yourself first – even in the smallest traits. If the characters remind you of someone you know, think about how you might act out that trait.

Also, though you may primarily be one PS, it doesn't mean that you will be prone to every trait listed in it. We are combinations of each PS and the existence of a trait in another PS may cancel out a trait in your primary PS. Notice if you tend to act more from your tragic or comic side. Make note of the tragic traits you routinely use in each Performance Style and how it affects your productivity.

SCENE 4 THE TRAGIC MENTAL PERFORMANCE STYLE (MPS) – FREEING YOUR CREATIVE BLOCKS WITH CREATIVE CHOICE

There is nothing either good or bad, but thinking makes it so.

~ Hamlet

One of the MPS's major motivations is to demonstrate superior intellect. We need facts; we want proof to validate our thinking. We are direct, practical thinkers. But when we come at this from our tragic side, we often seek it by coldly criticizing the intelligence of others. We always need to be right and smart, plus we like acknowledgement from others. Here are some of the most relevant tragic performance traits plus the LPPractices that will help you redirect these creative blocks into creative skills.

TRAGIC TRAIT: JUDGE-MENTAL

How would you be, if He, which is the top of judgment, should but judge you as you are?

~ Measure for Measure

Standing on facts, the MPS enjoys being argumentative and dismissive of other people's opinions or creative input. The need to be right (always) can make us hypercritical of others, creating a negative mental ambiance across our mindstage. We form solid opinions of others and hold on to it as though it is written in stone by the hand of God *(guess who plays God?)*. Rather than getting the agreement we seek, we push people away as they don't like verbally engaging with us for fear of arguments or being judged. Our opinion being the ultimate expertise makes it hard for anyone to change our mind.

Contemplative Practices

1. Ask yourself, is this how I choose for people to think of me? Do I like interacting with friends, colleagues and family in this way? Why? What's my reward?

2. Go to the mirror and tell yourself that you are stupid – express what you don't like about yourself. See how it feels. The next time you catch yourself being judge-mental, check your motivation. Are you normally this hard on yourself? Can you self-correct without punitive attitudes?

3. Go to the ESA. Put the following questions up for viewing on your mindstage. Try approving, helpful, or supportive characters.

   - Do I have good reason for holding to my viewpoint?
   - Why do I always need to prove my point?
   - Am I actually hearing the other person's viewpoint?
   - Do I automatically discount other people's opinions?
   - Muse over these questions and rehearse MPS creative skills – kindness, understanding, etc.

TRAGIC TRAIT: WORRY, WORRY, WORRY

> *Where care lodges, sleep will never lie.*
> *~ Romeo and Juliet*

As an MPS, we can get focused on one thought theme and find it hard to clarify, assess and make decisions. Instead, we worry ourselves with bothersome ideas that turn into angry and inflexible feelings.

Habitual worry is Self-Harassment. Constant "thought looping" of an aversion puts the distasteful image front and center on your mindstage, eventually magnetizing it into play. In the same way that we hold a desire or goal in our mind and work toward it, we hold our worries. It allows us to proclaim, *I knew this would happen!!!* And lo' and behold, we take pride in being right in our self-fulfilling prophecy. So carefully notice your worries. You have the mental power to make them your reality or…choose to think more creatively.

Contemplative Practice – Ask yourself:
1. Who in me chooses to harass myself? Why?
2. What is "The Worrywart" in me getting out this?
3. Who in me deserves to be harassed in this way?

4. Will worry help control my concerns?
5. Is worry a character habit? Notice.

Muse on these thoughts with honesty and you will find a new approach to worrisome ideas. Are you locked in your mind's little Black Box Theatre?* Notice any Character Residue or Thought Looping. Go to the ESAwareness and *think clarity*. Try opening to new ideas.

Performance Practice – Creative Play
1. Imagine yourself as a worried squirrel, frantically gathering acorns and hiding them in a tree. You worry that other squirrels will find your stash. You worry about your survival. Act it out.
2. By acknowledging worry as an animal instinct; by playing a little squirrel, you can identify with its character of worrying.
3. After being the squirrel, you might be able to release attachment to your worries and find another character in you to handle your Worrywart's concerns.
4. Now speak all your worries out loud. Though our storylines are different, all creatures worry.
5. The point here is not to get so established in a tragic thought, that it becomes your Obstacle Character. There is always another part of you who can take center stage and change the ending.
6. If the worry habit persists, get creative with this practice and choose another animal or person that better exhibits your worries. The more you consciously play out your worries, the less you will have them swimming in your head causing headaches.

Tragic Trait: Anger – The Sharp Tongue

> *I understand a fury in your words, but not the words.*
>
> *~ Othello*

Anger arises when our concepts of right and wrong are invaded or challenged. Our angry character starts resisting, resenting, rejecting, refusing, denying and disproving. Because we are right and feel wronged, we become irritable, sardonic and downright negative. When we negate, we become rigid, put up barriers and stop the flow of incoming positive energy.

Anger has a lot of heat, so if we suppress our angry characters, they move into our bodies and can develop various types of inflammatory diseases. Depending on the different degrees of anger, from mild annoyance to malicious verbal abuse, our body holds the heat of our angry ideas.

For the MPS, anger arises when we feel out of control, aren't acknowledged properly, or when we are made to feel wrong or stupid. When anger becomes the tragic mental's habit, we can be vicious. If someone insults our intelligence, we will catch every cue to insult that person with our greatest weapon – our tongue. Resentment surges when we have been offended. Like a child throwing a temper tantrum, we furiously snap at others trying to make them feel wrong or stupid.

Anger can also result from not having the inner resources to get the acknowledgement or position we want in life. It's a creative crisis. Our self-dissatisfaction can vent in contemptuous attitudes toward others. And then when we can't take it anymore, we suddenly explode.

Those of us who can't control things, use anger to regain control. Since the MPS usually expresses anger verbally or thinks up some kind of plot against someone, here are a few LPPractices.

> **Contemplative Practice – Ask yourself**
> 1. Do I have to use cutting remarks to get acknowledged?
> 2. Who is the real target of my ongoing anger?
> 3. By making others wrong and stupid, does that make me right and smart?
> 4. Am I hurting people with my sarcastic remarks? How do they react to me?

5. How long can I hold resentment in my heart? Who is it hurting?

6. Practice catching the tragic moment and pre-empt it.

Don't try to figure out your self-queries. Muse on them. Watch how your thoughts and words make you feel. Satisfied, arrogant, superior? Do you want to change?

Performance Practice – How do I look when angry?

1. When you feel a surge of anger coming on, see yourself as an angry crocodile snapping at everyone. Watch yourself crawling through the office with biting words for your co-workers. Soon you will become bored with yourself and see how stupid you look – and we don't like to look stupid, do we?

2. If anger surfaces in public, you can also just picture yourself as a big angry bear, croc, pit-bull, vulture or werewolf – whatever works. If you are prone to habitual anger, this practice should work. If it doesn't, then, as Mentals are prone to do, you are taking yourself far, far too seriously.

3. Develop your sense of humor. You have a clever way of seeing things.

TRAGIC TRAIT: RIGHT AND WRONG

To do a great right, do a little wrong.
~ Henry VI, Part Two

MPSs often think in *black or white.* We have a lot of concepts about how people and how things should or shouldn't be. Things must be one way or the other. Therefore, our thoughts become verdicts about what's right or wrong, good or bad. Life becomes locked in black box theatre thinking and can influence everything we do in life. "I" must always be right. We can't handle being wrong, and yet, we can learn the right way from our wrongs.

Contemplative Practice – Ask yourself

1. Why do I insist on always being right?
2. Can I let someone else be right?
3. What is my need? What do I want?
4. Don't try to make yourself right or wrong. Listen to the information with interest in learning.

Contemplative Practice – Coloring in the box

In this practice, we look at the colors within the black and white spectrum. The objective is to find less rigid ways of seeing ourselves, others, and situations.

1. While performing your day, notice the colors in people's clothing and the lively inflections in their voices. Notice shades, textures and shadows in the scenery around you and intensities in people's performance. Be aware of interesting variations in light as passing hours change things around you. Ask yourself if your own thinking has this kind of interest and variation?
2. Imagine what new ideas and experiences could come if you opened the color spectrum between your black and white thinking. Hear other people's view and listen without negating.
3. Investigate colorful, creative thinking.

TRAGIC TRAIT: OVER-THINKING

Faster than springtime showers comes thought on thought.

~ Henry VI

Most of us don't even realize when we are thinking. Too much thinking can confuse our state of mind and affect the condition of our body in the long run. Imagine running your car's engine 24/7 for 75 years straight without turning it off – ever... and even gunning it every morning to give it more power. Yes, it will wear out or break down if you don't give it an occasional rest. But that's what we do to our brain. Even in our dreams, the continuum of thought prevails.

And most of us gun up our brain with a stimulant in the morning and/or some kind of downer in the evening. We treat our brain as if it will run perfectly forever. It's not our collective habit as human beings to slow down the brain's obsessive activity. Though we never know our ultimate fate in life, we can take steps to enjoy greater mental health for our future. So, here is a practice for us Overthinkers.

Contemplative Practice – Overthinking

Notice when you are mentally chatting with yourself or an imaginary someone, or when you are just running benign scenarios on your mindstage. This can be viewed as overthinking. When you catch yourself overthinking, breathe some space into the cracks between thoughts and slowly expand into the ESAwareness.

Contemplative Practice – Brain Breaks*

1. Observe when you have useful thoughts – functional thoughts, junk thinking or imaginary musings.
2. Notice how you use your head as an entertainment center; make note of the shows you are playing (serials or one-time specials?) How do they make you feel?
3. If Brain Babble* confusion, try going to the ESA.
4. In the same way you might take a coffee break to release tension, try taking a Brain Break to release overthinking and ease into the ESAwareness of your mind.
5. Inevitably showers of thoughts will begin again. So, whenever you notice or catch yourself stressing out, repeat this practice.
6. Slowly but surely, by remembering the mental health rewards, you will cultivate an on-growing awareness and soften the hard edges of day-to-day mental pressures.

TRAGIC TRAIT: SMUGNESS

The fool doth think he is wise, but the wise man knows himself to be a fool.

~ As You Like It

Because we always need to be right, we have trouble recognizing our self-righteousness. We can get stuck in mental concepts that may be impressive to us but not necessarily to others. The habit of smugness is the only reason we struggle with change. We don't need to change – we're perfect.

The best concept to maintain is playing the moment with Genuine Presence. It also takes rehearsing our comic characters to break tragic ones. We can learn to break the habit of smugness or other tragic attitudes. However, we must really see the harmful effects of these mindsets and want to change them.

There are many times during a day when we wish we could change a thought or attitude. Some part of us knows we are behaving badly, but out of habit can't stop it. The following practices are meant to help you break the habit of perpetual thinking, junk thinking, and brain babble.

Contemplative Practice – Thought Themes

Tragic MPSs have ongoing thought themes. Things like, *"Jerry is so stupid. And his wife is a real idiot."* Or, *"I could figure that out in a second!"* Even though you don't say or think those exact words every day, you've memorized the lines for instant recall. These thought themes take character and create a smug attitude.

So, listen to who in you is talking. What is your character trying to express? If it is causing obstacles, practice *Calling Cut* as instructed below.

Performance Practice – Calling CUT!

1. First identify your thought. Are you thinking someone is stupid or lesser than you? Is it making you act arrogant or negative toward them?

2. Notice when unwanted thoughts and attitudes arise. Learn to sharply and loudly say, "Cut!"* (Of course, you should

do this when you are alone, unless you want to startle your co-workers and make them stop their thoughts too.)

3. In the same way, a film or theatre director calls CUT! and the action on stage immediately stops, the same will happen when your inner director stops action on your smug thoughts. The more you notice what you are thinking and when, the easier it will be to clear your mindstage and open into Genuine Presence.

4. You will soon be able to *Call Cut* quietly to yourself. With practice, you will become aware of the time-saving, face-saving and refocusing benefits it provides.

5. This practice can also be used to turn off certain annoying thoughts or stop the incessant Brain Babble. Cut and go to the ESA.

As you read the following scenarios, watch your reactions to the characters and their actions. Imagine how you would play it.

Take 1: A Tragic MPS Scenario – Can't you see I'm working?

My thoughts are whirled like a potter's wheel;
I know not what I am, nor what I do.

~ Henry VI

THE SCENE: Kenji's home office. Dinner time.

Kenji, a computer programmer, is obsessed with his work. Following Steve Jobs' lead, Kenji has a wardrobe of black t-shirts, so he doesn't have to waste time thinking about what to wear. He throws on his black shirt and jeans every morning, grabs his black rimmed glasses, downs a cup of coffee and muffin, and off he goes to the office — very early! Ken thinks he has to write more coding and work longer hours than anyone else in his workplace in order to stay ahead. He is driving himself loony and his girlfriend, Emiko is unhappy with their relationship.

Emiko
*(At the door to Kenji's home office. Vying
for his attention with a sexy voice)*
Kenji, dinner is ready.

Kenji
(Totally engrossed at his computer)

Emiko
Ken?

Kenji
(Typing and not answering)

Emiko
(Waiting for him to answer)
Ken?

Kenji
(Talking to the computer)
Huh? What the hell?

Emiko
(Louder — getting annoyed)
Ken? Kenji! Dinner is ready!

Kenji
(To Emiko, but still nose to the computer)
Hey, what's up?

Emiko
(She walks into his office, cups her hands on his ear and says)
Hey, Wizard of Odd. Dinner is served!

Kenji
(Glancing at her then back to computer)
I'm in a weird math situation here. Coding is very detailed.
Can't figure it yet. Sorry…I can't stop right now.

Emiko
Kenji, I've just coded out a dinner — one that you love.
Beef and nourishing vegetables……over noodles.
(Waits for a response…he doesn't answer. Feeling
hurt, she stares at him like never before. Standing
there, she suddenly comes to an AHA moment.)
Kenji, this isn't working for me. I've
given this a lot of thought.
(pause…he ignores her)
Ken, I'm leaving you. This is Goodbye!
(She turns to leave and stops at the door)
Your dinner will still be on the table at breakfast.
Cold…but on the table.

Kenji
(Not really hearing her)
Umm…thanks.

Emiko
(Sadness in her voice)
I mean it Ken. This time I mean it. And by the way,
your mother is worried about you. Call her.

Kenji
(to himself)
Damn…this is pissing me off. Why can't I figure this out?
(Half to Emiko)
Got to get this tonight!
That new guy at work said he could do it in a flash!

Emiko
(Deciding she wants her parting words to be heard,
walks back to his desk. Shouting at him.)
Ken, Listen to me!!!

Kenji
(Looks at her.)
What the hell are you yelling about!

Emiko
(Heartsick and half-crying)
I know no other way to get your attention! I love you.
NO, I don't love you anymore. There is no one there to
love! You have no love. You are a machine! I can't take
it anymore. So, for my sake, I have to leave you.

Kenji
(Getting angry)
Look, I don't have time to deal with your needy outbursts.
You look ugly when you act like this! If you can't handle my
workloads, then maybe it is best for you to get out. I have
enough stress from my boss. I don't need it from you too!!!

Emiko
*(Shocked and stung by his reaction, she
stares at him and walks out.)*

Kenji
(Keeps banging it out at his computer)

Emiko
*(Later, all packed, Emiko is leaving. She sees his iPad on
the dining room table and sends him a selfie and a note.)*
"Poor Kenji…I pray that you will not die a lonely old man.
Maybe you can instruct the funeral parlor
to cremate you with your computer."

CURTAIN

READER'S Q & A NOTES
- Can you remember a scene in your own life when you performed like Kenji?
- Review it and note what you might do differently to bring about a better outcome.

KENJI'S PERFORMANCE EVALUATION
- Performance Style: Mental
- His Creative Blocks: Overthinking and anger
- His Roles: Computer Programmer and Boyfriend

- His Character Choice: Intensity and anger
- Motivation: To be the smartest programmer at work
- Intent: To stay focused without disruption

How Kenji's Tragic Character Traits Might Affect…

- His Health?

Kenji's health is very much at stake here. It is said that some computer programmers work so intensely that it sends them over the edge. And it doesn't have to be a programmer – this can happen to any MPS who works so stridently on their projects that, other than coffee, they don't eat, sleep, hydrate, pay attention to hygiene, or relate to anyone. This may be fine for a robot, but what can this do to a human being?

In the beginning, tension brings worry, fret, and impatience. This affects brain function and creative clarity. We saw Kenji go from irritation to anger, which if repressed, could lead to mental disturbances and even rage. It is documented that anger, worry and mental disquiet often caused by "stress" can lead to high blood pressure and heart disease. Kenji might also develop inflammatory dis-eases, skin rashes and acne due to excessive heat in his system.

- His Relationships?

We saw how Emiko finally had it. How can you have a real relationship with someone who is never there? Living in the same house with Kenji and hardly ever connecting with him is difficult for Emiko. It's not easy to sustain love and support when there is no end in sight to his self-absorption. Kenji's intensity is the character he gives to both his roles. How long would you hang in? Kenji's main relationship is with his computer.

- His Creativity and Productivity?

Kenji thinks he can be both creative and productive by putting in long hours or hard, concentrated work. Unfortunately, the business and corporate bottom line often drives people into this work-style. This unreasonable demand is not only disrespectful to the human instrument, but it creates a lifestyle that negates the very thing we are all seeking – happiness and security. In fact, it creates just the opposite, unhappiness and fear.

Still, some executives and business owners think this intensity and drive keeps the wheels of productivity rolling. For Kenji, it instigates a mind filled with a thicket of thoughts – financial concerns, extreme deadlines, unfriendly competition, personal disengagement and total loss of self. Question is, can creativity and productivity really flourish under such conditions? And if your answer is yes, then the question remains…at what cost?

Director's Notes

Kenji's first priority is his work. As a young man trying to get ahead he thinks concentrated, hard work will get him there. It's what you have to do to survive and get noticed. However, if he continues on this path, his tunnel vision may miss greater opportunities for expansive vision.

Though many companies, large and small, are trying to change old stressful ways of doing business, the money-driven motivations of big business focus on big profit. Sadly, employees like Kenji involuntarily suffer from work overload and unnecessary stress to meet the corporate bottom line.

Like Kenji, most all of us must follow the fold in order to make a decent living. Kenji's motivation is to become a Real Programmer with intent to work long hours until he is acknowledged. However, living in worry and edginess about his livelihood with little human interaction is not natural. Something will have to change if he wants a life.

In the last scene, Kenji took Emiko for granted and in general, dismissed her love. In a replay of the same scene, can he find places in the scene where he can let her know how much he appreciates having her in his life? Showing love and kindness of character can make up for his absence at dinner.

If Kenji cares about Emiko at all, I would direct him to initiate a heartfelt talk with her and try to save their relationship. He must try to understand that his friendship and love is what matters to her. That means to (at least sometimes) turn his head away from the computer and enjoy her presence. Advice: Kenji, take a Brain Break and go to the ESAwareness.

Retake: A Comic MPS Scenario — Give me ten?

A woman would run through fire and water for such a kind heart.

~ The Merry Wives of Windsor

THE SCENE: Kenji's home office. Dinner time.

Kenji, a computer programmer, is seriously into his work. Following Steve Jobs' lead, Kenji has a wardrobe of black t-shirts, so he doesn't have to think about what to wear. He throws on his black shirt and jeans every morning, grabs his black rimmed glasses, downs a cup of coffee and a bowl of oatmeal Emiko made, and off he goes to the office — very early! Ken wants to write more coding and feels he sometimes has to work long hours. He knows he is compromising his relationship with his girlfriend, Emiko, but is making an effort to enjoy time with her and still achieve his own goals.

Emiko
(At his home office door and hoping to get
his attention with a sexy voice)
Kenji-chan, dinner is ready.

Kenji
(Totally engrossed at his computer)

Emiko
Kenji?

Kenji
(Typing and not answering)

Emiko
(Waiting for him to answer)
Hey, Kenji?

Kenji
(Talking to the computer)
Huh? What the hell?
(Stops and turns around)
Sorry Emiko, what did you say?

Emiko

I said dinner is ready!

Kenji

Oh wow, can you give me half an hour?

Emiko

(understanding)

I guess I could keep it on a low flame.

Kenji

(Glancing at her then back to computer)

I'm in a weird math situation here. Coding is very detailed.
Can't figure it yet. Sorry…I can't stop right now.

Emiko

Okay, but I've just coded out a dinner that you love.
Beef with nourishing vegetables over noodles
(Waits for a response…)

Kenji

(Turns around again to look at her)

Umm…thanks. That sounds really good! You're making me hungry.

Emiko

(She smiles)

Okay. I'll be back in half an hour.

Kenji

(to himself)

Damn…this is pissing me off. Why can't I figure this out?
Got to get this tonight!
That new guy at work said he could do it in a flash!

(Half an hour later)

Emiko

Kenji-chan, time for dinner.

Kenji

(Looks at her.)

Wow that was a fast 30. I need another 10.

Emiko
(Disappointed she sighs)
Oh Kenji, always another 10.

Kenji
(With patience)
I know, but I promise I'll be there in 10. It's going
to be a long night for me, so having one of your
nourishing meals will help me get through it.

Emiko
(Feeling encouraged, she leaves.)
*(10 minutes pass and even though he is not at a good stopping
place, Kenji stops and saves his work. He takes a quick
moment, breathes in, clears his mind and opens his heart.
Getting up from his desk, Kenji heads to the kitchen.)*

Kenji
(To Emiko who is watching TV in the living room.)
Umm…smells good in here. Let's eat.

Emiko
Oh, I'm sorry Kenji, can you give me 10?
This program will be over then.
*(She flashes a flirtatious smile at him. They both laugh. He
sits down next to her on the couch and puts his arm around her.)*

CURTAIN

READER'S TAKE

Did you identify with Kenji's Creative Blocks or his Creative Skills?

Performance Challenges

1. Seek relaxed concentration & avoid extreme intensity.
2. Relate to others by showing appreciation.
3. Notice the world around you and how it serves you.

Performance Practices

1. Go to places where you can interact with others – a bar, clubs, volunteer work, etc. Don't have time? Think of it like working out a math problem only working out social matters instead.

2. To build confidence in social interaction, start with people you feel most comfortable with, whether family, close friends or strangers.

3. Start a conversation on a topic you know and notice how long you hold people's interest. Try to keep them engaged. Ask questions and be curious. This is a necessary practice for those MPSs who are stuck in their head.

SCENE 5 THE TRAGIC EMOTIONAL PERFORMANCE STYLE (EPS) – FREEING YOUR CREATIVE BLOCKS WITH CREATIVE CHOICE

> *To be or not to be…that is the question.*
>
> *~ Hamlet*

Who to be or not to be…Good Question. We have all heard the saying, *"Just be yourself."* Whenever I hear this I always ask, *"Which self should I be?"* The fact is, we have many emotional choices to display our inner cast of characters.

I had a man friend who when we went to bed at night would set his alarm for 6:00 a.m. to give himself time to go for a run in the morning before getting dressed for work. One morning as he rolled over and turned off the alarm. I said, *I thought you wanted to go for a run?* Muffled under his pillow, he said, *"The guy who set the alarm last night is not the same guy who just turned it off."*

We all play many parts and often don't realize it. You may have heard yourself say, *I don't know, one part of me wants to go to the party and another part of me wants to stay home.* Given the many roles we play and the variety of emotional characters we give them, it is only natural that we have internal conflict and confusion. Recognizing whether you are acting from your comic or tragic side is very important to the EPS's ability to act with equipoise.

When you can identify the tragic character in you that is causing existing difficulties, you will realize it's not the whole of you that's to blame. You will dispense with damning yourself and know how to call on a more suitable part of you.

The challenge for the EPS is to gain command of our emotional range and become alert to our tragic mood-set so we have choice in changing it. Being in touch with your feelings is only the beginning. You can know you are angry but are unable to transition into emotions you would rather feel and convey.

Knowing how to access and play the emotion you need helps you make realistic character choices. Developing that creative skill requires you to explore the full emotional range and expand your character repertoire.

Next are some of the tragic EPS characters we tend to play along with LPPractices to help turn the creative blocks they cause into creative skills.

TRAGIC TRAIT: TALK, TALK AND BLA-BLA-BLA

> *Gratiano speaks an infinite deal of nothing.*
> *~ The Merchant of Venice*

One tragic performance routine the EPS has is a tendency to talk nonstop – mostly out of a need to communicate and connect with anything and anyone. The ongoing verbal chatter is likely an expression of feeling overwhelmed, unhappy, or needy. It's like we live in some ongoing trauma and need to talk about things – constantly. Whether real or exaggerated trauma, our habit is to unconsciously just keep talking. For example, when a friend is talking about an unfortunate experience they had, rather than empathizing with them, we will cut in on their story to talk about our own similar experience. This comes from our need to bond with them, but it actually short-circuits the connection.

We have to tell you every little detail about an event or issue. By talking we feel we are sharing, connecting and being sociable. We don't realize that we are actually disconnecting. What our tangential rant does communicate to others is our lack of self-awareness.

As an Emotional tragedian, our unfulfilled need is to be loved and accepted. Though friends and family may love us, unfortunately, our nonstop chatter can make people uncomfortable, bored or frustrated because they can't get a word in edgewise.

The Obstacle Character Practice, *Allowing #1*, is great for the EPS. It lets you consciously express the feelings of your Nonstop Talker without constraints or public embarrassment. If you approach your talkative character (or any tragic character) as a part of you in need, you can tend to its need and thereby break the character habit of nonstop talking. So, review Allowing #1. Use it and don't push your feelings away.

Contemplative Practice – Ask yourself
Why can't I stop talking when I get around people? Am I saying anything of interest to others? Am I uneasy? Do I get defensive about my talkative character habit?

Practice – Breaking Character

1. When you are with someone and catch yourself over-talking, stop suddenly and break character. Try saying to the person you are with something like…"*Excuse me, did you say something? I couldn't hear because my Motor Mouth was running.*" Hopefully you can both get a laugh out of it.

2. The idea here is to bust yourself instead of knowing that you are jawing but continuing anyway. You can get creative and make up your own lines for breaking character. Make light of it, as it is an easy habit to break if you just begin to notice your own Gabbing Gabe or Chattering Chelsea.

TRAGIC TRAIT: OVERACTING

> *Nor do not saw the air too much with your hand thus,*
> *but use all gently, for in the very torrent, tempest, and as*
> *I may say, whirlwind of your passion, you must acquire*
> *and beget a temperance that may give it smoothness.*
>
> ~ *Hamlet*

Our emotional tragedian will often overact to compensate for feelings of lack. If we can show-off, our insecurities and long-playing hurts won't be seen. Somehow overacting makes us feel secure and we want others to see us as confident and fun-loving. Besides, we love to perform, so we tend to indulge ourselves with high drama, whether comedic or tragic.

Reacting from our tragic side, we can make a huge dramatic scene out of a mere walk-on part. We are highly reactive and very excitable. We can easily get insulted, jump to conclusions, misinterpret facts and invent a scenario that is true only in our own mind. Often our personal feelings provoke us to redirect a situation that if left alone, could have been enjoyable. Instead we must embellish it, leaving everyone wondering '*what the f#^&k*' just happened?

Our need for love and approval makes us perform with exaggerated style. These antics can also trigger our highs and lows. We can be overly dramatic at both ends of the spectrum. On the low side, we can sulk in a corner bringing everyone around us down. On the high side, we dramatize our dissatisfaction by spewing displeasure into a room for all to feel.

For the EPS, practicing the ESA is absolutely necessary to help level our tendency to go off on one of the deep ends. In addition, learning to work with our emotional range through study and rehearsal in self-correcting ways is also essential.

Performance Practice – Balancing Your Act

As an emotional tragedian, we jump from sad to happy and often the result is pretense. This just reinforces our emotional ups and downs. In the following practice, use Character Choice to slowly and naturally transition emotions from reactive overacting to responsive acting. If you can, make a few copies of the Character Chart as you will be using it in many ways.

1. On the Tragic side, identify and circle, highlight or check the emotion that best describes your present character.
2. Now go to the Comic side and find an emotion that has the same energy level as the tragic emotion you are experiencing. *Example:* For instance, if your tragic character is "sad", (a low energy) go to the comic side and choose an emotion that has the same low energy but means something positive, like "gentle."
3. Visualize the tragic word, "sad" on your mindstage. Watch it transition or morph into the comic word, "gentle."
4. Now begin feeling gentle in place of sad. You are exchanging one attitude for another but not changing energy levels.
5. Stay with the positive, comic-side word for a bit. Perform any tasks or conversations with gentle on your mindstage.
6. Then, like working on a sliding scale, slowly begin to energize. Find another character on the comic side that is a little more energetic like "caring" or "friendly". Put that word on your mindstage and be with that for a while. Rehearse that feeling in a situation.
7. Keep energetically working your way up the Character Chart until you reach an emotional character energy that feels right for the activities at hand.

CHARACTER CHART

These are emotional characters we all play and are not listed as opposite emotions in the chart. The root of comedy is joy and love. The root of tragedy is hurt and fear. All other characters play from these root causes. The 3rd place to take our mind beyond comedy and tragedy is the ESAwareness.

COMEDY JOY & LOVE	THE EMPTY STAGE The 3rd place for the mind to go	TRAGEDY HURT & FEAR
CHARACTERS WE PLAY		**CHARACTERS WE PLAY**
CONTENT		SAD
WILLING		SELFISH
ACCEPTING		HATEFUL
COURAGEOUS		LONELY
HAPPY	CREATIVE RESOURCE	DEPRESSED
CONFIDANT		ANGRY
PEACEFUL		DOUBTFUL
GRACIOUS		GREEDY
GRACEFUL		HOSTILE
ATTENTIVE		ANXIOUS
FUNNY		FRUSTRATED
PLAYFUL		INSECURE
HONEST	CLEAR AWARENESS	SPACEY
BRAVE		SHAMEFUL
CHEERFUL		JEALOUS
GENTLE		NEEDY
SWEET		RESISTANT
BOLD		DEFENSIVE
DIGNIFIED		STUPID
PATIENT		SCARED
HUMBLE		JUDGMENTAL
CONSIDERATE	NEUTRAL GROUND	STUBBORN
CARING		IMPATIENT
RESPECTFUL		GLUTTONOUS

EFFICIENT		SPITEFUL
APPRECIATIVE	PERCEPTIVENESS	CRUEL
Charismatic		AGGRESSIVE
ASSERTIVE		ARROGANT
FUN LOVING		STINGY
INDEPENDENT		WORRIED
INDUSTRIOUS		HELPLESS
GRATEFUL		AVOIDING
GENEROUS		SUSPICIOUS
PASSIONATE		EMBARRASSED
ENTHUSIASTIC		CONFUSED
CAUTIOUS		DULL/FOGGY
VIVACIOUS		COMPLAINING
WITTY	SPACIOUSNESS	HOPELESS
MOTIVATED		GUARDED
DELIGHTFUL		DEMANDING
LOVING		ABUSIVE
DISSATISFIED		RESENTFUL
CHARMING		PRETENTIOUS
ENERGETIC		CRASS
EMPOWERING		CRANKY
THOUGHTFUL		IRRITABLE
KIND		DISHONEST
FRIENDLY		CHILDISH
SENSUAL	STABILITY	DISGUSTED
SEXY		DESPERATE
DARING		SARCASTIC
ROMANTIC		RESTLESS
INSPIRED		UNHAPPY
PERKY		NERVOUS
CALM		BITTER
AMIABLE	SANITY	TERRIFIED
FLEXIBLE		INCAPABLE
COMPASSIONATE		BELLIGERENT

Your Balancing Act

You can also do the *Balancing Act* Practice with feelings that are stronger, hi-energy like "Excitable" and work your way down the energetic chart. This practice helps you monitor your energy levels and self-correct trauma-related health issues.

This practice will slowly and steadily help balance your reality effectively if practiced. Since there are far more emotions than listed in the chart, if you do not find the emotional character that suits your immediate feeling, just add it.

Tragic Trait: Complaining, Blaming, and Feeling Guilty

Thou art the Mars of malcontents.

~ The Merry Wives of Windsor

Some of us are happiest when we are complaining about someone or something. It gives us a focus for our suffering and allows us not to face our own unhappiness. We usually don't see what we have wrought, so it's hard to take responsibility for it. Instead, we put the blame on others.

Complaining and blaming can lead to gossiping as well, and put us in a negative mind state. When negativity is what you dwell on and put out, negativity is what will inevitably boomerang* back to you.

Then comes the guilt. You start feeling bad about how you are acting and before you know it you strongly believe you are a bad ass person. But you must stop it. Feeling guilty is like carrying a piece of trash in your bag without anyplace to dump it. Simply change your Character.

Performance Practice – Talk to the Mirror

1. The next time you hear yourself blaming someone, complaining or gossiping, repeat it over and over in front of the mirror. Elaborate on it and exaggerate your feelings. Notice what you look like and what it does to you. Is this what you want to express and how you want to look?

2. Then complain in the mirror about YOU. Talk to the mirror as if you are complaining to a friend about someone you both know. Keep doing this practice until you understand

the unhappiness embedded in your complaints…or until you crack the mirror laughing at yourself.

3. Then go to the ESA, clear the complainer and rehearse JOY. Jump for joy! Do the same practice in the mirror and feel and see the difference. As a comic Emotional, you can spread joy. That's our comic EPS specialty.

TRAGIC TRAIT: SCATTERED

All is uneven. And everything is at six and seven.

~ Richard II

The EPS can get so over-extended that we spread out all over the place – like a circus jumping from one spectacle to another. This disperses the heart's priorities and causes hesitation – *"I don't know what I want."* Panic – *"OMG, where did I put the money I just withdrew?"* And postponements like, *"Sorry, too much going on – can we meet next week?"*

We want to give everyone a slice of our bigheartedness, but often we are not realistic about our time, take on too much and things don't get done. It also affects the very people we want to help who might be counting on us.

Practice – Character Check-in
Make a copy of the Character Chart and put it on your desk or some-place where you will see it frequently day and night.

1. Every hour or two, check-in and ask yourself, "Who's acting? What emotion am I feeling? How is that character driving my actions and attitude?"
2. Refer to the chart and put a check by the emotion you are using at that moment.
3. By the time you go to bed, you will see what emotions have been influencing your attitude and actions throughout your day.
4. If too scattered or confused, you will see it. If too focused, angry, happy, etc., you will be able to gauge your emotional

movement and the character needed for a more favorable transition will become clearer.

If you find you are living in tragedy too often, identify your tragic character(s) and return to the prior practice, the *Balancing Act* and slowly develop a better relationship with your comic side. Remember, as a Emotional PS you are naturally cheerful and loving.

TRAGIC TRAIT: BEING A WALKING WOUNDED

What a sigh is there! The heart is sorely charged.

~ Macbeth

Feeling weakened by accumulated hurt is a big creative block for the EPS. Our mindstage is darkened by hurt. Our emotional scars are so close to the surface that we are easily offended and get defensive if someone says anything that evokes the slightest old bruise. We need love and acceptance since many of our bruises come from real or perceived rejection. While a Physical PS may simply opt to try harder, the Emotional tragedian often takes on the role of the Walking Wounded.

Due to deep hurts (and most all of us have them to some degree), we develop character traits like low self-esteem and insecurity that act in reactionary ways. We lie to twist the truth in our favor. We indulge our pain by seeking pleasure wherever we can find it. We resist love for fear of attachment or rejection – only to trigger more rejection by our overly emotional reactions. We create a kind of self-fulfilling prophecy, "See…nobody loves me."

We are unaware of how much we pamper our hurt. We are psychologically hyper-sensitive and need to be eased into restored self-worth. For those around us, this can be exhausting. So, to ease the burden on others, try redirecting your Walking Wounded with the next practice.

Practice – Naming Our Character
1. When your 'Walking Wounded' character is performing, try separating this wounded part of you from the rest of your characters by naming it. It could be a silly name like "Wounded Willy" or "Mona Bemoana."

2. Who is it? Hear his or her complaints.

3. You needn't milk old wounds by continually interacting with ghosts from your past. As an actor drops his personal issues when he/she walks on the set, so too can you.

4. Recognize how habitual your wounded character is by not identifying with it.

5. When you name your wounded character, you will always know who it is in you that is acting. You won't mis-take that one part of you for the whole of you.

6. Discover your happier, more energetic characters who can counter-act your wounded one.

7. Notice how your wounded character acts from the habit of hurt. Use the ESA to release your hurt into open space. Sing your hurt out loud. Dance it into the ethers.

8. With more comic character rehearsal, you can develop the practice of creatively choosing who you want and need to be at different times.

9. The more we become aware of our transient nature, the easier it is to release thoughts, memories, feelings and actions that don't work for us anymore.

TRAGIC TRAIT: PICKING UP UNWANTED EMOTIONS FROM OTHERS

One fire burns out another's burning;
One pain is lessened by another's anguish.

~ *Romeo and Juliet*

Emotions are transitory energies that exchange from one person to the next. As an EPS, you are susceptible to feelings and the emotion you are feeling may not be your own. Just because you begin to feel anger or love doesn't mean it is originating from you. We exchange feelings through Emotional Osmosis* and reactively start playing the other person's emotion. It's what happens when we fall in love or when we are inspired by someone's character. It is very important to recognize whose emotion is whose and be aware enough to flex with it. This way you can choose whether to take on another's feeling or not.

Emotional Osmosis also happens when watching a movie or when reading an article. Just notice how the writer's story is affecting you and how the actor's performance moves you. Do you end up feeling sad, jittery or happy? The same thing happens in daily life. Even being in a crowd, we can experience other people's emotions. We are both receptors and transmitters, but not always aware of how we are affecting each other. All you know is that someone upset you or made you happy.

It's like catching a cold from sitting next to someone who's sneezing and coughing. If you are emotionally unaware or susceptible, you can catch it. But, if you know your constitution is healthy, you can be around the person without fear of catching their cold. It's the same with emotions. If you are aware of your susceptibility to certain people and emotional mood-sets, you can change it. You have the power to accept or reject the thoughts and feelings coming at you from outside influences. It's your character choice.

Practice – Emotional Equipoise

1. If you feel confused and don't know how to identify your feelings, Stop! Go to the ESA.
2. Once clear, ask yourself, Who's here? What emotion am I feeling?
3. Staying in the ESA, then try to identify the emotional character of the other person.
4. If their character is not the same as your own experience, then you know you are feeling what the other person is feeling.
5. If it is unsatisfactory, either choose a constructive feeling to act out and send back to them, or gracefully exit the scene.

No one can "make you feel" or do something. It has to be either your choice, or your fear and confusion that takes on someone else's emotional character. Separating what you are feeling from what another is feeling is important to your emotional equipoise. In the ESA, reaction turns to awareness.

TAKE 1: A TRAGIC EPS SCENARIO – ALL I WANT IS LOVE.

False face must hide what the false heart doth know.

~ Macbeth

THE SCENE: Hotel ballroom with buffet and dinner tables set around a dance floor. Evening.

Tasha is a big, beautiful young woman who has scored a first date with Jasen, the cute new guy in town. For the evening, she wears a sunny gold-colored formal dress with very trendy stiletto high heels and carries a jeweled evening bag. She is feeling high on herself, as she knows she's lookin' good!!! They are at her cousin's wedding reception in a classy restaurant and Tasha is trying to fill Jasen in on who's who.

Tasha
(Standing at the bar, she leans into Jasen)
That girl over there…her father owns a chain of fast food
restaurants in the area. I call them junk food joints, but
they are millionaires from flippin' cheap burgers. She's a rich
bitch. Miss Jolanda Jackson…good luck getting to know her.

Jasen
So how do you know the bride and groom?

Tasha
(With pride)
Oh, I'm sorry, I thought I told you. Marvin is
my cousin. He graduated with honors and is now a
neuroscientist doing research on Genetics.

Jasen
Wow, what made him decide on that profession?

Tasha
Alzheimer's runs in his family and so he wants to cure
it!!! We all put high hopes on him. I just hope he can
cure his wife's eating habit. Janelle lost weight for the
wedding, but she eats like a pig. I've been out with them,
so I know. He doesn't know how to handle her. I don't
know what he sees in her — but they say love is blind.

Jasen
(Changing the subject)
So, what about you? What are your interests? What is your work?

Tasha
(Almost apologetic)
I'm between jobs right now. I haven't decided what I want
to do next. Everyone tells me I'm very artistic, so I
know it will be something creative. I may open a beauty
salon or a clothing boutique. I think it would be fun to
shop for all the merchandise. Do you like my dress?

Jasen
Well, yes, I do.
(pauses)
You know, running a business of any kind takes a lot of
financial and marketing skills. Are you good at business too?

Tasha
(Avoiding the question)
I have friends.
(Calls out to someone)
Oh, Robert, come over here. I want to introduce you to someone.

Robert
(Waves hello and yells back)
I have to help Marvin right now. I'll catch you later.

Tasha
(To Jasen)
That's my Uncle Robert. He's Marvin's father. He's a nice
man…I just hope he doesn't drink too much tonight.
(She gives Jasen a look that implies Uncle Robert is a drunk.)

Jasen
(Starting to feel uncomfortable)
So, who are your best friends here?

Tasha
Oh, you'll meet them — don't you worry.
Are you ready for another drink?

Jasen

Not yet.
(Noticing a smartly dressed young woman across the room)
Tasha, who's that woman over there?

Tasha

(Seeing his interest in her)
Oh, she's my banker cousin, Lorene. She has some position at
Alliance Bank downtown. Her boyfriend is at the bank too. I
don't think he is very good to her. Or, so I've heard. She has
a better position and he must not like that. She was pregnant
but had a miscarriage. I'm sorry, but I think it was a blessing.

Jasen

Too bad, she looks like a nice lady.

Tasha

I don't see her very much. I hear she takes a lot
off him, but then you never know what goes on behind
closed doors. You know, she could be the nasty one.

Jasen

Seems like a lot of pretty challenged people in this crowd.
(Looks at her with curiosity)
Tasha, do you have anything good to say about anyone?

Tasha

(Blindsided — takes a pause)
Well…of course. I was just telling you about everyone, so you
would know if you want to make friends with them or not.

Jasen

Well from what you've told me, I'm not
sure I want to know any of them.
(Seeing her defensiveness, he backs down)
I'm sure you're right about everyone, but I would like
to hear about someone you like. Tell me about yourself.
What do you like to do? What's important to you?

```
                        Tasha
        (Having punched her low self-esteem button,
                she's hard-put to respond)
    Oh, if you ever get to know me, you'll find out.
          (Fighting off tears, she fondles her hair)
Excuse me Jason, I need to go to the restroom and freshen up.


                        Jasen
                    (Awkwardly)
          Certainly, I'll just wait here.


                        CURTAIN
```

READER'S Q & A NOTES

- Can you remember a scene in your own life when you performed like Tasha?
- Review it and note what you might do differently to bring about a better outcome.

TASHA'S CHARACTER EVALUATION

- Performance Style: Emotional
- Her Issue: Approval and acceptance
- Her Role: Single, unemployed woman
- Her Character Choice: Needy and Dissatisfied
- Motivation: Desire to be special and loved
- Intent: To make Jasen fall in love with her and make others seem less than her in his eyes.

HOW MIGHT TASHA'S TRAGIC CHARACTER TRAITS AFFECT…

- Her Health?

Not feeling supported by others and not receiving the acclaim and approval she seeks can bring up a number of issues related to self-support. Not being able to stand up for herself may cause back problems. Suppressing long-held anger, fear and disappointment in herself might show up as skin conditions. (See Dr. John Sarno, *Healing Back Pain*) Though she expresses her feelings, it is done in unaware, inappropriate ways like gossiping or dissing others, and usually followed by lows of guilt, shame and blame. Living mostly as an emotional tragedian, her ups and downs could also make her prone to emotional breakdowns.

- Her Relationships?

Tasha depends on good feedback from others and upbeat situations to make her feel good. When she gossips and talks about the faults of others, she doesn't realize that she is reflecting her own faults and cravings. By gossiping about the faults of others, Tasha was indicating to Jason that she is a better person than those people she was dissing.

When people call her on her shortcomings, or see right through her, as Jason did, she gets defensive or takes an emotional dive. In truth, others are mirroring how much she dislikes herself. When she feels good about herself she performs in fun-loving ways, but when she feels bad about herself she behaves haughtily or retreats in shame. The quality and tone of her relationships is dependent on how she feels about Tasha.

- Her Creativity and Productivity?

Tasha feels inadequate and her low self-esteem has difficulty developing her talents. She needs approval and seeks applause yet fears that her talents won't be liked or good enough. Despite her creativity, she has developed the character habit of "I'll try." Because of her ups and downs, Tasha has never played her "I can" character long enough to experience the wealth of her talent. Therefore, she has no experience of productivity. I would direct her to not take herself so seriously and try things out without so much expectation – have a playful attitude and see what works for her.

Director's Notes

Tasha lives in a creative crisis. Creative frustration can impact all of us. And in truth, regardless of our primary PS, most of us experience some degree of emotional imbalance from time to time. If Tasha can use the ESA to see herself, she will be able to create some balance and confidence in her life. She has developed habitual "go-to characters" that have never really worked.

Tasha is seeking love but because she hasn't experienced the brighter side of her talents, she doesn't love herself. She continues to believe she is capable of more but is afraid to apply that part of herself. She fears she can't live up to her imaginary self-image.

Her future depends on her ability and willingness to take a good hard look at her feelings and embrace them, especially the tragic ones. Because she views others in such disparaging ways, she takes her own character flaws too seriously. Too feel better about herself, she needs to learn how to creatively critique. For Tasha to become the woman she wants to be, requires her to discover and rehearse parts of herself that can counteract the Tasha she's ashamed of.

RETAKE: A COMIC EPS SCENARIO – LET'S LOVE ONE ANOTHER

Love sought is good, but given unsought is better.

~ Twelfth Night

THE SCENE: Hotel ballroom with buffet and dinner tables set around a dance floor. Evening.

Tasha is a big, beautiful young woman who has scored a first date with Jasen, the cute new guy in town. Going out that evening, she wears a sunny gold-colored formal dress with very trendy stiletto high heels and carries a jeweled evening bag. She is feeling good and looking forward to the evening. They are at her cousin's wedding reception in a posh restaurant and Tasha is trying to fill Jasen in on who's who.

Tasha
(Standing at the bar, she leans into Jasen)
That girl over there is Jolanda Jackson. Her father owns a chain of fast food restaurants in the area. I don't know her very well. I'd like to, but Jolanda has a different set of friends.

Jasen
So how do you know the bride and groom?

Tasha
(Delighted to tell of Marvin's achievements)
Oh, I'm sorry, I thought I told you. Marvin is my cousin. He graduated with honors and is now a neuroscientist doing research on Genetics.

                              Jasen
              Wow, what made him decide on that profession?

                              Tasha
       Alzheimer's runs in his family and so he wants to find a cure!!!
       We all put high hopes on him. His wife, Janelle, is over there.
                      She's a big support in his life. I've
                      been out with them, so I know.

                              Jasen
                        (Changing the subject)
       So, what about you? What are your interests? What is your work?

                              Tasha
       Oh Jasen, that's sweet of you to ask. Actually, I'm between
       jobs right now. I haven't decided what I want to do next.
       I'm very artistic and love to work with clothing design and
       hair so I may open a beauty salon or a clothing boutique.
       I think it would be fun to shop for all the merchandise.

                              Jasen
              You know Tasha, running a business of any kind
              takes a lot of financial as well as marketing
                      skills. Are you good at business too?

                              Tasha
                          (She laughs)
       Oh Lord no, I'm terrible with figuring out finances. So, I am
       looking for a business partner. I have a couple of sharp friends
           in sales who like my ideas and may want to work with me.
       I'm just starting to think about all this but would love
              to toss some ideas around with you if you're into it.
                        (Calls out to someone)
       Oh, Robert, come over here. I want to introduce you to someone.

                              Robert
                   (Waves hello and yells back)
         I have to help Marvin right now. I'll catch you later.

Tasha
(To Jasen)
That's my Uncle Robert. He's Marvin's father. He's a
wonderful man. And…he loves his bourbon, so every now
and then I'll have a Manhattan with him. *(She giggles)*
He calls me a cheap date — I only drink socially.

Jasen
(Laughs with her)
And yes, I'd love to toss some ideas around with you whenever
you're ready! So tell me, who are you best friends here?

Tasha
Oh, after dinner, I'll take you around
and introduce you to them.

Jasen
(Noticing a smartly dressed young woman)
Tasha, who's that woman over there? Is she a friend of yours?

Tasha
Oh, Lorene is a cousin — she has a good position at Alliance
Bank on Elm St. midtown. She is a terrific lady. I don't
get to see much of her because she works long hours.
(Noticing he might be interested in her)
You might want to meet her boyfriend too. He
also works at the bank. He's over there with
her. I'll introduce you to them later.

Jasen
Great! I'd love to meet them.

Tasha
(Poised & secure)
But meanwhile…Do you like to dance?

Jasen
Yes, I do.

Tasha

Well, when we get out on the dance floor you'll meet a lot of
my relatives and friends. You can tell a lot
about people when they're dancing. You can see
if you want to make friends with them.

Jasen

(Not sure what she is getting at)
Now what can you tell about someone dancing?

Tasha

(jokingly)
You can tell if they like to have fun or
if they're a stick in the mud.

Jasen

It sounds like you are a better judge of people than I am.
(Taking her hand)
Hey, let's sit down. Tell me about yourself. What
do you like to do? What's important to you?

Tasha

(smiling gently)
Oh, if you get to know me, you'll find out.
(Looking at him tenderly, she fondles her hair)
You know Jason, I'd like to know more about you too.

Jasen

Well, we'll just have to do something about that, won't we?

CURTAIN

Reader's Take

Did you identify with Tasha's Creative Blocks or her Creative Skills?

Performance Challenges
- Self-approval – who's insecure?
- Developing empathy* for self and others
- Breaking the character habit of gossiping

Performance Practices
1. When out in public, notice if you look for the faults in others.
2. Develop new friendships based on appreciation for their creative skills.
3. See the reflection of other people's tragic characters in yourself.
4. Notice that part of you who is unhappy – incomplete.
5. Commit to help your unfulfilled character as you would any friend in trouble.

SCENE 6 THE TRAGIC PHYSICAL PERFORMANCE STYLE (PPS) – FREEING YOUR CREATIVE BLOCKS WITH CREATIVE CHOICE

Suit the action to the word, the word to the action, with this special observance, that you o'erstep not the modesty of nature.

~ Hamlet

The Physical PS represents our material presence in the world. We use our body to accomplish things in life, to make physical contact with each other. We have this incredible vehicle, this complex human instrument we play from every day. For each of us, the winning factor is in how we use it, how well we coordinate all our parts. As a Physical, we can live on our tragic side, being destructively abusive, obstinate, and brutally competitive, or we can use our bodies to heal, be helpful, flexible and adaptable. We can also foster team spirit and fair play.

Our physical actions influence our health. If we misuse our body in negative ways, whether stuffing it with food, drink and drugs, or not giving it proper exercise, or if we use it to harm others, we are only cutting the health of our own life short. Ultimately how we treat our self affects our ultimate bodily power.

On the comic side of our physical character we can do wonders. We are the part of our earthly presence that gets things done. As PPSs, it's our choice to help or hinder, to heal or to abuse. We are capable of doing so much for the glory and health of life.

These are some of the typical PPS tragic characters and LPPractices that can help you turn physical creative blocks into creative skills.

TRAGIC TRAIT: STUBBORNNESS

You stubborn ancient knave, you reverend braggart, We'll teach you.

~ King Lear

Our resistance to doing something comes from our discomfort with what we are being asked to do, and/or the person giving the command. Some of us don't easily step out of our known physical routine. If we are asked to be or do something we don't know how to do, it makes us feel incapable. And often we are unwilling to learn about something that sounds different or out of the accepted mainstream. Unwilling to step out of our safe boundaries, we often prevent ourselves from experiencing new things, even if it could help us or bring more joy in our life. We doggedly refuse.

We can also be a bit insensitive to social civility and personal boundaries. If someone accuses us of stepping over that boundary, we stubbornly refuse to admit that we have done anything offensive. We like to feel as if we know what we are doing, as "doing" is our thing. If someone is crying or upset, we stare at them – not knowing what to do.

Contemplation Practice – What Can I Do?

1. You take pride in what you do. Yet, if you use stubbornness to defend your actions and can't stand to be corrected, you cause resistance in others.

2. Then the first thing to "do" is realize that there is no shame or blame in making a mis-take.

3. It's all about your attitude. Instead of counterattacking the accuser and jumping into defense mode, see if the situation can take a healthier turn.

4. Even if you are wrongly accused, your attitude is still the defining act.

5. Is an apology in order? Ask what you can do to rectify the situation.

6. Ask yourself, "What about this is a valuable performance practice?"

7. If need be, call out your brave character and swallow your pride. Put your natural goodness to work. Move into the situation with the willingness to bring goodwill back to the situation.

8. Learn how to "do it" better and self-correct. This is a winning action.

TRAGIC TRAIT: JEALOUSY

> *O, beware, my lord, of jealousy! It is the green-eyed monster, which doth mock the meat it feeds on.*
>
> ~ *Othello*

Jealousy is an instinctive tragic character trait of the Physical PS because it triggers aggression. It arouses actions of hostility, combativeness and violence. As Othello strangled Desdemona out of jealousy, a jealous person will go for the throat.

Jealousy arises when deep down inside we don't feel as good, fortunate, skilled or attractive as the next person. We become fixated on a group or person that embodies what we lack. We want what they have, and that fixation can quickly lead to aggression and assault.

The problem with jealousy is that most of us who harbor it are blind to our own actions, dumb to our thoughts and numb to our feelings. As a result, we just keep rehearsing that Green-Eyed Monster without any awareness until it becomes our character habit. Then we covet, protect, and defend our own jealous actions thinking at worst, we have a bad temper.

Defensively we hold jealousy as our sword, swatting at the very thing we want to win, keep or earn. In counterproductive ways, we fight those we believe to be our rival, but without realizing it, this perceived enemy is our own lack reflected in our face by the abundance of others.

Practice – Green-Eyed Monster

1. Find a safe environment to let your Green-Eyed Greg or Greta act out.
2. As if facing your rival, roar, shout, call him or her names, strike the air with your fist or hit a punching bag.
3. Let your jealous character do and say whatever it needs. This is not a "get-it-off your chest" exercise. That is spewing your toxic waste onto others. This is a practice in awareness.
4. Listen to the part of you that has been yearning to accomplish and hasn't been able. Learn what that Green-Eyed Monster really wants.

5. What are the character qualities in others that make you jealous?

6. Are they actually qualities you would like to be recognized for? Might you act them out differently? Rehearse the characters you envy.

7. Notice how jealousy steals your energy and weakens all your efforts.

8. Breathe into the ESA – clear your mind, ground your body and expand your awareness.

9. Now refocus your energy. Choose and rehearse Physical PS comic characters that can counteract jealousy. Caring? Cooperation?

Be really great at what you do best, and that Green-Eyed Monster will not need to occupy center stage. If and when he/she reappears on your mindstage, take it as a cue to creatively revisit your sense of lack and repeat this practice.

TRAGIC TRAIT: ABUSIVENESS AND AGGRESSION

> *O, it is excellent to have a giant's strength but*
> *it is tyrannous to use it like a giant.*
>
> ~ *Measure for Measure*

Every Performance Style has its way of being abusive. However, the abusive character of the Physical PS can get forcibly violent, kill or do substantial harm to others and our self. The abuse takes form in our body by continually rehearsing characters such as laziness, hostility, anxiety, brutality, resistance and others. With longtime play, they can create painful illnesses.

Sometimes self-violence is slow-acting such as in overeating, doing excessive drugs and drink, poor hygiene, and even down to picking at our pimples or biting our fingernails. Because the effects don't always manifest quickly, we don't see it as a violent act. But the results you are accumulating through your actions add up. These tragic traits are poisons to our wellbeing and cause us much harm in the long run.

Like diagnosing any ailment, the sooner you identify your abusive character, the sooner you can begin the healing and transition process. There are times too, when your character has done physical damage and needs to seek medical help.

When it comes to sexual abuse, we feel so inept and/or so filled with self-hate that we have an obsessive need to shame and devastate another, while pleasing ourselves. Though we may be sexually abusive with one character trait, we have other comic character traits that we present to the world, such as being a brilliant Mental PS, or a generous Dynamic PS. This is how we surprise friends, coworkers and family when we pull a Jekyll and Hyde. When our tragic, aggressive side suddenly acts out, we are seen as being out of character.

Self-abuse results from the habit of aggression that is easily projected onto others. We like to think others cause our feelings of hostility. Yet if we are honest, it usually has to do with our own failure to get what we want or be who we want to be. Out of touch with our own feelings of lack, this suppressed fury in our body makes us want to strike out at anything or anyone. Some of us play it tough, while others assume a high-functioning character to blow off steam.

Aggression is a way of acting that has many psychological components. There are many forms of illnesses, mental, physical and psychological that are associated with aggressive behavior. The causes are medically and physically explained, yet the emotional cause might be locked up in such obscured places in the body that aggressive and eruptive outbursts are the only expression. Though we have medical names for these behaviors, we tend to act and look like a caged animal trying to break free.

Self-abuse is potentially there in all of us. Our tragic side is capable of doing subtle harm, like stubbing your toe, or great harm by developing a death-defying dis-ease. Knowing the comic and tragic traits of our Performance Styles help us recognize our obvious character traits as well as the dormant characters we are capable of performing. Knowing your abusive character is only one part of you and that you possess other parts who do not want to be destructive, then you can transition more easily.

Using the following practice can begin a process that leads to greater understanding of your abusive character's dis-ease.

Practice – Bursting Free

Because our apparent abusive traits are easy to see, in this practice, direct your Badass Bart or Bitchy Betty character to noticing the small less obvious self-abusive actions. This is subtle inner research.

Before you begin the practice, name your characters 1) Abusive Abbie, 2) Aggressive Agnes, or whatever name suits you.

1. Notice when you trip over something and almost fall. Notice when you have tension in your neck or have heartburn.

2. Notice what you are doing at the time. Are you talking down to yourself, annoyed with someone, slightly unhappy with yourself, using abusive language, or spaced out? These are all signs that you are acting from your tragic side. Try to identify the emotional character acting.

3. When you feel these characters coming on, sing out your character's name. Using force, sing LOUD.

4. If you are not in a place where you can do this, just sing a song that expresses how you feel or want to feel. People will think you are either happy, sad or crazy. If they question you, just say… *"I'm singing away my frustrations. Try it sometime, it helps."*

5. Or, If you can, dance! Music is good, but you don't need music. Just allow your character to move and express!

6. The idea is to turn that forceful antagonistic energy into forceful creative energy.

7. If you have a big outdoor or studio space where you can energetically throw paint onto a canvas – do that! Create your antagonistic character's masterpiece. Let your killer instinct slay that canvas!

8. Pound out your feelings and thoughts on a keyboard – piano or computer.

9. Most importantly…Be Empty Stage Aware! Notice how your feelings and thoughts are creating your actions.

10. In the ESA, notice other characters in you. Who would you rather be?

11. With this awareness, can you transition from Abusive Abby to Assertive Andy?

This is one way to transition from abusive and/or aggressive character to a comic character of the same energy level. Awareness and willingness to change are the keys. Note: Always get professional help if your aggression feels dangerous.

Is Physical Pain a Character?

> *Each substance of a grief hath twenty shadows.*
> *~ Richard II*

Our performance habits physically take hold and keep us attached to tragic self-images that are hard to recognize, let alone change. Though a character trait may be uncomfortable, sad or downright painful, we still see it as ME and don't know how to acknowledge or change it. So, we let it fade into the distant past or keep playing it until we get really good at it, adding emotional and mental suffering to physical suffering. Then we complain as if we had nothing to do with the results.

We treat pain as an invader – separate from ME and accept it as something that just happens to us. We blame our condition on genetics or some physical event and otherwise have little understanding of it. If it is a simple cold, we become annoyed with it never noticing who in you was susceptible. If it is a chronic pain, we drug it or divorce ourselves from it. We try to kill the blood-sucking parasite with distraction therapy – becoming a workaholic, shopaholic, use entertainments, or more drugs – anything to make it go away.

If a death-defying dis-ease, we fight it – as well we should, yet rarely do we fully address the emotional component. Sometimes we are successful in reducing our suffering with diets, or holistic healing, but often the pain will reappear in a different form somewhere else in our body that we see as a different ailment. We forget that any pain occupying our body is an unhappy expression of an emotionally injured part of us. We ignore its storyline and forget to have compassion for our self at a time when self-love is most urgently needed.

Hopefully, for some, the challenge sends us deeper into self-discovery. As human beings, we have a choice: to continue ignoring those condemned unsavory characters in us or listen to them and find out why they cause us so much grief. Our Pain knows things that might be a key in freeing other parts of us held captive – the part who likes to function and accomplish things. The longer we let our pained prisoner scream without listening, the more we run the risk that our Abuser will do greater damage to our body.

Practice – Who is my Pain?
The following is an example of a process for getting to know your pain as an individual, existing part of you that has been ignored. Fill in your version of the following process.

Directions Part 1
What specific role does my Pain play in my life? Create your version of the following example:

1. Give your pain a title and role: Ex: CEO of Pain, Inc.
2. What is your CEO's job function?
   * In charge of my human instrument
3. What is his/her tragic motive and intent?
   * To shut down bodily operations
   * To take-over and suppress functionality
   * To distract and cause suffering
   * Block my comic characters from feeling good
4. What Performance Style would best describe your CEO of Pain, Inc.
   * Tragic Dynamic
5. What emotional character traits are at play here?
   * Hostility toward my body
   * Power over other parts of me
   * Possessiveness of my mindstage – pain is all I can think about
   * Self-anger – pissed off at myself for being sickly
6. What action does my CEO cause?
   * Slow functioning – can't work as well – no success
   * Lethargic – Loss of mind and spirit –

- Non-social – lack of desire to participate in things
7. What is my CEO of Pain's ultimate objective?
    - Defeat? Death? Punishment?

Directions Part 2

Now that you know your pained character's role, motive, intention and emotional character, let it be. As painful as it is, don't try to resist or change it, just give it space to be. Go to the ESA, relax and breath into it.

It is a part of you that needs understanding and compassion. Would you push away a friend who is in pain? Try the *Allowing Practices* (Obstacle and Hidden Characters) to hear its storyline. As long as you resist and hate your pained character, it will "Take-Over" your whole human instrument.

As you come to develop affection for all the parts you play, you will be able, given physical conditions, to recast your pain – create new roles for yourself and accomplish your objectives.

TAKE 1: A TRAGIC PPS SCENARIO – ALL PISS AND VINEGAR

Heat not a furnace for your foe so hot that it do singe yourself.

~ Henry VIII

THE SCENE: Evergreen Hills Senior Living. Late afternoon.

Carrie is a caregiver at an Old Folks Home, as she likes to put it. Though she is small, she is strong and well-built with a couple of colorful tattoos. She takes care of "her people" and likes to take them on outings. It is 3:30 on a sunny summer afternoon and Carrie is bringing five elderly live-ins back to the residence. She is looking forward to getting off at 4 p.m. when her boyfriend will be picking her up.

Carrie
(Standing at the foot of the van. Teasing a resident.)
Come on old poky. Do I have to come up there and carry you off?

Evelyn
(in a slow sweet voice)
Just wait till you get old and gray Carrie. Getting up and
down the stairs isn't as easy.

Carrie
Oh, I'm just playin' with you to get your adrenalin goin'!
Now come on down ole gal!

Ole John
(Poking Carrie with his cane)
I'd like to get your adrenalin goin', girlie.

Carrie
(Punching at him)
Believe me, Ole John, you do!

Ole John
(laughing)
Come on, I'll race ya to the door.

Jackson
(An aide walking out to the van)
Hey Carrie, do you need some help?

Carrie
Yah, Merle's gonna be here in 10 and I gotta do that report junk
and check out. Thanks!
(She leaves Jackson with "her kids" and goes inside the office.)
(To the head nurse)
June, do I have to fill out this shit every time I take them
out? Why can't I just write a report if somebody gets hurt?
(Looking at the papers)
Aw man, this is gonna take me another 20 mins!

June
(annoyed)
Carrie, just write it. Why do I have to fight you
every time you don't want to follow procedures?

Carrie

Oh, come on June, it's bullshit and you know it!
I'm not gonna take them out again if I have to do this.
(Getting heated — waving the report at June)
You fill the damn thing out — you know what happened.
They went to the park; they had fun and came back
to play freakin' bingo.

June

(Holding her temper)
It's your job to take them out and if you don't like
writing up reports, then find another job.

Carrie

(really pissed off)
Hell, you know you won't find anyone as good as me. I'd beat out
anyone you try to bring in. The residents here love me.

June

(reacting to Carrie's aggressiveness)
You're too rough with them. For your information,
there have been a couple of complaints.

Carrie

Who? Who complained? I'll slap 'em a good one.

June

You know I can't tell you that. Why are you always so resistant?
(Losing it)
You know Carrie, sometimes you're just a stubborn little…!

Carrie

(Aggressively raising her arm)
Shut up, June! I swear, if you were a guy, I'd punch you out!

June

(Upset and a little frightened)
Now calm down Carrie. No need for that!

(With tough guy swagger Merle enters the office.)

                                   Merle
                         (Sees the skirmish. To Carrie.)
                           Hey Baby, you ready?

                                   Carrie
                      (Throwing the report on the desk. To June)
                      I'll fill this out tomorrow. I'm outta here.
                          (Leaves the office in a huff)

                                   Merle
                      (Walking out of the building with Carrie)
                             You okay Babe?
                                (Pause)
                       I brought the Harley. You in the mood?

                                   Carrie
                      Man, I'm in the mood for a good hard
                        ride and a drink. Got a smoke?

                                   June
                         (Still in office. Seriously ruffled)
                      Yes, indeed Miss Carrie… you're outta here!

                                  CURTAIN

Reader's Q & A Notes

- Can you remember a scene in your own life when you performed like Carrie?
- Review it and note what you might do differently to bring about a better outcome.

Carrie's Character Evaluation

- Performance Style: Physical
- Her Issue: Competition and Aggression
- Her Roles: Caregiver and Girlfriend
- Her Character Choice: Combative and Defiant
- Motivation: Gratification
- Intent: To win the fight with June and get out

How Might Carrie's Daily Performance Affect...

- Her Health?

Carrie's defiance and aggression causes tension. She tends to relieve her tension by over-drinking, smoking and in general, pushing herself over the edge. As we all know, too much alcohol can cause loss of judgment, weight problems, and liver damage. A cigarette pack or more a day could lead to illnesses such as cancer, lung and heart disease, or emphysema. Being fairly young, Carrie doesn't think about these health issues, so she continues to play tough. But prolonged use of these abusive addictions can be serious threats to her health.

- Her Relationships?

She drives herself hard and often pushes others beyond their edge as she just did with June. Unless they are tough like Merle, she will probably loose people quickly and wonder why. Her "shoot from the hip" style of interacting may not work with everyone. She doesn't know how to relate to people whose style is different from her own. As a child, to win favor, she learned to play every scene with a competitive edge. Now, she is often offensive and loses favor.

- Her Creativity and Productivity?

Carrie's creativity is tied up in her aggression. It takes all her creative juices to maintain her level of belligerence. Though Carrie is productive, if she could turn her hostile character into one that has team spirit, she might gain more energy, more friends and discover more creativity. She might also develop a self-image that she secretly wants.

Director's Notes

Though Carrie has a heavy backstory causing her aggressive character to hold center stage, from a performance POV, she has choices. As an actor drops her personal character when entering the stage, Carrie, as life actor has the same ability to decide how she wants to play any scene in her life.

I would direct Carrie to notice the needs of others in a situation and their particular Performance Style capabilities. Presently she jumps to conclusions about people based on how they work with her needs. Carrie is caring, but her aggressive character automatically acts before any other part of her can assess the scene. Getting the job done is one thing, but her additional assignment is to rehearse concern for others. She is addicted to aggression and to break the habit, she must break character and rehearse a counter-part, like "considerate."

RETAKE: A COMIC PPS SCENARIO – HEY, HOW CAN I HELP?

Tis not enough to help the feeble up,
But to support him after.

~ Timon of Athens

THE SCENE: Evergreen Hills Senior Living. Late afternoon.

Carrie is a caregiver at a Retirement Home, as she likes to put it. Though she is small, she is strong and well-built with a couple of colorful tattoos. She cares about "her people" and likes to take them on outings. It is 3:30 on a sunny summer afternoon and Carrie is bringing five elderly live-ins back to the residence. She is looking forward to getting off at 4pm when her boyfriend will be picking her up.

Carrie
(Standing at the foot of the van. Carefully watching a resident.)
Do you need some help Evelyn? Do you need me
to come up there and help you down?

Evelyn
(In a slow sweet voice)
Oh, thank you Carrie dear. Getting up and
down the stairs isn't as easy anymore.

Carrie
It may take you some time to get down, but you still have some
adrenalin going! You're doing pretty well for a gal your age!
Maybe you can give me some pointers for when I get old and grey.

Ole John
(Poking Carrie with his cane)
I'd like you to get my adrenalin goin, girlie.

> Carrie
>
> *(Laughs)*
>
> Oh, I don't know, Ole John, you're doing a pretty good job all by yourself! I don't think you need any help from me.

> Ole John
>
> *(laughing)*
>
> Come on, I'll race ya to the door.

> Jackson
>
> *(An aide walking out to the van)*
>
> Hey, Carrie, do you need some help?

> Carrie
>
> Yah, Merle's gonna be here in 10 and I gotta write that report and check out. Thanks!
>
> *(She helps Evelyn down and leaves Jackson with "her kids")*
>
> *(Inside the office.)*

> Carrie
>
> *(To the head nurse.)*
>
> June, why do I have to fill out these reports every time I take them out?

> June
>
> It's procedures in case anything happens down the line we have a way of looking back at each resident's behavior patterns.

> Carrie
>
> Really? I never knew that. Thanks for explaining it. Now I know what to watch for. Frankly, I just thought it was a way of keeping me busy.
>
> *(Looking at June's desk)*
>
> You know I can organize all those files for you.

> June
>
> *(Surprised)*
>
> Thanks, but it's not your job to organize everyone's reports. Also, the file cabinet is old and jammed. Eventually, I want to transfer everything to digital documents.

Carrie
(wanting to help)
Look June, I don't want to do unnecessary time here,
but you need help and it's my duty as part of this
team to do what I can. You need a techie for the
digital stuff, but I can fix that cabinet — easy!

June
Okay, if you don't mind, that'd be great. I'll take
any help I can get! Carrie to the rescue! I knew you
were reliable but didn't know you were so handy.

Carrie
I'll come in a little early tomorrow and get to it.
And I'll fill this out tomorrow. Merle will be here any minute.

June
You know I shouldn't let you do that. You're supposed to write
it up when your mind is still fresh with the incident.
(She winks at Carrie)
You know Carrie, sometimes you're just amazing! I'm knocked
out by the discipline you have to get things done.

Carrie
(making light of the compliment)
Ah, if you were a guy, I'd kiss you!

June
Well, it was only a compliment, not a proposition.
(They both laugh)

(With cowboy swagger Merle enters the office.)

Merle
(Caught the interaction. To Carrie.)
Hey Baby, you ready?

Carrie
(Picking up the report. To June…)
Okay June, you win. I'll take it home and do it tonight.

June

Great! It'll save you time tomorrow.

(They leave)

Merle

(Walking out of the building with Carrie)

How's it goin' Babe?

(Pause)

I brought the Harley. You in the mood?

Carrie

(Stoked)

Oh man, you bet! Can we go to the Pier for a good fish and veggie dinner? They have a fresh fruit smoothie I love.

(stops Merle)

Let me say a quick goodbye to my kids.

June

(Still in office.)

Yes, indeed Miss Carrie…you're the winner!

CURTAIN

READER'S TAKE

Did you identify with Carrie's Creative Blocks or her Creative Skills?

Performance Challenges

- Admitting defeat and letting it be okay.
- Releasing the aggressive need to win. Learn to win without hostility.
- Helping others without fear of losing.
- Notice the effects of your actions.

Performance Practices

- Complete jobs to your satisfaction.
- Practice working with others in co-operative ways.
- Create team spirit.

SCENE 7 THE TRAGIC DYNAMIC PERFORMANCE STYLE (DPS) – FREEING YOUR CREATIVE BLOCKS WITH CREATIVE CHOICE

Tempt us not to bear above our power!

~ King John

As Tragic Dynamics, we don't always understand the magnitude of our power and can mistakenly use it against ourselves. Our desire to "be somebody" is so great that we spend much of our energy suffering "not being" the person we want to be. We want respect, prestige and power, yet our self-serving motivation acts out as greed, dominance, narcissism and other unbecoming characters who limit our success. We neglect to nurture our better parts. We are too busy trying to prove our worth.

In order to make confident changes we have to take a serious and honest look at our tragic traits and how these performance habits are affecting our career, loves and life goals. The following are a few Tragic Dynamic character traits and some LPPractices to help turn our creative blocks into creative skills.

TRAGIC TRAIT: ASSUMED NOBILITY

Nor I, nor any man that but man is, with nothing shall be pleased,
Til he be eased with being nothing.

~ Richard II

A major tragic character trait of the Dynamic PS is a sense of entitlement. We are simply "The Privileged." Because we are charming, daring, and commanding, others just can't help but idolize us. And we not only love it, but we feel we deserve it and are the first to tell you so! We truly believe we are special and deserve to be treated royally. However, this well-rehearsed cover character of sovereignty is a defense mechanism for our deeply embedded self-doubt. Because of our big display or position in life, others are duped into supporting our inflated sense of self. With this kind of encouragement, we believe we are invincible. Unfortunately, the pressure of power actually distorts our good sense. As a result, we are prone to misjudgments and public scandals. If we have not established our inner power, or think we have lost it, we need to show off, brag, and exhibit a contrived power. By disempowering others, we feel more powerful. We fear that if we let others show their power, we will lose ours.

Our biggest cover character is the con-artist. Whether it is in romance, business or family life, we are very good at making people believe we are the answer to their prayers. This overblown self-image lessens our dignity and integrity. Only when we know how to empower our self in honest ways will we be able to lead and empower others.

Tragically, some of us spend our lives in self-service, confusing dictatorial commands with true leadership. As Assumed Nobility, we have trouble admitting that we have character flaws. We all have character imperfections that we can't see or refuse to admit. The following practice can help us see our reflection in our inner mirror – and we Dynamics do love the mirror. We're just not as familiar with the inner one.

Practice – Turning Assumed Nobility into Noble Character

We assume ourselves to be important bigshots and talk big. It may fool some of the people some of the time but lose most of the people most of the time. As a dynamic tragedian, it may be difficult for you to even imagine that you need to do this practice, as you believe your own PR. However, it is urgent that you see how you look.

Directions Part 1

1. Go to the mirror and tell the person in the mirror how important you are. Recall impressive things you have said to people in the past. Talk really big about yourself – exaggerate.
2. Try selling the person a bill of goods – whatever you want them to believe or buy.
3. Notice how you look and sound. Are you impressing yourself?
4. Would you interact or do business with this person in the mirror?

Directions Part 2

5. If you are seeing your dishonesty for the first time, you might deny, ignore or become dejected and flip into the insecurity you are trying to cover up.

6. No need to go there. Though your habit is playing the con-artist, you have the power to see your MIS-Take and make character changes.

7. No need to dwell on parts of you that no longer serve you and those around you.

8. As a professional actor drops a character that isn't playing well and tries-out another, look in the mirror again, and try out various emotions that make you feel genuine and honest. Learn the difference between assumed nobility and true noble character.

9. Reassess your motivation and intent with less focus on "Great ME" and more centered on enabling others.

This character building process happens in us without deliberate preparation. We may have deliberate intent, but no awareness of what side of our character we are developing. Nor do we always have the performance savvy for taking useful action. We just go after it – assuming our superior attitude will make us look good and gain prestige.

One thing that is important with doing this practice is to define what noble character is for you. If you pay close attention to the consequences and the rewards of your character actions, you can discover the real meaning of noble character.

TRAGIC TRAIT: GREED AND GLUTTONY

> *I am not in the giving vein today.*
> *~ Richard III*

Our greed for power is insatiable and is born out of the fear of appearing lowly – of not being significant. Our motive is to gain status for ourselves and that desire is what drives us to act in selfish ways. Greed is also a feeling of not having enough – the need to cling to what you have, or to grasp insatiably at anything you want. Once you have established the character habit of needing more, it is very hard to change.

Greed makes us treat others poorly and act in such ugly ways that even those who love us will eventually turn away. If we don't know how to nourish ourselves properly, how can we nourish others?

The counter-character to greed is generosity, yet open heartedness is hard for the Tragic Dynamic. However, if you really want to secure your fortune, it is important to share your sense of abundance with others. The quality of character you are building daily will determine the quantity of your prosperity. If you are thinking that hoarding will secure your future, then think again.

For those of us who would like to change the focus on self-interest, our new practice is to see, feel and reach out to the bigger picture. Our tragic style is to ignore the needs of others and take what can benefit ME. We don't understand that the more we have, the more we can give – and the more we give, the more we get.

Performance Practice – Eat Your Gluttony

1. If you have a greedy or gluttony character, imagine yourself as a wild boar tearing into a piece of meat. Find a place where you can act it out. Feel the desire to consume whatever is in sight.
2. What is motivating this voracious beast in you? What do you want that you are not getting? Why can't you satisfy your greed?
3. If you allow yourself to really feel this insatiable craving and grasping at money or power, you will see how your greed is eating you up.
4. Awareness of your greed is the first step toward change.
5. Practicing a counter-acting* character, such as generosity or enabling others is the second step.
6. Every time you feel the need for gluttony – make an offering to someone else.

TRAGIC TRAIT: UPSTAGING*

He will steal, sir, an egg out of an oyster.
~ All's Well That Ends Well

In theatre, when an actor upstages another actor, he or she is trying to steal the other actor's moment on stage and bring the audience's attention to him or her. Also, known as *scene stealing*, the cast does not look upon this kindly.

In daily life, upstaging is a classic Dynamic Tragedian move. It is an out and out Take-Over – stealing the limelight from another person and taking command of the situation. The Tragic Dynamic automatically upstages without a thought or care of others. In business, it could be your partner who takes credit for things that you did. In a life partnership, it could be your spouse dominating the conversation when you have guests. It's inconsiderate, rude and can be insulting to anyone who had the so-called floor. But it's the DPS's tragic insensitive habit to own and rule.

This Take-Over Character can be seen in the grocery line butting up in front of you, or speedily passing your car from the wrong lane, or reaching over you to grab the sweater you were about to buy. No "Excuse me" is necessary for an upstaging move. It's an instinctive "ME FIRST" way of acting. We just take what we want.

Common decency is an obsolete concept in our world. We don't have time for people who are slow and uninteresting. Worst of all we don't see how obnoxious we look to those who experience our rudeness. Unaware of our self, we suck up all the space in a room.

Only a mature and genuinely self-empowered Dynamic will say, *"Oh don't let me interrupt the conversation...please continue."* The self-empowered comedic Dynamic knows that his/her turn will come when the time is right. The possessive need to upstage comes from a dread of not being seen or heard. Almost all the character traits of a Tragic Dynamic are born out of a fear of not being special – not being noticed. Yet, the Comic Dynamic has genuine power.

Practice – Upstage Yourself
1. The next time you cut in on someone, notice their reaction.
2. Is it your intention to interrupt or disturb the other person's spotlight?
3. If you feel it is necessary, explain your motivation to them.

4. If it's just you being you, then cut in on yourself. Upstage your own need to take over.
5. Go to the ESA and be present to what the other person is doing and saying.
6. Then, in the right moment, respond.
7. Your presence will be far more powerful in this way.

TAKE 1: A TRAGIC DYNAMIC PERFORMANCE STYLE SCENARIO — I'M THE BOSS HERE!

> *Third Fisherman: Master, I marvel how the fishes live in the sea.*
> *First Fisherman: Why as men do a-land. The*
> *great ones eat up the little ones.*
>
> *~ Pericles*

THE SCENE: High-Rise, posh office building. Early afternoon.

Griffin is an adventurous entrepreneur in his early 30s, with an attraction to the high life. He plans to make a lot of money with his new venture, Interactive Theme Restaurants. His first restaurant, *Elsewhere ~ Dining in Future Worlds,* is a huge success. He is in his office with Jorje Rodrigues, a probable big investor, discussing the plans for his next restaurant village, *The Magic Gate ~ Dining in Mystical Lands.*

His associate, Timothy Barnes, came to Griffin asking him to partner his idea. Timothy is the creative brain behind what Griffin now calls HIS ventures. Griffin, as the executive producer, does have a large investment in this project; however, he doesn't acknowledge Timothy as the concept creator and architectural designer.

Griffin
(Playing it suave and commanding)

So, Jorge, I'm glad you liked *Elsewhere* because The Magic Gate is the same concept but gives the diner a different theme. While *Elsewhere* takes the adventurous diner to Future Worlds, The Magic Gate takes you into mystical lands. Jorge, which worlds did you visit at Elsewhere?

Jorge
I first went to 'Condos in the Cosmos'! Fascinating! I enjoyed
choosing the foods I would eat in that world and having
the Chefs create amazing dishes out of it! Then I went to
'Mars, the Red Planet' and as I walked around savoring each
morsel, I was "fired up" by the sets, costumes and the themed
interaction with the chefs, waitpersons, and other patrons.
It was a surreal movable feast. In fact, that's what I liked
about the concept — it's a surreal dining experience.

Griffin
Thank you, Jorge, I'm glad you like my concept. I am
very good with creative ideas and development.

Timothy
(Gives Griffin an incredulous look)
It's brilliant! You're a genius Griffin!

Griffin
(Ignoring Timothy's glares)
Timothy, get Jorge a cup of coffee and some of
those tidbits on the table over there.
(Timothy's insulted, as he is NOT the Gofer, but obliges anyway.)

Jorge
Griffin, this will be the new Disneyland — only
in a restaurant village. Each venue within the
restaurant village is a different culinary ride.

Griffin
(Playing him)
Jorge, you are just the kind of investor I like
to work with…smart, creative and enthusiastic! And
it sounds like you are quite the gourmand!

Timothy
*(Eyes rolling, but not letting anyone see him,
brings over a tray of coffee and sweets)*

Jorge
(Patting his belly)
Thank you. As you can see, I love to eat! You know, I
have always wanted to get into the entertainment business
and this might just be the ticket. But before I get too
excited, tell me about The Magical Gate. Where will it
be, how will you execute it, and what is your budget?

Griffin
Well, here is where I will turn it over to Timothy.
He has taken my ideas and put them on paper. He has
written up my plan for the entire project. Tim?

Timothy
(Upset by no proper introduction from Griffin, he says to Jorge)
First of all, Jorge let me introduce myself. I'm Timothy
Barnes, Griffin's Co-Producer. I have a degree as an
architect and have enjoyed sharing in the creation and
success of 'Elsewhere' alongside Griffin. And though I
may not look like it, I am a gourmet chef also.

Jorge
(Surprised)
Oh, wonderful news! Did you……?

Griffin
(Cutting in and dismissing Timothy's
attempt to "promote himself".)
Tim! Why don't you stand near the screen?
We can hear your presentation better
over there. And hit the lights.

Timothy
(Annoyed at Griffin as he walks to the light switch.)
Certainly…

Twenty minutes later ~ presentation complete

Timothy
So, Jorge, what do you think?

Griffin
Thank you, Tim, I can take it from here.
(To Jorge)
As you can see, I have covered every angle.
*(Timothy decides to leave with his iPad notes
in hand. Griffin gets annoyed.)*
Timmy don't leave. Jorge may have some questions for you.

Timothy
(Holding back his hurt and anger)
I have another meeting Griffin.
(To Jorge)
It was very nice to meet you Jorge.
I look forward to seeing you again soon.

Griffin
(To Timothy)
Well, then you better leave me your iPad with your notes.

Timothy
Sorry Griffin, but I need it for my next meeting.

Griffin
*(Shooting Timothy an "I'll deal with you later" look.
Then irritated, he waves him off.)*

Griffin
(To Jorge)
So, what do you think? Any questions?

Jorge
Not at the moment Griffin, Timothy did a great job presenting
the project. You're lucky to have him by your side.

Griffin
(Discrediting Timothy under his breath)
Sometimes I wonder if he is by my side. He
seems to forget that I am the CEO.
(To Jorge)
Well, Jorge, it sounds like I don't have to convince
you to invest in The Magic Gate. How about meeting
next week and talking with my financial officer?

Jorge
(Aware of the interaction between Timothy and Griffin)
I like your project Griffin. However,
I need to do some thinking
and get with my advisors before we meet again.

Griffin
(Walking Jorge to the door)
Sounds good. I'll give you a call early next week.
*(Jorge leaves and Griffin motions to his assistant to come in
as he walks back to his desk)*

Griffin
Where's Mr. Timothy Barnes? What kind of important
meeting does he have that he has to walk out on me?
He needs training in people skills, that ungrateful
smart ass. Tell him I want to see him. Now!
(To himself)
I'll bet Rodrigues drops out after the way Tim treated him.

CURTAIN

READER'S Q & A NOTES
- Can you remember a scene in your own life when you performed like Griffin?
- Review it and note what you might do differently to bring about a better outcome.

GRIFFIN'S DPS CHARACTER EVALUATION
- Performance Style: Dynamic
- His Issue: Greed and Self-importance
- His Role: Financier & Tycoon
- His Characters: Narcissistic & Domineering
- Motivation: To be important and be very affluent
- Intent: To exhibit his CEO title and control the business

How Might Griffin's Daily Performance Affect...

- His Health?

Griffin lacks the courage to face the truth of his real talents and develop them to the best of his ability. Instead, he greedily grabs at what is not his. He puts all his energy into "acting important" rather than "being important" in his own right. He weakens and drains his power by tragically trying to be what he is not. He is dissatisfied with his own talents and consequently lacks self-love. Instead of enhancing his skills and growing new ones, he secretly plays into his fear of being unimportant. His disappointment can be disheartening, causing much heartache. His heart health is at risk here – from aortic sclerosis to hi-blood pressure. Courage to see the truth of his character is what's needed.

- His Relationships?

Griffin demands respect from his colleagues, yet since he uses people, the respect he thinks he is getting is not genuine. In fact, most people don't really like him because his main objective is to profit himself. Some of his relations, like Timothy, are in so deep, having invested so much time and creativity in him and his company, that to provoke him or pull away could mean ruin for them as well.

At some point, Timothy will get so disgusted with Griffin that he will have to confront him. He will not only resign his position in their restaurant projects, but he will have to call Griffin on his unethical sense of power, lack of integrity, and cruelty to others. Unless Griffin can wake up to what his greed is creating and give Timothy his due, he will never really be powerful or respected. Griffin doesn't have self-respect, only a self-inflated image, so he can't offer respect and won't receive it.

- His Creativity and Productivity?

Griffin's creative talent is wasted on hiding his lies, stealing Timothy's Intellectual Property (IP) and who knows what else from countless others. His resourceful energy is spent in manipulation. So what creativity he has is wrapped up in other people's ingenuity. To Griffin, he uses his title as a creator/producer to boast of his possessions. He doesn't see his talent in the correct light – as a way of bringing and keeping talented people together and showing the leadership skills for producing high quality projects. That talent is insignificant to his desire for celebrity status and affluence.

DIRECTOR'S NOTES

Narcissism is a hard character to change because we cling so tightly to our ego stance that we don't see our own performance failures. In Griffin's view, others are creating obstacles for his company's progress. He doesn't see that "He" is the obstacle character. Griffin is strongly attached to the self-image he has created in his mind. His greatest fear is the loss of that image. He assumes his influence is wanted and accepted by everyone. However, to develop real self-esteem, Griffin will do well when he respects his given talents and cultivates them. So, I would put him to the mirror and look at himself as others might see him.

RETAKE: A COMIC DPS SCENARIO — IT'S GREAT WORKING WITH YOU

> *Greatness knows itself.*
>
> *~ Henry IV*

THE SCENE: High-Rise, posh office building. Early afternoon.

Griffin is an adventurous entrepreneur in his early thirty's, who has an attraction to good living. He has a passion for his work and as a side effect financing seems to come naturally in his new theme-based venture, Interactive Restaurant Villages *(IRV)*. His first restaurant, Elsewhere ~ Dining in Future Worlds, is a huge success. He is in his office with Jorje Rodrigues, a big investor, and Timothy Barnes, his Artistic Director and Associate Producer of IRV. They are discussing the plans for the next restaurant village, The Magic Gate ~ Dining in Mystical Lands. Timothy is the creator and architect and Griffin is the CEO and executive producer of the interactive dining company.

Griffin

(Charming and commanding)

So, Jorge, I'm glad you liked Elsewhere because The Magic Gate is the same concept but gives the diner a different theme. While Elsewhere takes the adventurous diner to Future Worlds, The Magic Gate will take you into mystical lands. Jorge, which future worlds did you visit at Elsewhere?

Jorge

I first went to 'Condos in the Cosmos'! Fascinating! I enjoyed choosing the foods I would eat in that world and having the Chefs create amazing dishes out of it! And how did you create the impression of that asteroid zipping by? Then I went to 'Mars — The Red Planet', and as I walked around savoring mysterious Martian wilderness delicacies, I was amazed by the fiery mountain sets, robotic desert costumes of the waitpersons and chefs. I loved the sensation of Mars as a desert-like city under glass! It was a surreal, movable feast.

Griffin

Thank you, Jorge. I'm happy to know how much you liked it.

Jorge

It's brilliant! You're a genius! This will be the new Disneyland — only in a Theme Restaurant Village. Each venue in the village is a different culinary ride!

Griffin

Well, Jorge, I'm not the genius behind it. I'd like to introduce you to the man who IS responsible for the concept, Timothy Barnes. Timothy is the creator, architectural designer and Creative Producer of ITRV. He's the genius! I'm just the barker trying to bring in the people, the money and put the project together.

Timothy

(Timothy thanks Griffin and walks over to shake hands with Jorge.)
Don't let him kid you Jorge, without Griffin's empire-building talents, none of this would be happening.

Griffin

(Smiles at Timothy…then)
Jorge, would you like a cup of our "Future Worlds Coffee"?

Jorge
Oh Yes, thank you.

Griffin
(Opens the door to signal his Assistant
Clarence to bring in the spread.)
Jorge, you are just the kind of investor we like to work with.
The description you gave of your experience at Elsewhere told me
that you appreciate the hard work and creativity that went into
it. And it sounds like you are quite the gourmand yourself!

(Clarence brings in a tray of coffee and exotic refreshments)

Jorge
(Patting his belly)
Thank you. As you can see, I love to eat! You know, I
have always wanted to get into the entertainment business
and this might just be the ticket. But before I get too
excited, tell me about The Magical Gate. Where will it
be, how will you execute it and what is your budget?

Griffin
Well, here is where I will turn it over to Timothy.
Since it's his conceptual designs, he has the
prospectus for the entire project. Timothy?

Timothy
First of all, Jorge, just so you know my expertise
regarding this project, I have a degree as an architect
and have enjoyed sharing in the creation and success
of Elsewhere alongside Griffin. And though I may
not look like it, I am a gourmet chef also.

Griffin
(in a booming voice to Jorge)
His expertise as chef is the inspiration for Interactive
Theme Restaurant Villages! He put his architectural
skills together with his culinary love and Voila!

Jorge
(Surprised)
Oh, wonderful news! How ingenious and exciting!

Griffin

Timothy, why don't you stand near the screen? We can hear your presentation better over there. I'll get the lights.

Timothy

Thanks Griffin.

(He begins his presentation)

The Magical Gate provides us with a fantastical setting, the latest projection mapping, holographic technology and boundless imagination that will take the diner into……

Twenty minutes later ~ presentation finished

Timothy

So, Jorge, what do you think?

Jorge

(In awe)

Why I think it will be amazing — if you can pull it off! I'm held speechless by your talent and the ingenuity that went into this.

Griffin

(To Jorge)

As you can see, Tim has covered every angle. Do you have any questions?

Timothy

(Looking at his iWatch)

Griffin, Jorge, I hate to do this, but I have another meeting. And it is very important — it's my daughter's recital at her school! This unfortunately can't be rescheduled. I'm late now. Will you please excuse me?

Griffin

(Loudly to Timothy)

Well, then you better leave me your iPad with the notes.

Timothy

I need it for the school meeting. But I will send the notes to Clarence right now and he can print them out for you.

(He hits "send")

                         Griffin
Well, sorry to lose you, but we understand, don't we Jorge?

                         Timothy
                         Thanks.
                  (To Jorge and Griffin)
It was very nice to meet you Jorge. I look forward
        to meeting with you again very soon.

                         Jorge
Enjoy your family Timothy. Griffin and I will set some
   time up for next week to move this further along.
          (Timothy nods favorably and leaves)

(Clarence gives Griffin a hard copy of Timothy's notes)

                         Griffin
                   Thanks Clarence.
                     (To Jorge)
       So what do you think? Any questions?

                         Jorge
Not at the moment Griffin, Timothy did a great job presenting
    the project. You're lucky to have him by your side.

                         Griffin
     Yes, I am very fortunate that he came to me
   with this project. We work well together, and I
     foresee an enjoyable and profitable future.
                      (pause)
Well, Jorge, if you have no questions right now, here's
Timothy's prospectus you can take to review. You can
  look through it and give some thought as to how you
  might work with us on The Magical Gate. We can meet
   again next week and get with my financial advisor.

                         Jorge
   I like the project very much Griffin. However,
  yes, I need to do some thinking and get with my
       business advisors before we meet again.

Griffin
(Walking Jorge to the door)
Sounds good. I'll give you a call early next week.

Jorge
It was a pleasure.
*(Jorge leaves and Griffin motions to Clarence
to come in as he walks back to his desk)*

Griffin
Thanks for your help, Clarence. Please text Timothy and tell him, "Great job!" But next time we need to make sure there are no conflicts in scheduling. Worked out fine, but I would like to schedule it, so Tim can be here for the full meeting. But, it's lookin' good — Jorge seemed enthusiastic.

CURTAIN

READER'S TAKE

Did you identify with Griffin's Creative Blocks or his Creative Skills?

Performance Challenges

- Not needing to be the all-important one
- Show interest in others – they are also in the room!
- Giving others the creative nod
- Learning how to use your voice and influence

Performance Practices

- Practice self-control and humility (look them up in the dictionary).
- Develop ESA (learn Genuine Presence).
- Practice generosity (not just with money, but with giving credit where it is due).

SCENE 8 THE TRAGIC SPIRITUAL PERFORMANCE STYLE – FREEING YOUR CREATIVE BLOCKS WITH CREATIVE CHOICE

*Art thou not, fatal vision, sensible to feeling as to
sight, or art thou but a dagger of the mind, a false
creation, proceeding from the heat-oppressed brain?*

~ Macbeth

The Spiritual PS excels in sense perception. Learning the difference between sensing, imagining, and thinking is key to understanding how to best use your human instrument. You know you are lost in thought when the outside world goes away, and you are in the little black box theatre in your head. When we become creatively blocked, we lose our sense-ability and often fly into fear.

Though we all use our sensory mind, many of us aren't sure what it is or how to willfully access it. We aren't practiced in deliberately turning our thinking brain off in order to sense something. Whenever we analyze, contemplate, follow imaginings, or question something to come to a conclusion – that's acting and thinking. When we stop the brain babble and look, listen, taste, touch and smell, we can have a direct experience of something – that's being and sensing.

Sensing requires a mind free of congestive thought themes; a mind alert to the outside world. If your thoughts don't interfere with what you are observing, you can receive clear information about it. The mind isn't cluttered by the brain's chatter. Thought can come in later and evaluate it, but to sense something first saves a lot of "figuring it out" time.

There is always interplay between thinking and sensing. It happens so quickly that we don't notice. Most of us hold many layers of thought themes that cloud our perception. If we know the differences, we can cut out the seesaw of doubt and see the reality of the moment. Below are a few Spiritual PS tragic traits we play out and practices to help avert them.

TRAGIC TRAIT: ISOLATION, DETACHMENT AND GLOOM

I am gone tho I am here.
~ Much Ado About Nothing

A SPS likes to be alone and yet, if we are not a practiced comic spiritual, capable of envisioning a bright future, we can get pretty dispirited. We misinterpret our senses. This tragic side of us sees and hears things that are not necessarily true. Our taste turns to a darker palate and our sniffer seems off. As opposed to the light and bright touch of our comic side, things touch us in fearful ways. Gloomy characters monopolize our mindstage – and most of them choose despair and distancing instead of interest and engagement.

The late cosmologist, Stephen Hawking joked, *"If you feel you are in a black hole, don't give up. There is a way out."* But the spiritual tragedian gets sucked into loneliness and hopelessness, so escaping a black hole can seem close to impossible. Like any strong beliefs and sensations, we can become committed to them. As a protection against fear of the outside, we take comfort in seclusion and refuse to venture out.

In such despair, compassion for our self eludes us. We lose appreciation of just how precious life really is. Wasting away in gloom without the light of self-awareness, we have no way to come to our senses. In fact, we've lost our good senses and don't know how to retrieve them. As a tragic Spiritual PS, we can find our way out of isolation by changing our perception from fear to creative potential and return to a compassionate overview, which is our specialty.

Contemplation Practice

The meaning of compassion is to have such deep concern for human suffering that we develop a strong desire to eradicate it. If we want to use our life to help bring compassion and awakened awareness to others in the world, we first have to apply these elevated ideals to our own suffering.

Why is it that we can feel compassion for others but not for our self? Do we not see and hear our own sorrow? Dare we not touch our painful core, taste our own tears or smell our own grime? For the SPS, it is vital that we do not take our 5 senses for granted or use them in unsafe ways but experience them in-depth and learn how to use them to our benefit.

First, it is important to notice how you use your senses.

- When you **smell** something good, do you grab and devour it?
- When you **see** something you want, do you buy it even though you don't need it?
- When you **taste** something you don't like, do you get surly about it?
- When you **hear** a compliment does it feed your ego? Or do you reject it?
- When someone **touches** your heart, how do you relate to that person?

Just notice your reactions. Practice using the five senses and notice how your reaction makes you feel. If you have a bad reaction, use the ESA to rebalance. Notice any character residue. Can you let go of a bad experience? If you have a good reaction, notice what you do with it – do you maintain goodness? Where do you take it?

To have sincere compassion for yourself, practice the ESA and find comfort and support in awareness.

Tragic Trait: Being Lost in Space

> *Of all base passions, fear is most accursed.*
>
> *~ Henry VI, Part One*

A Spiritual Tragedian may have a hard time being in the here and now. In fact, we have a fear of being present. As some PPSs are afraid of too much space, we are afraid of the ground. Landing means we will have to function. So, don't try to pin us down or we will fly away into the ethers. Not that we get anything accomplished in the ethers, but that's the point. We just like hanging out there. No pressures. No fears.

However, there are times when because of family, friends or work obligations, we need to come down to earth and be actively involved. This makes us feel pressured and we bolt when pressured. We become wishy-washy not knowing which way to go. To others, we look bewildered, deluded or distant. We seem to be searching for something, wanting but not finding, doing but not doing. Sensing that something is missing in our life, we become frightfully insecure. We search for the missing link somewhere out there. Though we may have an optimistic outlook, we can spend a lifetime searching for the secret to life.

However, when we are grounded in the ESAwareness, we can be based in reality, yet with the spatial freedom to move in and out of situations with calm independence. Our comic side wants to know space and use it resourcefully, not get lost in it. We choose to develop a secure "sense-ability" and use the empty stage of our mind wisely.

Practice – Understudying a Physical PS

1. Daily practice of the ESA is essential for the SPS to get familiar with space and understand how to use it. To gain balance between spatial freedom and groundedness, your Spiritual Tragedian might need a little help from the Physical PS. Our Physical can bring us in for a landing – help us with touch down. However, we may need a little coaxing. We need to be reminded of the good we can do on the ground.

2. Understudy a Physical PS that you admire. What about that person's physicality is attractive to you? Notice their character traits. Notice their motivation and intentions. Understudy the character traits you see in them that you want to develop in yourself and rehearse them.

3. Start some physical practices, like taking a walk and touching the leaves on trees or feeling the ground under your feet. Try a physical exercise that appeals to you. Begin appreciating your physicality. Slowly begin to enjoy your body by doing positive things in the physical world.

Tragic Trait: Avoidance, Procrastination, and Indifference

Man's nature cannot carry the affliction nor the fear.

~ *King Lear*

The Spiritual PS is the tender, most sensitive Performance Style of our human instrument. Our tragic side turns sensitivity into insensitivity and we can become paralyzed with fear. So, up pop characters of avoidance, procrastination and indifference.

Because our heads are often in the clouds, we have trouble seeing things on the ground. As a result, we procrastinate and avoid doing what is necessary. We fear what's necessary. We avoid people for fear of having to interact; we avoid situations for fear of having to face the cruel, hard world. Thus, as spirit, we are easily pulled off our point and fly off to something more pleasant.

We are afraid of losing our freedom in spite of the fact that we don't know what to do with it. We develop the character habit of looseness (a mis-take for freedom) and by choice we are slow to act. We have no committed ambitions because any goal represents stress and we can't handle pressure. It means completing some-thing by a certain time, in a certain way. So, our motto is, *"Whenever."*

Because we are not tracking our actions, we leave a trail of undone situations and relationships. We become indifferent to the physical needs and cries of frus-trations from those who live and/or work with us. To them, we seem out of touch and uncaring, living only in the safety of our own imaginary world.

But flip the mask and our comic side is appalled by this behavior and desper-ately wants to serve others. We don't want to avoid. We like being awake to the needs of others and have an altruistic desire to help serve in the world.

Practice – Facing Life

When you want to fly away from a situation that requires you to do something you don't fancy, try finding a single point of interest to help you do it. Make it into an art. Find what is motivating, fascinat-ing or feels good about the project to get your body into it. If it is exercise you avoid – sense the body stretching or swimming, or… how about a little sexual activity with the one you love.

Low-energy character habits, such as procrastination, can become our Character Sclerosis. Yet, there is that part of us that wants to experience a radiant light and emanate it out for others to enjoy. The practice that follows is aimed at revitalizing your life force.

1. When your energy is non-functional, go sit in the light! Go outside if it is a sunny day or turn on all the lights in the house and walk, sit or work in the light.

2. If possible, paint your room a bright, happy color or hang a colorful photo or painting that is cheerful.

3. Use your sense of sight to experience how the light is affecting you. Notice how things look in the light. Get into the light!!!

4. Recognize if you are stuck in an impassive character who is hogging your mindstage. Hear what you are telling yourself.

5. Even though your tragedian doesn't give a damn, if your comedic side wants a life, force yourself to turn a bright spotlight on your mindstage! Visualize it.

6. Let your senses bring you back to life. Look beyond your dreary character, hear the sounds going on around you, taste your food, smell the roses (so to speak) and most of all touch in regularly with those you love.

7. If it is the sight, sound, taste, touch and smell of things around you that are depressing, then sense what you need or want and create it.

8. Keep coming back to the ESAwareness.

9. Discover what can be done from your bright side and allow the light to touch you. Life is too short to avoid it. Face what is and give it light.

Take 1: A Tragic SPS Scenario – Did you see that?

He takes false shadows for true substances.

~ Titus Andronicus

THE SCENE: At the front door. Nighttime.

Bill and Denise Cummings just moved into their new home early
that morning. Denise has been waiting on the front porch for Bill
to show up. He arrives…

                    Denise
       Where have you been? I've been waiting out here
          for the last 20 minutes? It's cold and dark.

                     Bill
          I'm sorry Honey, I have no sense of time.

                    Denise
        That's not true Bill, you have no sense of
              others! You're off in dreamland.

                     Bill
             (Fumbling for his house key)
            Denise, do you have your key handy?

                    Denise
        No, Mr. Space Cadet. You were going to have
          some extras made but never gave me one.

                     Bill
        (He finds his key and opens the door)
             I'll get the extras made tomorrow.

                    Denise
        *(She walks into the entryway but can't find
        the light switch. The house is dark and empty
            with only a few pieces of furniture.)*
                Bill, where's the light?

Bill
Denise? Where are you?

Denise
I'm right behind you. Where's the damn light?

Bill
Shush! Did you see that?

Denise
See what?

Bill
(He freezes. Whispering…)
I wouldn't be surprised if this old house was
haunted. All day today I had a sense that
something bad was going to happen here.

Denise
It's not haunted. It just needs repairs and a reno…
(They both see a willowy shadow in the bedroom.)

Bill
(Still whispering…)
Now be still Denise. Something's not right. Don't you sense it?

Denise
No.

Bill
Where are you?

Denise
I'm being still behind you.
(Pause)
Bill, did you have the electric turned on today?

Bill
(Walking carefully in the dark toward another room)
I just felt a strange sensation run through my body.
(Mumbling to himself)
This house gives me the creeps. But she
had to have the old-world charm.

Denise
(Bumps into a chair. Annoyed…)
Damn it, Bill, did you have the electricity turned on?
*(She hears a big crashing noise. Denise
Squeals. Bill is groaning.)*

Denise
Bill? Are you okay? Where did you go? Bill?

Bill
(Faintly from another room)
Oh-o-oo.
(Moaning in pain)
I'm in the bedroom.

Denise
Bill, this isn't funny. What's going on?

Bill
(To Denise with fear in his voice)
There must be some entity in here playing with us. You know that
big chair we brought in earlier? …they moved it. I fell over
the damn thing. Shit…I think I broke my ankle. Ohhh, man…the
pain. I was right. I knew something bad was going to happen.

Denise
*(Standing near the open doorway she
feels her way into the room.)*
Bill, I moved the chair. You saw me move it this morning.

Bill
All day I sensed something bad would happen. I intuit things.

Denise
Where's the light! I just want to turn on the lights.

Bill
Can't. I didn't call the electric company.

Denise
I asked you to call them this morning before I left for
work. *(Feeling her way in a cabinet, she finds the flashlight
and flashes the light around to find Bill on the floor.)*
(Sarcastically)
But you had the gas turned on!

Bill
(Totally deflated)
Denise, this is no time to make me the bad guy. Please,
help me up. I needed the stove to make coffee so I
called the gas company and they came right out.

Denise
(Helping Bill up) So why not call the electric co. too?

Bill
I got busy setting up my office, so I could
work on the design for my client's new building.
I'm on a deadline. I hate deadlines.

Denise
(Shaking her head in disbelief)
Well, here's another deadline. Get the electricity
turned on first thing in the morning or you're
gonna intuit a really bad Denise!
(Finding a candle in the cabinet)
Honestly Bill, there is nothing in this house
for you to be afraid of…really!

Bill
(He stumbles away groaning and mumbling…)
Okay, when I redesign this place, I'll
exorcise any signs of entities.

Denise
(Lighting candle)
Not if it costs extra!
(Sees him limping)
Are you still in pain?

Bill
Yes. Think I better go to the emergency. I knew
this would happen. Where did I put my phone?

Denise
Bill, I love you. You're a talented, wonderful man…
but I just can't take all this booga-booga stuff anymore.
You aren't the guy I married when you act like this.

Bill
(Sidetracked. Pointing to a box on the floor.)
Oh, look Honey, I found the box of
candles. We'll need them tonight.
(Back to Ghost Stories)
I still say this place is haunted.

Denise
*(Holding a lit candle under her chin to make herself
look spooky, she turns to him and howls…)*
BOO!

Bill
(He jumps.)
That's not funny Denise.

CURTAIN

Reader's Q & A Notes

- Can you remember a scene in your own life when you performed like Bill?
- Review it and note what you might do differently to bring about a better outcome.

BILL'S SPS CHARACTER EVALUATION

- Performance Style: Spiritual
- His Issue: Procrastination and fear
- His Role: Husband and new homeowner
- His Characters: Fright & avoidance
- Motivation: Insecurity
- Intent: Not to take responsibility

HOW MIGHT BILL'S DAILY PERFORMANCE AFFECT...

- His Health?

Bill's interest in ghostly manifestations indicates a fearful attitude in life. Unlike the Comic Spiritual, whose fascination with the unknown stimulates curiosity in optimistic ways, Bill torments his nervous system with fearful imaginings.

Also, Bill's tendency to forget essential things and to get spacey might cause at the very least, a hazy mind. That character habit could possibly lead to dementia or at least, forgetfulness. As a SPS, being so focused on any fear producing beliefs can also produce a weak constitution. Fear can trigger the desire to check out socially or develop dis-eases that disable functionality. It can disconnect our body from our mind. Fear can be a killer.

- His Relationships?

Bill's focus on the supernatural has gotten worse and Denise gets exasperated with his dark phobia. Despite her protests, he continues to invest his time in it, creating a barrier of contention between them. She notices how the "spook" or fear element weakens his overall character, which might eventually affect her feelings for him. Also, his lack of attention to everyday needs really annoys her since she is the one who winds up handling the practical things. The love she once felt is slowly waning.

If Bill performs at work as the absent-minded architect, he may have difficulty meeting his client's needs. Though he may not bring his supernatural interest to the office, the fear issue and avoidance is rooted in his PS. He might doubt his work and feel insecure around his colleagues. His friends and family may just think he's weird.

- His Creativity and Productivity?

Bill is a talented architect but his dislike of deadlines triggers procrastination and feeds his fear of not meeting the client's timeline. He can't take pressure, so he takes flight in escapism and avoidance. As an architect, he deals with lines and space, yet as a Spiritual Tragedian, he doesn't understand how to establish lines in his life and use space with awareness.

DIRECTOR'S NOTES

Bill's fear actually attracts disaster to him. The sensation he was feeling all day invited a self-fulfilling prophecy. That sense-sation was his own growing fear and he created a frightful storyline around it. Ill at ease, he made himself unstable and insensitive to the actual world around him. So as a natural chain of events he became accident-prone.

If he can begin to focus on being present to reality, he could accomplish much more in his work. And he and Denise would have a more enjoyable relationship. Were it not for his trepidations about everything he could be quite successful.

RETAKE: A COMIC SPS SCENARIO – THIS OLD HOUSE

Be not afraid of shadows.
~ Richard III

THE SCENE: At the front door. Night time.

Bill and Denise Cummings just moved into their new home early that morning. Denise has been waiting on the front porch for Bill to show up. He arrives…

Denise
Where have you been? I've been waiting out here
for the last 20 minutes? It's cold and dark.

Bill
I'm sorry Honey, I picked up some Chinese, so we could have
our first dinner in our new home. I thought I texted you.

Denise
Well I don't think so. I kept texting you,
but you weren't responding. Guess you were
picking up the food. Great. I'm hungry.

Bill
(Fumbling for his house key)
Denise, do you have your key handy?

Denise
No. You were going to have some extras
made but never gave me one.

Bill
(He finds his key and opens the door)
Here's yours.
(hands it to her)
I had them made this afternoon.

Denise
(She walks into the entryway but can't find
the light switch. The house is dark and empty
with only a few pieces of furniture.)
Bill, where's the light?

Bill
(Walking passed her in the entryway and sets the take-
out food on the floor — muttering to himself…)
Denise? Where are you?

Denise
I'm right behind you. Where's the light switch?

Bill
Shush! Did you see that?
(He carefully and quietly walks into the next room.
His sensory antenna is searching every room.)

Denise
See what? Is someone in the house?

Bill
(He freezes. Whispering…)
Something's weird. Don't know what it is.
(Heart beating…he keeps walking)

Denise
Just old house noises. We have a lot of reno to do you know.
(Suddenly they both see a willowy shadow. They freeze.)

Bill
(All his senses go on alert. He listens
for clues. Still whispering…)
Wait here, Denise.

Denise
Okay. Be careful.

Bill
Where did you put the flashlight?

Denise
In the hall cabinet by the bedroom.
(Pause)
Bill, did you have the electric turned on today?

Bill
(Feeling his way carefully in the dark to
the cabinet — finds the flashlight)
Got it.

Denise
Okay Bill, where did you go?

(Again, they see a willowy figure from the far end of the
living room. Denise Shrieks. Bill's interest is now peaked.)

Bill
(Bumps into a chair. Annoyed…)
Damn!

Denise
Bill? What was that?

Bill
(Faintly from another room)
Nothing, but just stay there.

Denise
Bill, what's going on?
Please, turn on a light!

Bill
Can't. I didn't reach the electric company today.

Denise
No electric but you had the gas turned on?

Bill
Shh…Hush
(whispering to her from other room)
I scheduled both for today and the gas people came early.
Called the electric company but couldn't get through.
I got busy setting up my office when they didn't come.
I'm on a deadline. Then I ran out to pick up dinner.
(Bill's now at the bedroom door. He flashes the light around.)

YIKES!!! I can't believe my eyes!
(He quickly shuts the door and pauses.)

Denise
What is it?

Bill
(Speaking softly)
Denise, just stay there. I'll come get you.
(Walking into the living room to take Denise's hand.)

Denise
(Distraught)
Okay, what's in the bedroom, Bill? I saw something moving.
(They start walking slowly.)
Where are you taking me? What's in there?

Bill
(whispering at the bedroom door)
Sweetheart, now be still. Don't be scared. I'm right here.

(He slowly opens the door. The full moon is shining through the open window illuminating the old sheer white curtains. The wind is blowing them wildly to and fro, making an eerie whooshing sound and giving the distinct impression that there is a ghost in the room. Twirling his flashlight around for special effects, Bill makes the room seem to spin.

Denise shrieks out with nervous laughter and runs into Bill's arms for protection. Bill picks her up and makes hissing sounds like a vampire. He throws her on the rickety old brass bed left by the former owners and kisses her neck.)

Denise
(Still laughing)
Oh Bill, this is so much more fun than when you
thought you actually saw ghosts and vampires.

Bill
(Rolling over on his back...takes a beat)
You know, it's funny. Guess I was letting fear
play me. Now I can play the fear.
*(Getting up from the bed, he goes to a
box on the floor. To Denise)*
I was actually glad that the lights didn't get turned
on today. I found our box of candles and imagined
us having a romantic first night here together.
(He lights the candles and smiles lovingly at her.)

Denise
(Winking at him)
Come here, Count Dracula.

Bill
(He moves toward her playing the vampire...)
Don't be afraid my little pretty.

CURTAIN

READER'S TAKE

Did you identify with Bill's Creative Blocks or his Creative Skills?

Performance Challenges
- To break the character habit of fear and avoidance
- To live in the reality of the moment
- To turn interest from the macabre into a sense of creative exploration

Performance Practices
- Notice your tendency to fly away...come back!
- Go to the ESA to determine what's factual and what's not.
- Distinguish between fear-based insecurity and fears that are actual.
- Notice how you idle away the time. Whatever the task – do it now!
- Understudy someone who is a PPS to find grounding.

Though you may be primarily one or two Performance Styles, everyone possesses and use all five of them. So, it is important to honestly check these tragic character traits in yourself and learn to recognize how they all affect you, others and your daily performance.

SCENE 9 USING THE **ESA** TO MAKE BETTER CHOICES

There's small choice in rotten apples.
~ The Taming of the Shrew

I f life is a self-written play and we are all actors in it, we effectively become what we rehearse the most. Although we rely on our habitual characters with their feelings and routines to maintain a familiar path through life, we also need to have choices.

Yet, unknowingly we act out all kinds of tragic character traits to handle a variety of negative situations. Sometimes we get lucky and they work, but most of the time they cause more challenges and problems. Our poor character choices have one thing in common – lack of awareness. We go numb and dumb. We are not in the habit being aware of ourselves. In self-defense of our unconscious actions, we pull out the proverbial excuses like, *My dog just died, and I was sad...I hadn't eaten or slept, or I wasn't feeling well.* We apologize with – *I'm sorry, I didn't mean it. I wasn't thinking straight.* It is our human habit to excuse our tragic flaws.

There is but only one excuse – *I wasn't awake.* You were, "rounded by a sleep," as Shakespeare's Prospero says in *the Tempest.* Sleep-walking through life is an age-old, human dis-ease that causes accidents, misunderstandings, daily stupor and much, much unhappiness.

Now however, in the 21st century, with so much at stake personally and globally, it is time to honor our power of awareness. Whether in shock, fear or stupor, with ESA practice, you can recognize the character in you who is susceptible to illness, shock or any other issue. Like recognizing a disease to heal it, recognizing your tragic character is critical to transitioning from stupor to awareness.

Practice – Tragic Character Awareness

1. When in the ESA, you have cleared the thicket of thought themes that cover your mindstage, focus your eyes into a steady view ahead. Feel that steadiness sink into your body. Rest there a few minutes until you are stable minded.
2. Acknowledge the tragic character(s) that are causing creative blocks.

3. Allow them to speak out loud. Give them the stage and they won't steal your mindstage causing pain, illness and disturbances.
4. If necessary, while allowing your tragic characters to take stage, simultaneously rehearse counterparts that can help you transition into more constructive characters.
5. The ESA gives you a home base, a clear space to review your choices.
6. Your mindstage is a place where you can storyboard your needs, imagine different takes on any issue, then try them out to see how they play in real time.

By identifying with the ESAwareness as your true self and the source of your creative nature, you will have a home base for balance and clarity. You can stop identifying with each transitory character that enters your mindstage, stays for a moment to perform, and then exits. You'll recognize all of them, the catastrophic to the subtlest, as the passing parade of comedy and tragedy that come and go on-cue.

The ESA is a lifetime practice and usually develops in stages. The beauty of it is that we can practice it anywhere – at a tense business meeting, in a stressful interaction or a joyful wedding. It can relieve ordinary pressures of daily living and help us do things that we often complicate with overthinking. With this level of mental freedom, we can act with more enjoyment and self-trust.

ESA is the hardest and most important thing a person can achieve. It gives you a flexible center as it does not fix your view as life situations change. When we maintain a firm center, self-centrism comes into play. We act to complement our self-image, validate personal interests and long-standing beliefs rather than acting with awareness of the present reality. ESA can level the deflated or exaggerated ego and give you the ability to adapt into whatever is needed.

I must emphasize here that without the ability to access a calm and steady space within our mind, we will always be wandering, searching and caught up in the quagmire of emotional, spiritual and mental gymnastics. We will always be subject to outside influences without much choice. Confusion will prevail with only periods of clarity and enjoyment. Being grounded in spacious awareness keeps us awake and genuinely present throughout our life story.

You are who you rehearse.

Act IV

Character Development –
Rehearsing Your Comic Characters

There are so many life scenarios in which we have opportunity to stand in the light, but don't. Act 4 is devoted to helping you rehearse and strengthen your comic characters until they become a part of your go-to instincts. When you see yourself automatically acting out your tragic traits you can then quickly access and use them. Knowing your motivation and intentionally playing a well-rehearsed comic character, you can avoid any creative blocks. In the end, it comes down to the following: *You are who you rehearse!* So why not rehearse your creative skills till they become second nature to you?

SCENE 1 EVERYTHING WE DO IS AN ACT OF CREATIVITY

The lunatic, the lover, and the poet, are of imagination all compact.
~ *Midsummer Night's Dream*

In your home, business, or social life, do you act from your tragic side? What do you do when you know someone is gossiping about you in unjust ways? Do you retaliate in like-kind? Do you accuse others of wrongs for which you are guilty? Do you act defensively towards someone who doesn't like you? If you ask a colleague to do something for you and he screws it up, do you resort to anger, belittling him or lessening his value around others? If you were to act from your comic side instead, you might forgive him a Mis-Take and with a helpful attitude, encourage him to try Take 2,* empowering him to do better. That action would certainly make you both feel better, while easing the situation. By playing tragedy, we are simply rehearsing and perpetuating our negativity and undesirable characters.

Overall, your objective is to identify and choose character traits that will bring about a happier and healthier lifestyle for you. Rehearsing some of your best character traits in each PS can help you develop your creative skills so that you don't give in to your tragic habits as often as you might. In fact, by neglecting to strengthen your creative skills, you are effectively rehearsing and strengthening your creative blocks.

You may immediately think, "I don't have any creative skills," or "I am just not creative." But everyone has the gene within them that produces their creative skills. However, don't mistake *creativity* with being *artistic*. There is a difference. Art is about living and producing beauty, or crafting thought-provoking and poignant works, whereas creativity uses imagination to come up with something totally original. Though people in artistic professions use their imagination to create unique works of art, artistic people are not the exclusive holders of creativity.

While not all of us possess talent in the Arts, all of us are creative. Indeed, as life actors, we are creating every moment of every day. Everything we do is an original act. You are the only one creating the scenes and relationships in your life. How we treat ourselves can form conditions for good health or ill health. So why not use our originality to enhance our lives?

Too often, we may thwart our own talents by making up stories of self-lack. Ironically, this is where many of us can actually get very creative –inventing creative blocks and stopping ourselves from enjoying the positive results that we could have. For example, I was once teaching LPP at a Los Angeles University and one guy in the class insisted he was not creative. I recall how he spent 20 minutes giving me a slew of self-justifying reasons for his creative lack. I listened to his tale of woe and when he had finished, I said, "What a fascinating story – and very creative!" I pointed out that his story was quite imaginative, but he just hadn't applied his imagination in positive ways to his personal goals.

Once you label yourself as "not being a creative artist," the idea of being a creative person stops. When you make up disparaging stories about yourself, your latent creative talents stay locked within you. Instead, by rehearsing your underdeveloped comic character traits, you can consistently learn to turn creative blocks into creative skills.

The creative process* starts with an idea that suddenly appears in the open cracks between thoughts and moves into the challenging stages of mental and physical development. And then after great effort, to see your work completed as reality can be an exciting adventure. There is also a reverse creative process that results when what we developed dissolves and transitions into something we don't want – like a barn burned into ashes, or an apple fallen from its tree to decay back into the earth. But whether the results are good or bad, that is the creating process.

If you look at things in the right spirit, everything you do can be an expression of your creativity. Working with difficult people can create patience where you have been impatient; unbearable situations can create courage where you have been frightened. To master the creative process, understanding how to use space and learning to accept the transient nature of the creative process is our saving grace.

204

SCENE 2 DEVELOPING VALUABLE CHARACTER TRAITS

I have touched the highest point of all my greatness.
~ Henry VIII

Learning to live on the Empty Stage, your awareness begins to act as Genuine Presence. To enhance that presence, however, the following character traits are invaluable to your progress. To become a well-rounded life actor, these foundational characters will help you in a wide variety of settings, regardless of your Performance Style.

TO DEVELOP PATIENCE

Be patient, for the world is broad and wide.
~ Romeo and Juliet

The biggest requirement for being present is to rehearse the character of patience. No one can be present when his or her mind is impatiently busy. Patience implies endurance – having the ability to see things through with a calm acceptance and willingness to work with the way things are.

Patience Performance Practice

First, take an inventory of your capacity for patience. Notice your tolerance level in different situations. What is your motivation for acting impatient? What role are you playing? What needs are not getting met? Is impatience making you feel better? Is it getting the job done faster? What is that character doing to your relationships? How is it affecting your health?

To develop patience, start noticing your character tendencies like annoyed, irritated and greedy when they arise. Slowly diminish those traits that set up feelings of impatience – like the inability to communicate with someone or the sensation that you can't do something. Begin to rehearse patience and notice the response you get from others by displaying your creative skill. If that old habit keeps taking center stage, don't give up. The root of impatience is intolerance, which can keep you from being genuinely present.

TO DEVELOP DISCIPLINE

I am a kind of burr, I shall stick.
~ Measure for Measure

Genuine Presence cannot exist in a person who is too busy, scattered, or rigid. When we are like that, we are either out of our mind or too set in our ways to be truly present to the people around us. It takes discipline to develop such presence.

Discipline Performance Practice
Every morning upon rising, practice the ESA for 5 min. (Okay, get your coffee first if you must.) After a week, increase it to 10 minutes, then up to 15. This will help set your day with clarity of purpose and make you less prone to assume one of your tragic characters. Maintaining this consistent discipline will help you develop Genuine Presence during your many daily activities.

TO DEVELOP GENEROSITY

My good will is great, though the gift be small.
~ Pericles

We think of a generous person as someone who is financially charitable. If money is your generous inclination, it is good to check your motivation for giving. Do you need a tax write-off, or do you sincerely want to help others? It is said that true generosity comes when a person overrides his own needs in order to help another. That means "give even if it hurts."

If you are truly present to a situation, you are willing to give of your mental expertise, physical assistance, emotional support, and of your spirit. In addition, it is wonderful to give of your time and influence when needed. Having a sense of presence allows us to know why, when, and to whom you should give.

Generosity Performance Practice

In each of your Performance Styles, notice how, when, and where you can find an opportunity to give of yourself – especially in places where you might not even consider it. Notice your motivation and intent. Then practice generosity from the ESAwareness and act with Genuine Presence.

To Develop Empathy

> *Are you like the painting of a sorrow, A face without a heart?*
> ~ *Hamlet*

Presence requires us to identify with the needs of others without judgment, fear, or estrangement. When we have conflicts or mis-takes with one another, it is because we have hardened our POV* and are unable to experience each other's needs. If you can't relate to others as you would to yourself, you are not present. You may be looking at them with judgment or pity.

Not experiencing the joy of others is another way we turn our backs on opportunity. Learning to enjoy the happiness of others, even if you don't like them, may be difficult, but it is a good practice. In this way, you not only develop empathy for others, but presence and deeper love.

Empathy Performance Practice

The next time you don't understand someone or have an argument, stop and put yourself in the other person's skin. What is their motivation for acting like that? Might they be hurt, scared or needy? Then, see if you can find the empathetic character within you that can support both of you.

To Develop Ethics

To thine own self be true.

~ Hamlet

Each of us must, in our own way, have a set of values that we live and work by and it is important to know what they are. Don't just keep them floating around in the back of your head, but state them out loud – or even write them down as your own directives. Knowing your values gives you the courage to move forward with integrity and dignity. Maintaining presence, ethics also gives us our code of conduct.

Ethics Performance Practice

Most of us have a conscience that tells us when we're off-track. If your conscience nags, don't avoid its cues. Listen, not just to the people and situation around you, but as Polonius said to his son Laertes in Hamlet...*To thine own self be true.* Know your set of ethics, be true to them and the nags will come less often. Your mind will have the freedom to be genuinely present.

SCENE 3 THE COMIC MENTAL PERFORMANCE STYLE — INCREASING YOUR THINKING SKILLS THROUGH REHEARSAL

Thought is free.
~ The Tempest

- Performance Objective is to use our intellect to advance humankind.
- Our Talent is innovative thinking, technology, education, and mentoring.
- Our Comic Traits are that we can be kind, sharp-witted, and hold the genius to advance the ideas of others as well as our own.

If you are sincerely working to develop your MPS creative skills, becoming aware of your thinking is the first step. In general, unless we are deliberately thinking things out, we allow our thoughts to run amuck giving little attention to how they are affecting us and people around us. Consequently, we are thoughtless to what we are thinking and doing.

Yet, we can have greater control over how and what we think, and learn to maintain a healthier brain function. The sanity that we are all looking for comes when the brain and the mind are in sync. Like polluted air, our mind can become smoggy and dimmed by too much negative thinking. As many have experienced, our brain can malfunction when overworked, stressed and pressured. To create healthier brain function, take more Brain Breaks and become aware of junk thinking and other modes of thought. Free up relentless thinking.

The following list identifies modes of thinking that either favorably or unfavorably affect our brainpower and the quality of our life performance. This list is meant to help you identify your thought patterns as useful or not useful and help you self-correct if necessary.

COMIC MODES OF THINKING
- *Logical thinking* is when we are capable of correct and valid reasoning based on substantial facts. Our mind is rational and alert. We are thinking in a purposeful way.

- **Concentration** occurs when we are deeply absorbed in something like reading a book or engrossed in a topic or a conversation.
- **Focus** is having single pointed attention on a topic, person, or thing.
- **Blue sky** is innovative thinking, coming up with interesting new ideas. It is open-minded, creative thinking about life situations, artistic or business projects. The sky's the limit of this thinking mode!
- **Musing** is contemplative thinking. We quietly and privately reflect on a situation to find the right approach in logical or creative matters.
- **Quick witted** is having a clever sense of humor. This displays our resourcefulness and ingenuity.
- **Brain Breaks** help us stop overthinking and open into the ESA allowing space to clarify the mind.

TRAGIC MODES OF THINKING

- **Daydreaming** takes our thoughts off into fantasyland. It is usually a form of distraction. This can lead to being spaced-out in nowhere land.
- **Junk thinking** is just that – unimportant storylines that take up head space with no purpose or result – an energy zapper.
- **Brain Babble** is confusion – too many thoughts and images running amuck in your head.
- **Black Box thinking** is like being in a small theatre with black walls, ceiling, and floor. It is analogous to being in your head with your own thoughts, your inner lighting (how you color things), and special effects (your elaborations). To others, you seem self-absorbed.
- **Thought Looping** happens when something has upset you and has a mental hold on you. Trying to understand or justify the situation, you repeat the same thought-lines over and over.
- **Double Features*** happen when you are trying to focus on something, but another scenario starts running across your mindstage and your attention gets split.
- **Caustic Thinking** such as sarcasm and pessimism often hurts and offends others. It mostly displays your hurt and negative view of life.

By identifying the type of thinking you are using, whether you are coming from your comic or tragic side, you can choose to use your brain in more functional and creative ways. With greater awareness, you will be able to redirect your thoughts in more consistent, constructive, and inventive ways. You can choose to stay on the brighter side more often.

Just as unplugging certain appliances not in use saves environmental energy, releasing any type of tragic thinking into the ESA saves brain energy. Developing your ability to hold the ESA as a backdrop on your mindstage also helps you develop attention during those spacious moments. By noticing what mode of thinking is occupying your headspace, you can clear your mind into a moment of well-being.

There are many practices for expanding and developing the MPS creative skills. However, the best way to develop any Performance Style skill is through "Improv." It's what we all do every day and don't even think about it. Life is an improv and the better your improvising skills, the more equipped you are to handle all kinds of situations. If you are interested in subduing your over-active tragic character traits, like too intense or judgmental, or you want to promote new mental skills like focusing or listening, here's one way to use improv in daily activities.

Improv Practice for the MPS

Review the MPS Orientation listed in Act II, and choose a talent, creative block, skill, or enjoyment you would like to explore for yourself and either fix or enhance.

Let's say your objective is to improve your focus and mathematic talents and you are motivated to subdue your negative judgment when you work. So, your intention might be to rehearse "kindness" as your character choice. Because your character habit has been "judgmental," look up "kindness" in the dictionary and begin rehearsing it to counteract your tragic trait.

Next, create or find a mathematical situation like figuring out your monthly budget or a physics problem. First play the scene alone as if it is actual. Go to the ESA to clear, ground and expand your awareness. Use your imagination and practice playing out this scenario with patience.

Now, to test how you would interact with others in this scene, imagine a family member or colleague being involved. Imagine how the other character helps or hinders. Focus on their character mood, their names and what they are wearing. Imagine they are teaching you and you have to focus and listen. Or, you are teaching a difficult person to work a math, computer or other problem. Watch your tendency to be overly critical and judgmental. While you are improving your math and practicing kindness, you are also stretching your visualizing powers. Make up your own thought-provoking situations to play around with and keep increasing thoughtful creative skills.

SCENE 4 THE COMIC EMOTIONAL PERFORMANCE STYLE – INCREASING YOUR SELF-EXPRESSION THRU REHEARSAL

Our loves and comforts should increase
Even as our days grow.
~ Othello

- The Performance Objective is to gain equipoise, happiness, and self-love.
- Our Talent is emotional discipline, communication and self-expression.
- Our Comic Traits are that we can be loving, warm and cheerful. We express ourselves beautifully, communicate and interact with ease.

The EPS expands their creative skills through Character Study, which involves studying people who exemplify various emotional characteristics you wish to cultivate in yourself. Rehearsing both comic and tragic character traits is valuable for recognizing emotions and expanding your character repertoire. It also involves developing emotional discipline – the ability to see who in you is needed in a given moment and making a quick change when necessary.

Just as a painter has an extensive palette of colors, or a mechanic has a wall full of tools, the professional actor has an extensive range of emotions to play in order to communicate their feelings. They spend a lot of time working to understand, develop, and stretch their emotional range. The more an actor investigates, the larger the character repertoire they have to draw from when performing a role. This study is a large part of what makes someone a great actor. They cultivate versatility in their stage performance.

As EPS life actors, we have the same opportunity to stretch our daily skills by expanding our character repertoire. In Character Study, we get to explore our human ability to express ourselves safely and honestly. By studying, rehearsing, and experiencing emotions unfamiliar to us, we are better able to deal with all kinds of people (including ourselves) because we have a wider range of emotions to draw from.

You can stretch your self-awareness by noticing how these feelings affect your relationships and creativity. Watch how quickly negative emotions arise when you are in reaction to someone. Notice how long you stay in that negativity. Can you quickly access an emotional character that pulls you out of the funk? Can you truthfully play the feeling you want when you need it?

Most of us get stuck in a situation because we don't know what to say or do. When you rehearse new emotions, your emotional body gradually learns to feel each emotion with honesty and you become more versatile. You'll also be able to access your feelings instinctively without confusion or effort. You develop an awareness of how to interact in relevant ways with all kinds of people.

If you are having difficulty working or being with someone, try acting out the emotions you see in him or her when you have a private moment. You might find you know that character in yourself better than you think. We are just reflections of each other to different degrees, so often we don't recognize ourselves in someone else's conduct.

In LPP we not only find ways of using our emotions for greater expression but also learn not to suppress our feelings. Instead we express them in safer, more creative ways. This change and growth in emotional discipline can only be gained if we rehearse feeling these emotions honestly. Otherwise it is just playacting or blowing off steam.

By expanding your emotional (character) repertoire, observing, rehearsing and performing a fuller range of emotions, you instinctively gain more character choice. You don't just keep playing the same ole run-of-the-mill Me. You can open up to using more of yourself with educated experience. Try out new character options and see what it feels like. Remember, nothing is set in stone, so have fun with it. Here are practices that help you expand your EPS creative skills.

Practice – Character Stretching

The goal of the following practice is to gain emotional understanding and versatility. Use the Character Study Chart in Act 3 in the section on EPS.

- Solo Work – If you are in a tragic mood, go to the ESA to clear your mindstage. Notice the energy level of your character, high, low, etc.
- Then, on the comic side of the chart, choose an emotion similar to the energy level you are already feeling. This allows

you to slip into your comic character choice more easily. For instance, if you notice you are feeling fairly good one day, you might easily be able to practice being bold or humble. Whereas if you are feeling insecure, it might be more difficult for you to conjure bold or humble in honest ways.

- Once you have chosen an emotion to practice during your day, look it up in the dictionary. That will not only clarify its meaning, but it often gives clues as to how to live the emotion.

- Then imagine your day ahead and start playing that emotion in the role you must perform that day. Watch how you play out certain feelings, how people react to your character and how you react to others who encounter you. If it seems awkward at first, just stay with it until you make it your own. See how it feels when you consciously play it. This is character study, not play-acting; so have fun, but value and respect your study.

- Take notes if you like but explore and notice how that emotion makes you feel.

- When you feel complete with studying that character, go to the ESA to dissolve any Character Residue. Recognizing the ESA as your true character, rest there and act from Awareness.

You may choose to play two or three different characters during the course of a day. If there is more information to be gained there, you may want to stay with one emotion for a day or more.

As you try out each emotion, watch your act as if you are watching a movie. Re-adjust your focus from outward to inward – not in an ego-affirming or self-effacing way, but in interested, curious ways. Don't try to change anything you see or feel. Just stay with it and be aware of who, what emotion in you is acting. Ask yourself, what is my motivation for acting like this? What is my intent? What do I want to gain in this situation?

Mirror Practice – Who's acting?
This practice helps you identify who in you is acting.

PART 1 – Talking to your character
Go to the mirror and say hello to the character in you that is in the mirror. If you don't recognize your character, then ask, Who's here?* Talk to your character as if you are talking to a friend. If you recognize Grumpy, talk to Grumpy as if you are conversing with someone who is cranky and cross-tempered. Ask Grumpy questions. And…who in you is asking the questions? Name both characters. The idea is to get to know and learn to communicate with all parts of you. This helps make it easier to get to know and communicate with others in aware and creative ways.

PART 2 – Self-Love and affection
Go back to that mirror and repeat the process. This time look at your image and feel affection for the image in the mirror, regardless of who it is. If you can't spontaneously feel affection for your image, then express things about yourself that are worthy of a caring friendship. All emotions are changeable energies, so express and act out who you would like to be. Talk to that image with love.

Keep developing self-love, appreciate the things you do for yourself – like cook a meal, clean your house, enjoy the beauty you create. Soon your entire chemistry will change. You will feel and emanate affection and appreciation. When you love and accept yourself, others reflect that love back to you. You will also develop deeper empathy for those who feel unlovable because you will know the feeling in yourself.

About Social Media and your Life Performance

Social media is today's main artery of communication, so your Emotional PS skills must extend into this part of your life as well. It reflects your personal feelings and professional image. Since it is not reality facetime, but cyber air-time, you can rehearse new comic characters and develop great creative skills without having to show up LIVE.

How you use media depends on your motives – what you want to get out of it. Some of us need emotional reinforcement while others rebuke flattery. Some of us are voyeurs while others go online every day to share some tidbit. Celebrity or not, many of us post our best angle enjoying the online spotlight. The age of social media posts has become a means of expressing ourselves, sharing our most fancied moments, our business and social adverts...and, we want to be seen and heard.

The Internet is a great tool for communicating, learning, study, and re-search. It can also be misused and abused if we aren't aware of our motives and intentions for posting. Since just about anything we want to know can be accessed, there is the tendency to pull up data that is basically gossip, junk adverts, or fearmongering propaganda.

If overused, these types of websites and apps will waste your mental pro-ductivity, confuse your judgment and stabilize emotional traits that you don't necessarily want in your character repertoire. Online socializing can have the same character impact as a personal meeting or phone call. Are you projecting a phony online persona or a truthful one? Do you spread your hate and misery or offer vision and inspiration? Know your comic and tragic choices.

Notice how you feel every time you post a message or picture. Who in you is messaging? The Political Informant? The Bad or Good News Person? Environmentalist? Mother? Preacher? The Jokester? What's your motive for posting? Love? Neediness? Anger? Fear?

Be aware that every time you post, you are sending out a show-and-tell revealing your innermost needs, desires, hurts, fears, powers and beliefs. Because social media has immediate impact, it's good to do a character check-in before posting. Make your social media presence part of your LPPractices.

SCENE 5 The Comic Physical Performance Style – Increasing Your Bodily Skills Thru Rehearsal

I never did repent for doing good.

~ Merchant of Venice.

- The Performance Objective is to heal hurts, take action, and fix what's broken.
- Our Talent is body awareness, agility and functionality.
- Our Comic Traits are that we can be a healer on our comic side rather than physically abusive on our tragic side.

Some Physical PSs are constantly active and find it is hard to slow down. Trying to rest when there are things to be done (and there's always things to be done) can bring on anxiety. The excess energy will make us tap our feet at the dinner table, or restlessly go for a run to burn it off. Keeping busy represents accomplishment to us. We think, "If I am not doing something, then *what good am I?*" Saving our energy in healthy ways is a lesson to be learned for the comic PPS.

Because of our need to stay active, the Physical PS has come to understand that the ESA is the best source of energy we can acquire. We have learned to use the ESA to both save, maximize and extend our energy for action. Here is our favorite way to get into the ESAwareness.

Practice – Walking into the Empty Stage

If you don't have time to sit quietly to move into the ESAwareness, then use physical activity to enter it. In other words, use your physical nature as a creative skill.

1. Put on your walking shoes and prepare to go for a walk outside. Notice the thoughts in your head – about friends, phone calls, work, family, lovers, social events and things you have to do when you get back.
2. With your shoes on, get up and feel your feet on the ground. As you walk toward the door, keep your focus on your feet

contacting the ground. Eyes looking forward, open the door and walk out into ESAwareness – see the world with energetic clarity.

3. Become aware of the space around you. Notice the scene taking place in front of you, the traffic on the street, people, etc. If anything distracts, note it and keep your attention on space and the sensation of your feet. If you can, pick up the walking pace.

4. The air begins to clear your head. Take a deep breath in, let it travel into your brain and clear your mind. Ground your body as you walk and expand your peripheral vision. Keep walking into the Empty Stage Awareness. Stay in the ESA... as you walk.

5. Do you begin thinking of things that make you anxious? Do you pick up speed? Do you think of things that make you feel good, happy, sad? Notice the synchronization between your thoughts, feelings and your body's speed, pace, posture and action.

6. Whatever comes up, remember to keep walking into the ESA. Stay in the open awareness while feeling the space around you. If something unexpected happens, you will be more alert to tend to it.

7. Anytime your mind begins to wander into scenarios at work, at home, or other things, let your awareness keep you from getting edgy. Think about these things if you choose, yet hold spacious awareness as you walk. Stay present.

8. You can't stop thoughts from coming, but you can always find places in your life where you can walk into the ESA. There's the backyard, the balcony, or porch, even the bathroom. Wherever there is space – you can walk into the ESA.

TREATING YOURSELF WELL?

The critical thing to remember about the PPS is that although our tragic side can be abusive, we can work miracles as healers on our comic side. If you have ever noticed how you look when you have the flu or when you're being resistant, you will see how the change of character energy can affect your physical appearance. If our character energy can change our outer appearance, imagine what it might do to our body organs. Our comic side understands this and is ready to come to the rescue.

The natural earthiness of the comic PPS instinctively knows how to treat the body with moral and healthy respect. The body is our domain and our energy can be used to take helpful action. If you or someone you know is prone to physical abuse, whether beating up on themselves or someone else, know that we all have the potential to heal ourselves. As life actors, we can improve the ways we use our bodies. I'm not talking about body building as physical strength and prowess only, but also from the point of view of your character.

To develop the PPS creative skills, the following practice can be useful and lots of fun.

Practice – Shaping Your Character's Body
This practice is imaginative body work.

Directions Part 1 – Create Your Body's Performance Routine
Activity is the PPS's nature, so it is important to notice our movements. How are you holding your body when you walk, sit or lie down? Is it graceful, easy going, awkward, imposing, comfortable or uncomfortable? Do you stand rigid? Do you flail your arms about? Walk too fast or too slow? Notice your physical rhythm and listen to your footsteps during activities. Notice the timing between movements, your physical responses and reactions. Do you need to slow down and breathe, see the sights around you, or speed up to accomplish more? Self-correct your performance routine.

Directions Part 2 – Rehearsing Your Body
In this part, you will stretch your physical capacity. Example:
- Having evaluated your physical routines, you find that you have been somewhat awkward and klutzy and would like to rehearse being more agile.

- Choose a character you would like to develop and give it a name:
  – Graceful Gracie? Sophisticated Sophie? Smooth Smith? Elegant Alton?
- In the beginning, practice this character around the house. Just work with the physical development of your body. Use your imagination to visualize your body moving as you would like it to move.
- How would your character 1) walk 2) turn around 3) bend down to pick up something 4) brush your teeth 5) eat a meal at the table 6) eat at a hot dog stand 7) take a run 8) get in bed, etc.
- Start rehearsing your body to take on the character of grace or smoothness or easy-going. Rehearse in ways that make you feel good. If one way doesn't feel or look good, try it another way.
- Use the mirror to see your body tendencies and changes.
- Slowly your character's movements will begin to feel natural – and so will the whole of you.

Your character can influence your physique and how you are seen. There are those of us who are not very attractive and yet there is something about us that is engaging. It's character. And there are those of us who are quite attractive, or try to make ourselves so, yet something about us is off-putting. It's character. If you're sincerely interested in shaping your character, notice how your body posture, pain and mannerisms match your character.

Practice – Recasting the Character of Your Pain
Remember the CEO of Pain in Act 3? You can recast your CEO by giving that role another job function like "to make the body healthier." Choose different emotional characters like "nourish" or "encouragement." This automatically creates different feelings, action, and results.

Example:

1. Role: CEO of Health, Inc.
2. Performance Style: Comic Dynamic – repossess my sense of wholeness
3. Function: To find ways of creating balance and wellbeing
4. Motive: to feel healthy and happy
5. Intent: to develop methods for healing and comfort
6. Character
    *   Appreciation of my body – grateful that I have it to take care of
    *   Energetic, active and good-hearted
    *   Self-love – know my goodness and my strength
7. Action
    *   Eat well.
    *   Stop unhealthy habits that perpetuate any dis-ease.
    *   Find people who can help me if I can't do this alone.
    *   Rehearse comic character emotions that are healthy.
8. Goal
    *   Complete recovery, or at least a greater ability to live happily with what I have.

The more you rehearse feeling healthy and happy, regardless of your actual physical condition, the more you will learn to maintain a healthier attitude.

SCENE 6 THE COMIC DYNAMIC PERFORMANCE STYLE – INCREASING YOUR VOCAL SKILLS THRU REHEARSAL

Tell truth and shame the devil.

~ Henry IV

- The Performance Objective is to magnanimously enable and contribute to the overall welfare of family and society.
- Our Talent is our voice and our power to influence and lead others.
- Our Comic Traits are that we can be great and trustworthy. Knowing our true inner power, we are empowering to others.

Power is having the self-command to manage people, situations, and ourselves, while charisma is having that "something special," that indescribable quality that can magnetize and influence. You can have power without charisma or charisma without power. However, when you put power and charisma together, you have a dynamic person who has command accompanied by charm, truth, and persuasion.

As a comic Dynamic, we are clear about what we want. We have the ability to magnetize things we want and use our pull unselfishly. We trust our instincts to use our power with integrity, and don't easily shy away from challenges.

But the biggest obstacle for some Dynamics is that we equate power with success and safety. The more successful we are, the more powerful we feel, and the safer we imagine ourselves to be – assuming riches and power provide a safety net. This safety, however, is deceptive because power is nothing more than transient energy. How we choose to use it makes it destructive or constructive.

Thus, it is very important to distinguish between the two kinds of power we have available to us. First, there is *common power*, the obvious kind that most all of us long for because it looks and feels like success. It is achievable through hard work, nepotism, or good luck. With common power, the tragic dynamic displays success through possessions, luxury homes, expensive cars, designer clothes, and by being seen in fancy restaurants. We buy pricy toys and lavish gifts for loved ones and people we want to impress. This kind of power sports the high life – demanding respect by a show of affluent appearances. We don't notice that we are simply inflating ourselves and with inflation comes deflation. Common power seduces our tragic side into grasping at our swelling desires.

Immersed in the illusions of common power, we might ask: *Don't you know who I am?* We expect adoration and special treatment. But this kind of power has its revenge; if we abuse common power too long, it abuses us back. If others don't see through our disguise, the law of common power makes us face the mirror every time. Think of the saying: *"The higher you climb, the harder you fall."*

But for the Comic Dynamic, there is also *uncommon power* – the noble, unassuming kind that is motivated by courage and confidence. It is uncommon because fewer of us have experience performing in this way when we experience success. But if we possess it, we are freed of craving for the bling of common power.

With uncommon power, we are grounded in Genuine Presence and make the best of what life brings. This kind of power does not diminish or surge with the comings and goings of life events; it is a steady confidence within. Feeling secure in uncommon power, we welcome opportunities to empower others so that they too can have this level of self-trust.

Having uncommon power helps us live an unpretentious, down-to-earth lifestyle. Our character is rooted in common decency. We may have a large home, an expensive car and other refinements, but we don't need to flaunt them or possess in excess. We give for the sake of giving without seeking anything in return. That integrity has remarkable power. We aren't afraid of being common and in fact, feel as ordinary as the next guy. Without focusing on ourselves, this ordinariness gives us greater magnetizing powers.

When tragedy strikes, though we may feel the movement of sadness or fear reverberating in us, we don't lose ourselves in the misfortune of the situation. Instead, uncommon power supports broader understanding, maintains clarity, patience, and appreciation of life, despite the ongoing scene changes. On an everyday level, self-trust is the basis of a secure and self-reliant person. The Comic Dynamic can give control to another person and still feel in control. Our security lies in trusting that if you give something away, you have a never-ending supply of manifesting power.

Many of us today rely on the false hope of common power. Well-rehearsed in our chosen tragic Cover Character*, we parade around believing we are voicing our power. Because many people can't see through us, they misinterpret our performance as self-confidence and jump on our bandwagon trusting that we know the way to success. The comic dynamic does not allow this to happen because we are always in check with our motivation and intent. We use our power honestly and responsibly whereas the Tragic Dynamic isn't very different from the Wizard of Oz – fabricating special effects while hiding behind a glitzy curtain.

With our uncommon power, the comic dynamic has the gift to empower our personal world and the greater world stage for the better. We pay exceptional attention to how we use our power. Take your cues from the Tragic and Extreme Tragic Dynamics in history as a warning! Note how their gluttony for power and need to take-over lead them to ruin.

Trust only in your motivation and intent to inspire the best in us all. This is how we can bring long-term success to our lives. This means success that outlives our lifetime, that has legacy and legs into the future of our planet.

Performance Practice – Rehearsing Uncommon Power

If your routine character is Assumed Nobility, or another tragic character, try this rehearsal practice.

Scenario: Imagine yourself in a leadership position. Think of a troubling issue at work, at home, or elsewhere that is at stake.

Character: Choose a Comic Dynamic emotion, such as "confidence" to give character to your role.

Action: Now, with sincere interest in their answer, ask various people for their opinion about the issue following these steps.

1. First, go to the ESA. Clear, ground, and expand your awareness.
2. Taking the leadership role, ask those involved what they think of the issue. Ask what they suggest as a plan of action.
3. Listen carefully; make little or no comments. Ask questions if you speak at all. This puts your awareness on others and off your tendency to be self-centered.

4. Notice your character in having power over others. How are you holding your body to express your character? How does it make you feel? Powerless? Powerful? Is it a humbling experience? A learning curve? Watch your impulses and attitude.

5. Notice their character. Are they uncomfortable around you? At ease? Do they feel confident expressing their POV to you?

6. After listening, if you are the decision-maker, thank them for their expertise and suggestions. Let them know that their input will help you in your decision-making.

7. Now when you speak, your voice will be more powerful. You haven't betrayed your purpose with your usual "big talk."

8. This helps you enable others while simultaneously feeling your own power in a subtler, but genuinely present way.

Remember, you are empowering them to empower you to do the best job. This makes you a valuable leader who respects the views of others and is respected in return. Empowering others is extremely enriching. Ask any great leader.

CREATIVELY USING YOUR VOICE

As a Comic DPS, our magnetism also comes through our voice. Call it star power or charisma, we have an impressive vocal capability and using it beneficially is our mission in life. Learning to hear emotional character in the sound of your own voice is important. Listen to your tempo. Do you talk too fast, too slow or too clipped? The tone of your voice echoes your attitude. Is it melodic, caustic, thunderously loud, shrill or too subtle? Do you pronounce your words, mumble, or drop sentence endings leaving others to imagine what you meant? Your voice is your power and paying attention to how you use it gives you self-command.

The sound of your voice magnetizes as it resonates through space. Since all sounds are fleeting, the only thing that lasts are the impressions you leave. Whether you are a powerful speaker or soft-spoken, have a hi-pitched, loud, or gravelly voice, your voice speaks for you. And whether you are speaking from your comic or tragic side, the Dynamic PS voice will still attract. Therefore, to magnetize who and what you want into your life, choose your words and hear your tone, pitch, and volume when speaking. We get back what we send out. It's in the tone of our message. It's not only what you say, but how you say it.

With practice, you will come to see how your voice can be your greatest asset. Regardless of the quality and importance of your voice, to know and speak in skillful, powerful ways, use the following practices for turning creative blocks into creative skills.

Performance Practice – 3 Levels of Vocal Practice

1. Warm-ups

Breath Power Practice: Your voice is carried on the power of your breath as you inhale and exhale. To build strength in your breathing passages, the diaphragm and lungs must be clear and open, so the air can pass easily in and out of your nose and mouth.

- Go to the ESA and focus on the breath. On the in-breath, the outside air is taken in through the nose and sent to the brain to clear out the fog.
- As it passes through the throat and down, don't use it to expand your chest, but let it flow into your belly like blowing up a balloon. This opens up your diaphragm and expands the rib cage, stretching your capacity for air.
- Now hold the air in your belly for as long as you can.
- Then, while savoring that air, slowly release it through your mouth.
- Repeat the process at least 3 times. This steadies and fortifies the power of your breath.

Sounding Off Practice: Warm-up exercises that actors use before going on stage are useful for anyone when faced with a presentation, social event or interview. These situations are where our Dynamic PS can excel. Here are some helpful standards.

- Using your mouth, tongue and jaw recite aloud the vowels A, E, I, O, and U, using different pitches. Say them fast, normal paced, and slow.

- Now recite consonants aloud, like Pah, Pah, Pah, Ma, Ma, Ma, Da, Da Da, Ga, Ga, Ga, Kah, Kah, Kah, Bah, Bah, Bah, etc. Do these with different speeds and emotions.
- These will warm up your speaking instrument. Try various letters of the alphabet.

2. **Vocal Development**

Today we are in competition with a noisy world. Everywhere we go there are sounds bombarding our ears and consciousness. In addition, many of us lose our power by not speaking clearly. We drop the end of our sentences, speak under our breath, slur our words, use slang, talk too fast, too monotone, too high-pitched, too soft, too loud, and a multitude of other slights to the English (or other) language. Because of these mostly self-induced limitations, we are misunderstood, not heard, and sometimes rejected.

However, it is a simple fix. But it does require interest in developing a clear and good vocal effect when speaking anywhere. If need be, you can do your own research on this or find a voice coach.

For the purpose of developing your DPS voice, the categories below can help you explore vocal skills. These practices are good if your voice is too big, too soft, unexpressive or overly dramatic. Use the following to train your voice as you need.

- **Vocal Range** – on a scale of 1 to 10, some of us speak within a range of 3 to 6 pitches from low to high. The wider your range, the greater your resource for expression.
  Practice: Sing out as high as you can and slide down as low as you can. Slide up and down each time stretching a little higher and a little lower.

- **Intonation** – The tone of your voice involves vocal range and emotion. Working on intonation helps you learn to use highs and lows, volumes and attitudes for greater expressiveness in communication. Be aware that your tone of voice accurately displays your feelings and attitude.

Practice: Go online and find any play or movie script. It can be comedy or tragedy – try both at different times. You can also use any narrative that tells a story. Start reading it aloud, noticing if your voice has any interest or animation in it. Then reread it, emphasize the words that you wish to give special meaning. Do try-outs until you get it to sound as you would like. You can record and playback to get a good sense of your voice and what to work on. Practice this often until you begin to get a flow in emphasizing words and meaning in various sentences. This will bring interest to your voice when talking with anyone.

- **Pace, Rhythm, and Timing**
  We can create harmony when we are speaking naturally or dissonance when we are talking too fast or too slow. If you want to connect with your audience, whether it is one person or one hundred, by working with pace you can develop a rhythm of speech that is magnetizing. This also teaches you timing. You will become aware of when you need to pick up the pace, slow it down, add excitement, take a beat, or be silent.

  Pace Practice: If you talk too fast, notice the pace and movement of your jaw, your mouth, and tongue. They are probably going a mile a minute. Now, stop, and try saying the same thing without moving your jaw or changing the speed. Undoubtedly it will slow you down a bit. Practice this until you can find a composed yet confident speaking pace, then add use of your jaw and mouth.

Rhythm Practice: In music, there are enchanting rhythms that attract you to the dance floor; so too in our speaking patterns. We create a rhythm that can either attract or repel. Is your vocal pattern a lively allegro, or is it staccato – clipped, disconnected? Are you a smooth talker? Are you lyrical when you speak? It is great to have access to all these speech tempos to be used as needed. So, find something to read aloud and practice sounding it out in various rhythms: lively, animated, smooth, easy going, lyrical and graceful. In addition, listen to people whose speaking voice is attractive to you and learn how to make similar rhythms your own.

Timing Practice: Notice if you are in the habit of talking over someone or speaking out when someone else is try-ing to make a point. That is bad timing. We all do it every now and then. Practicing silence is a hard one for most of us. However, if you are at a party or meeting, try being silent throughout. You will begin to notice those cracks in conversation when the timing is right to get your point across. Notice when the time is right for something and when it is not.

- **Diction – Articulation, Enunciation, Volume & Delivery**
  Articulation demonstrates how well you formulate your thoughts and put them into words for others to under-stand. If you learn to think before you speak, this is easy. Practice restraint when you haven't formulated your ideas. When your ideas are clear, words come naturally.

  Enunciation is the art of speaking clearly and pronouncing your words distinctly. To enunciate is both a kindness to others as well as the art of being understood. Notice how you pronounce words. Do you say the K in kale or does it sound like, *I'm onna make some ale?* How about the H in hair or does it sound like, *I'm onna brus my air?* Notice if you have a lazy tongue – do you slur words? Practice enunciating clearly. In the beginning, over-emphasize your words and with rehearsal it will soon become a natural flow. Being well spoken is important everywhere, especially in business.

Volume is not just about how loud or soft you speak. It has to do with projecting the sound of your voice in the most effective manner. People can't understand you if you drop the end of your sentences, as in, *"I put it in the little thingy over there by the…"*

Then there are those who always speak under their breath. This uses no energy or breath and produces little more than a whisper. What little sound there is comes from the mouth. When I tell someone that they are talking under their breath, they often begin shouting their words as if they are being harassed. But really, it amounts to putting some life into your words by using your breath and diaphragm.

The opposite issue is over-projecting your voice when it is not necessary. Some people seem like they are shouting at you when they are actually standing right next to you. In this case, they probably have a big voice to start with and never noticed how loud they sound. These vocal issues require the practice of modulation. Awareness of how you sound and making the necessary changes will give you more influence in communicating and presenting yourself anywhere.

Delivery displays your style, your ability to deliver a message or concept with self-command. If you practice all the above, you will become a stronger communicator in everyday dealings. A great delivery requires developing the talent to put all the elements of voice and diction into a powerful and colorful package – a Dynamic You.

3. **Knowing your voice**
   - To know your own voice is to know your own mind. If you keep your mind open and clear, you will know who in you needs to speak and when. From a performance POV, knowing your voice is to be steady of mind and versatile in your emotional character. It is to be confident in your ability to perform well from all 5 Performance Styles within you. When you know yourself in this way, your will know your own voice.
   - If influenced by someone else's voice, make sure that person(s) voice is in sync with the things you want in life. No matter how important someone seems, let their voice ruminate within you before deciding if it can speak for you.

THE POWER OF DYNAMIC PRESENCE

The Comic Dynamic's objective is to express our power without throwing it around – be powerful but not overpowering. With poised confidence, our unique power is genuinely present in any situation. We identify with Genuine Presence as our true character and are able to perform with a keen understanding of situations and people. The side effect is natural charisma.

This is not the chest-extending star presence you might see in some Dynamic Tragedians. It is a lionhearted magnetism, a generous and courageous presence that enriches those with whom we interact. Because we feel and know our own power without the need to inflate our self-image, we can empower others by our very presence. This is empowerment in its highest sense.

Practice – Rehearsing DPS Presence

On our comic side our presence instinctively empowers others. Knowing the difference between being self-empowered and being deluded with self-importance is our greatest skill. Use the following hypothetical scenario or make-up your own situation to practice empowering presence.

1. You are going out with your family for a fun day of togetherness.

2. You know it will not be a day for you to relax and do your own thing. But it's not about ME.

3. Before engaging…go to the ESA. Choose to be genuinely present to the family and enjoy being totally with them.

4. You give them a choice between going to the park and playing outdoor games, going to a movie, or go swimming.

5. Their choice may not be your choice, but you like to let them make decisions. You ask them questions to help them make their choice and don't influence with your preference.

6. They choose a movie. You get there and make a pact with the kids. You will give them money to pay for their own ticket and in turn they will help with cleaning up after dinner tonight. A deal's a deal.

7. They want popcorn? Hot dogs? Candy? What can they do to earn the money? Sweep the porch? Make their own bed? You make this into a fun game rather than playing the authoritarian.

8. Your partner wants to sit in the back with you and let the kids sit closer to the screen. You let him or her know that is what you'd like too.

9. After the movie, you may go for an ice cream or drive. You do not talk about your work, your personal worries and/or disagreements with people. You are living in the moment, enjoying the scenery and events happening around you. Mostly, you are staying present to the people who mean the most to you.

After practicing, create your own scenario based on your real-life situations. Rather than family, it can be something in your community, being with a friend, or interacting in a business meeting with colleagues. The practice is to "be" with people, not show off, or lord over them. Empower others, maintain the ESA, be generous, hold confidence, composure, and affection as your creative skills.

SCENE 7 THE COMIC SPIRITUAL PERFORMANCE STYLE –
INCREASING YOUR SENSE PERCEPTION THRU REHEARSAL

And as the morning steals upon the night, melting the darkness, so their rising senses begin to chase the ignorant fumes that mantle their clearer reason.

~ The Tempest

- The Performance Objective is to hold a perceptive overview that sees all beings with compassion.
- Our Talent is sensory awareness and intuition.
- Our Comic Traits are that we have an expansive overview in our awareness. We have a fearless freedom of spirit and compassion for all.

Studies show that fish receive underwater communication from other marine life through sound waves. Birds and forest animals receive airborne signals of danger through their acute sense of sound and smell. So, might it be feasible (if not logical) that we, especially Spiritual PSs, can also receive distant sensory signals from other human beings? As in, *OMG, I was just thinking of you and my cell rang!! How freaky is that!*

Yet, why is it that most of us cannot receive remote images and messages that travel through space? Is it possible the human mind, unlike other animals, is too desensitized with fears and cluttered with brain babble to connect with people, events, and information existing out there in the universe?

As Comic SPSs, our training is to clear our minds long enough to receive spatial messages and are open to learning new and unique ways to communicate with each other. From our experience, we understand that for everyday purposes, keen sense-abilities are badly needed. Yet, our senses are the most overlooked, under-studied, and unemployed asset we have available to us as human beings.

As Comic Spirituals, we maintain an inner ambiance of awareness and release any mood-sets and thought themes that fog our ability to perceive. We enjoy being free of "junk thinking" and instead being actively receptive to what's happening. We use our sense perception with practiced wisdom.

We've learned through practicing the ESA that the five senses – sight, sound, taste, touch and smell – all feed sensory information to our brain. When the mind is undisturbed by brain babble, the five senses are astute, and intuition is awakened. At that time, the SPS becomes more sensitive to the environment, as well as to people's character. In short, we can intuit things more quickly.

However, as spiritual tragedians, we are susceptible to sensory overload, which often makes us sick. We are not grounded enough to relate to strong sensory input. This lack of sensory education leaves us vulnerable to grim imaginings – from self-predicting an upcoming illness or a terrible accident, to fearing werewolves on the full moon. We sense that some thing "out there" is about to get us. However, what we are really sensing is our own deep fear. We don't understand how to use our sense perceptions and therefore misinterpret our fears as intuition.

Developing our comic sense-abilities can protect our well-being. There are many things out there that we can't see, such as dust particles, germs, microorganisms and other creepy-crawlies. Then there is our spiritual belief in the presence of fairies, monsters, devils, angels, and beings from other planets. And many of us sense the existence of God, Gods, or Goddesses. Though they may or may not exist, all these things have no substantial appearance, yet our sensibilities can either choose to believe in them or not.

Spiritual PSs must be careful with imaginings as they can develop into fearful insecurities. Learning sensory awareness gives us more acting power because it comes from direct perception as opposed to our fancies, beliefs, and opinions that vary with circumstances. Our senses play a huge part in our lives and it serves us well when we awaken our senses with awareness.

Knowing Your Five Senses

Coming to your senses is important training for the SPS life actor. Each of your five senses connects with one of the Performance Styles. Studying sense-ability actually helps you build creative skills not just for your SPS, but for all five PSs.

Sight. We see so many things in our world today – our family at home, neighbors, people at work or in the news. We are bombarded by countless sightings – pleasant and unpleasant, wholesome and threatening during the course of a day. Our mindstage is, in general, flooded with a multitude of visions.

The Mental PS relates well to the sense of sight formulating ideas and opinions based on what we see in the world. We formulate our attitudes, self-image, create ideas, opinions and strong beliefs based on what we see. So, ask yourself if you are seeing things as they actually are through your sense-ability or whether you are seeing things colored by your beliefs and judgments. Knowing the difference is useful to making effective decisions. As a Comic MPS, allow your point of view to see the good in situations and figure out ways to create the best of what you see.

Sound. The Dynamic PS relates best to the sense of sound. Our power is transmitted in the vibrations and tone of our own voice. Sounds penetrate our being and if well-meant, can have a strong effect on our wellbeing. Sounds can adversely be malicious and affect ill-health.

Listen to your inner voice. What character is speaking and what message is it sending? What sound is vibrating in your core? By purposefully listening and learning its needs, you can speak from your heart and let integrity resound from your sound stage.

Smell. The Spiritual PS relates best to the sense of smell as it is used to detect the nature of things by its scent, literally and metaphorically. We also use other senses to perceive information, but because we associate scent with the idea of "being on to something," the SPS uses scent to intuit.

Notice whether are you are actually intuiting something or imagining it to be so? Dispense with junk thinking and sink into your sense-ability. Discern things accurately without assuming your suspicions are always right. When sussing things out about people and situations, use your keen overview to differentiate between assumptions and intuitive awareness.

Taste. The Emotional PS relates best to the sense of taste as we use it to separate our likes from our dislikes and to determine pleasure from pain. Our taste shows off our sense of style, our aesthetics, and choices in food and drink. Taste helps us determine what is fitting, harmonious, beautiful, or harsh and ugly.

Notice how your likes and dislikes make you happy or unhappy. Use your sense of taste to make people happy. Help yourself and others. Curb your appetite for cravings that bear little fruit. Develop a taste for things that bring you greater sustenance.

Touch. The Physical PS enjoys the sense of touch. The physical sensation of touch, the act of touching or being touched, and making contact with the physical world is natural for us. Touch involves sensations of pleasure or pain. We can be touched negatively or positively.

Notice if you like to touch and/or be touched. Notice how you are touching others. Do you rely on the touch of others to make you feel good? Do you allow others to touch you in toxic ways? Do you seek a sexual or loving touch? Do you cling to the effect of a touch – good or bad? Notice these things as you go about your day. Develop good and strong touchstones in life.

As a comic SPS, we use all our senses practically, yet with great wisdom.

AFFIRM LIFE WITH LOVE AND COMPASSION

Though the tragic side of the SPS has trouble facing our role here on earth, our comic side is all about universal love and compassion. Yet our tragic side carries an undercurrent of sadness that senses something is missing, that maybe we are not living up to our greatest human potential.

Not understanding this sadness, we often fly into fantasy or resort to despair. Yet, it is vital to recognize that this is only character habit. We can transition into our comic side and deliberately rehearse and expand our given talent for profound perception. This virtue is not the well-meaning do-gooder in us, but our innate sense-ability for creating light in the world.

Since the SPS's orientation is space, rather than spacing-out, our responsibility is to use our spatial orientation in everyday situations. To realistically ground ourselves in reality and not fly away from it, we must remind ourselves of the bright spirit we can bring to others if we put both feet on the ground.

Sense-ability is our strength and we need to practice our other Performance Style talents to bring us down to earth. As hard as it is to stay grounded, we can gain help by practicing emotional discipline. Physically we can practice taking action; mentally we can practice focusing, and dynamically we can practice confident presence. Our devotion to the greater whole then deepens with understanding and experience of all parts of our human instrument. For the SPS, this appreciation of the whole helps us work credibly with others in a truly spiritual context.

Grounding Practice for the Spiritual PS Creative Skills

Do the following practices to develop your other PSs and their creative skills.

- **Emotional Discipline**: When you feel yourself flying off to play the Space Cadet, go to the ESA and make a disciplined Character Choice. Try caring, warmth, enthusiasm and develop empathy for those around you by relating to their emotional issues with compassion.

- **Physical Action**: Notice people who need healing or help and do something special for them. They need your freedom of spirit.

- **Mental Focusing**: To bring your vision down to earth, find a task of interest, and focus on staying with it until its completion. Notice your tendency to fly away and bring yourself back with devoted effort.

- **Dynamic Presence**: Practice confidence in interactions with others. Be present to them. Listen to their needs, loves and joys. With magnetizing presence, you can offer sense perceptions that bring light to their world.

How Do You Use your Sense Perception?

Another way to expand our spiritual creative skills is to stretch our capacity for receptivity. Our vision is blocked if we are too sensitive to our fears. Our tragic side plays the boogeyman. We scare ourselves. Our comic side is real and sees things accurately. The openness needed to see and hear the big picture isn't obscured because we can separate physical realities from our own imaginings.

We know how to use space for practical purposes and are not seduced by the lure of the unknown, the mysterious and the eerie. We are able to receive sensory information that is available to us. Since we all possess the 5 Performance Styles to different degrees, real intuition is accessible. Try the following practice.

Practice – Assessing Your Sensory Awareness

Becoming aware of how the five senses affect you helps you make choices and avoid displeasure and spacing out. In the scenario below, imagine yourself as the main character. You will be given situations and choices that will affect your experience of the situation. Your results will depend on your observations and sense-abilities.

Scenario Practice

You walk into a restaurant to meet business associates for lunch. You rushed to get there and you're late. You feel a bit harried. It's lunchtime and the place is jam-packed and noisy. There is no host or hostess in sight.

You look around the room trying to spot the people you are supposed to meet. You don't see them. You wave down a staff person to help. They shout over the crowd telling you to wait. You wait…and wait.

Does what you see and hear make you feel agitated?
[ ] yes [ ] no

Are you more settled now that you are there?
[ ] yes [ ] no

You are now 25 minutes late and the restaurant is getting more crowded. You pull out your phone and text your associate… *"I am here! Where are you seated?"* The wait person signals someone behind you to follow him. In trying to get past you, the person bumps into you, touching your butt and making your knees buckle.

Does the physical contact piss you off?
[ ] yes [ ] no

Do you take it in good humor?
[ ] yes [ ] no

Finally, you see your associate coming toward you. You move through the tables to follow her. She greets you with a smile. You return the smile. She says something to you, but you can't hear her. She leads you into a back room that is slightly quieter and offers you the vacant seat. You apologize for your tardiness and sit down. They had ordered while waiting for you. Another colleague asks if you'd care for a glass of wine.

Do you accept, feeling you need a drink?
[ ] yes [ ] no

Do you say, *"No thank you,"* feeling you just want to relax with water or something else?
[ ] yes [ ] no

The wait person brings a dish to your colleague. It sure looks good – and it smells divine. Should you order the same? Should you look at the menu and see what else sounds good? The smell and look of the other dishes are making you hungry. You order what is fast and tell the others not to wait on you. Your dish arrives. It does not look as appetizing as the other dishes, but you don't say anything and begin to eat. It tastes worse than it looks.

Do you make a stink and send it back?
[ ] yes [ ] no

Do you eat it anyway and focus on the business conversation?
[ ] yes [ ] no

As you eat, do you gulp your food?
[ ] yes [ ] no

Or do you eat slowly, savoring the flavors while talking?
[ ] yes [ ] no

Now review your answers. Notice how your sensory responses make you feel? How do your senses make you act? Do your sense perceptions help or hinder the outcome of this situation?

When you can stay genuinely present in the ESA, you become calmly aware of how your senses play you. This helps you to monitor your reactions to them. You can use your senses to respond in less stressful and more helpful ways rather than automatically reacting to sights, sounds, tastes, smells and touch you encounter every day.

As you become more aware of your own sense-abilities, your sensory focus can then deepen into sensing the goals and needs of people and situations without so much thought analysis. Being intuitive is simply stopping the brain-train long enough to go "deep-see" diving.

SCENE 8 USING THE ESA TO LIVE FREELY

'Tis the mind that makes the body rich.
~ Taming of the Shrew

By identifying with the ESAwareness as your true self and the source of your creative nature, you will have a home base for balance and clarity. You can stop identifying with each transitory character that enters your mindstage, stays for a moment to perform and then exits. You'll recognize all of them, the catastrophic to the subtlest, as the passing parade of comedy and tragedy that come and go on-cue.

The ESA is a lifetime practice and usually develops in stages. The beauty of it is that we can practice it anywhere – at a tense business meeting, in a stressful interaction, or a joyful wedding. It can relieve ordinary pressures of daily living and help us do things that we often complicate with overthinking. With this freedom of mind, we can act with more enjoyment and self-trust.

ESA is the hardest and most important thing a person can achieve. It gives you a flexible center, as it does not fix your view as life situations change. When we maintain a firm center, ego-centrism comes into play. We act to complement our self-image, validate personal interests and long-standing beliefs. ESA can level the deflated or exaggerated ego and give you the ability to adapt into whatever is needed.

I must emphasize here that without the ability to access a calm and steady space within our mind, we will always be wandering, searching and caught up in the quagmire of emotional, spiritual and mental gymnastics. We will always be subject to outside influences without much choice. Confusion will prevail with only periods of clarity and enjoyment. Being grounded in spacious awareness keeps us awake and present throughout our life story.

Awareness is the real me.

Act V

The Quick Change Artist –
Becoming Whole

The ultimate goal of LPP is to help you become a Quick Change Artist (QCA) – one who has the versatility, awareness and quick change-ability to act in whatever manner is best for a given situation. In order to gain this unique life performance fitness, we must understand our human nature. It is not, as traditionally believed, our shared behavioral characteristics as I have described in Acts 3 and 4. In fact, those are simply our learned conditionings, age-old human habits that can change given circumstances or choice.

In Act 5, I will attempt to describe, according to my understanding of ancient spiritual texts, the naturalness of human nature and how it relates to the way we act in our daily life. Comprehending our true nature and putting it to good use is the QCA's resolve.

SCENE 1 THE PARADOX OF EMPTY SPACE AND HARD REALITY

And like the baseless fabric of this vision, the cloud capped towers,
the gorgeous palaces, the solemn temples, the great globe itself,
Yea, all which it inherit, shall dissolve,
And like this insubstantial pageant faded, leave not
a rack behind. We are such stuff as dreams are made
on and our little life is rounded by a sleep.

~ The Tempest

To begin with, confusion arises because we don't understand our true nature. We believe that hard reality is all there is. Yet, at our very essence, the transparent view of awareness is our basic nature. The Empty Stage Awareness represents this naturally radiant and present self in us all. Practicing this ordinary wakefulness daily gives us a stable mind – a clear setting on our mindstage for both observation and quick change-ability when necessary. Without stability, we can't see what is actual and will not be able to act with Genuine Presence in daily life.

If more people could gain this kind of self-awareness, we might have a less conflicted and violent world. Without our ability to see the creative potential of a sound mind, we continue to believe in the inner and outer struggle of war and peace. We see no end to the conflict and call it human nature.

During childhood, we haven't been given courses or training on how to use our human instrument for creating a world free of conflict. Consequently, most of us see that idea as Pollyanna's impossible dream. Yet, we aren't born with an "Instruction Tag" around our little toe, so few of us know how to operate productively and happily in life, much less understand how to get along with each other. Nonetheless, beyond our self-concepts of what's possible or impossible, is the vibrant, Empty Stage Awareness of our mind. It is where creativity can come alive, take form and change us.

Understanding the Paradox

So, if you are still wondering why anyone would want to live on an empty stage, it helps to examine our interaction between the invisible potential within transparent space, and what we assert as hard reality. We may feel validated and comforted by the notion of reality, seeing it as "the truth." And most of us appear indifferent or bewildered by "*this insubstantial pageant faded,*" as Shakespeare put it – the fleeting, intangible quality of our life scenarios.

Stuck in this paradox, many people have trouble with the feeling of being in limbo. We need for things to be certain. When the safety of our reality is disrupted, we grasp and get anxious or angry trying to force "things" into something "real" we can hold on to. We engage with everything and everyone as if we are "such stuff as rocks are made on," but in truth, we are only "*such stuff as dreams are made on.*" and "*we sleepwalk through our little life, ignorant of our expansive, transitional nature.*"

But, what if suddenly someone yells "Wake Up!!!" and disrupts your sleep walking? You might quickly remove your sleeping mask and begin to perform your life wide-awake. This is what living on the Empty Stage does for you. As a life performer, you have the infinite creative potential of space that allows you to bring your unseen, embryonic notions into physical reality. Once a reality, our possessions and associations only appear real during their lifecycle before they disperse back into the creative potential of space – a sort of cosmic recycling.

Given that interactive union between unseen potential and reality, we can't say that reality, which appears solid, really is solid. Nor can we say that the unseen is really a void. What we can say is that reality is dependent on the potential to create and the unseen potential is dependent on reality to take form. Reality and potential are therefore interchangeable because of the compliance of empty space.

If we don't realize that this mysterious coming and going – this illusive, yet renewable wellspring of life is empty space itself, we won't recognize its importance or know how to travel wisely and fluidly in it. Like a womb, the empty stage of our mind holds the creative seed that manifests all our happy and sad realities. If we know how to use it, spacious awareness is our condition for sanity; it can guide us through the inevitable entrances and exits in life. But if we don't recognize its presence, like an unsolved mystery, we continue to search for answers.

How the Quick Change Artist Lives the Paradox

For most of us this mysterious, uncomfortable feeling of emptiness inside is related to our inexperience with space. We have never harnessed the use of space for our own benefit. Misreading it as a personal void, we can fall into fright when we don't know how to interact with it.

By becoming a Quick Change Artist (QCA), however, we know our choices – either fall into the black hole or get creative! We know that empty feeling is not a cue for despair but a cue to go to the ESAwareness and revision our potential.

Typically, our performance habit is to develop certain character traits in order to ground our lives. This gives us something definite to be and do that provides us with a "sense" of self. It solidifies who we "think" we are – *I am this…and I am not that!* This idea of a solid "Me" makes life seem real.

However, our habit of trying to stabilize ME through repetitious behavior is like a bird in flight leaving faded impressions in the sky. Though we perceive our actions as real, they are only real in the moment. After all, every action we take fades as quickly as it is created, and we are left with but a past impression of a time in space – a momentary reality faded into a memory.

Stabilizing our roles and characters also give us something to love and something to hate. If we didn't have set roles and character habits to play, then who are we? Would we even exist? Would we just be floating in space? Well, it depends on how we interpret and play the paradox.

What causes us endless fear and confusion is that we interpret this paradox backwards. As a result, we play it in reverse. It's not our character that needs to be steady, but the space in our mind that we need to steady. Then our roles, characters and performance styles can become flexible and spontaneously chosen to match the demands of the times.

Imagine what it would be like if the space surrounding us wobbled and changed constantly. It would be discombobulating. Yet, whether you realize it or not, that is our collective state of mind. It's as if our mindstage is in constant strobe lighting – whirling, wobbling and free-floating all the time. We are hardly aware of the creative space in our mind, so the idea of stabilizing it doesn't even occur to us. By calming and focusing our mind, whatever character we choose or need to play will naturally be present.

The more you practice the ESA, the more your mind will relax and open to the space surrounding your thoughts, feelings and imaginings. Like an artist using a fresh, clean canvas instead of repainting over crusty old paintings time and time again, you will come to see the value of a having fresh, spacious mind. Slowly, you will want to steady the space of your mind into wakeful presence and act with accurate foresight.

To do so, studying and rehearsing how to effectively and fluidly use all our performing parts, rather than developing Character Sclerosis, is necessary. It's valuable to practice acting from our comic side more consistently, even having some go-to regular characters we can use in our daily performance (as the valuable character traits you learned in Act 4), so that our tragic side doesn't impulsively direct our daily actions. Basically, becoming aware of who in us is acting will help us avoid misfortune.

By developing emotional versatility, we can productively play any role with character choice, and we can put color, texture, and meaning into any scene. Like an actor effortlessly moving on and off a stage, we can readily move in and out of our life scenarios if we have an unwavering mindstage to perform from. Our fear of space and ignorance of our human instrument is what holds us back. The QCA has learned to be grounded in space and spontaneous in life performance.

SCENE 2 TRANSITIONS VS. TRANSFORMATIONS

Bless thee Bottom! Bless thee! Thou art translated.

~ A Midsummer Night's Dream

From the LPP perspective, we do not truly transform ourselves until we are *Living on the Empty Stage* – acting as Awareness without grasping to outcome. Transformation is the ultimate goal of the Empty Stage Practice. To prepare, the life actor practices emotional discipline, versatility and transitioning in order to be free of hardened character traits – comic or tragic.

There is a distinction between a transition vs. a transformation. In becoming a QCA, we learn to transition smoothly from one role, character and performance style to another when we adapt to various situations. Basically, anytime we change our persona, we are transitioning. These transitions can seem like transformation if we continually rehearse a positive character choice and we "feel transformed!" Yet, without the steadiness of mind that you get from living on the empty stage, you may not have self-command over whether old, opposing character traits will reappear and throw your chosen character off your mindstage again.

Transformation, on the other hand, is a totally different perception. It completely breaks through our dueling attitudes – the two sides of our character that live in opposition. Skilled in the Empty Stage Practice, the QCA has learned to see reality without fixed attitudes, beliefs, judgments, and attachments. It's not that we don't experience comedy and tragedy or have the good sense to think logically about things; we just don't harden our viewpoint into egocentric positions. We have the flexibility to change as things change. We have learned discernment rather than judgment, understanding rather than attitudes, and open awareness over attachments. True transformation only comes when we are firmly established in the ESA. Thus, for the QCA, *Living on The Empty Stage as Awareness* is our life's on-growing work of art.

THE BENEFITS OF ON-GROWING USE OF ESA

For the Mental PS...

- Clearer thinking
- Deeper insights
- Less anger and self-righteousness
- Better mental health in general

For the Emotional PS...

- Reality communication
- Emotional discipline
- Unpretentious, honest and artistic expression
- Better emotional health in general

For the Physical PS...

- Greater perseverance
- Increased energy for fitness and function
- Stronger healing powers
- Less anxiety and painful sensations

For the Dynamic PS...

- The power of self-command
- Diplomatic ability to empower others
- Embody dignity and integrity
- Advance noble leadership
- Charismatic vocal power

For the Spiritual PS...

- Stronger intuition
- Less fear and greater wisdom
- Compassionate overview
- Sense-ability in relationship with others
- An increase in purpose and functionality

How the ESA Helps Your Brain and Mind

To become a Quick Change Artist, your ESA practice helps you steady and focus your mental wandering and as a result, opens your mind to a clearer, bigger view. Once focus is established, spread that steadiness into spacious awareness. Establish that. Carry that awareness into all your daily activities.

For example, when you notice your attention gets caught up in an overexcited scenario, be aware that that feeling is only one side of your character expression. Go to the ESA and balance excessive excitement into the beauty of awareness and bring up an enduring enthusiasm. When your attention gets caught up in a fearful, miserable scenario, be aware that that feeling is only one side of your character expression. Go to the ESA and level that despair into the beauty of awareness and bring up gentleness or curiosity. No matter what you are thinking and feeling, emptying your mindstage will allow insights to arise in that free space and help you self-correct any existing character issues.

Living on the Empty Stage, we learn to let realities stream through us. ESAwareness allows us to be present and play the moment instead of allowing Character Residue to hold onto things unnecessarily. Awareness lets us love without grasping, give without expecting, and stay in the stream of life. We become more confident during uncertain times, knowing that, if we stay open, we have creative abilities regardless of life's changes.

The QCA has become accustomed to ESA as a third place for the mind to go – independent of comedy and tragedy. In fact, as our backdrop, we know the ESAwareness is our safe haven and is always present as our true identity. Adjust your mind to the perception that everything is transitional; that all realistic things are transitory and that you are a creative, transient being.

Of course, The QCA still has relationships, jobs, special interests and all the comic and tragic issues that arise from living life. But now, because we are moving freely in and out of daily scenarios, we are using our human instrument with newfound motivation and intent. The difference is that we deal with the issues in resourceful ways based on our sense of presence. This understanding is what it takes to become a Quick Change Artist in an ever-changing world.

SCENE 3 THE QUICK CHANGE ARTIST'S SUPPORTING ROLES

I do perceive here a divided duty.

~ Othello

Awareness is at ease with having no self-image. Though we are acting out our roles, our characters, and performance styles, we don't cling to them to support our significance. The Quick Change Artist is who we can be as human beings if we sincerely practice the process. If we don't, then we simply collect a lot of ideology about who we want to be and often wind up pretending to be.

Life Performance Practices is not an easy solution for the person who is looking for a quick fix. Because we have such aversion to our ugly, destructive side, we refuse to look at our inner characters that cause obstacles. Most of us have never really acknowledged our tragic character traits with clear intent to change them. Instead, seeing ourselves in others, we deflect our character flaws into them. However, we can't keep playing the same negative characters and expect positive results. The QCA works hard to gain a stable mind and rehearse character traits that feel honest and valuable to others. It's not about being perfect; it's about being connected to the best choices in you.

In the process, we can have fun developing three main supporting roles that are essential allies to the QCA's greater functionality and service in the world: 1) *The Well-Rounded Life Actor,* 2) *The Director,* and 3) *The World Player.* Like good friends, each of these roles within us supports the other, providing greater power to your QCA.

I. The Well-Rounded Life Actor

With a working knowledge of all parts of our human instrument, we become a Well-Rounded Life Actor. That wealth of self-knowledge develops out of a deep devotion to cultivate self-love. Through study and rehearsal, we know our comic and tragic sides. We develop compassion for our character flaws that often manifest in bad behavior and/or emotional and physical pain. We have come to appreciate the value of using our comic talents to the best of our ability instead of reactively defaulting to our tragic side. The Quick Change Artist is effortless in action because of the accomplished support of the well-rounded actor.

In this new era of technological interfacing, being well rounded increases our capabilities. By dedicating yourself to becoming the best you can be, by training your body, intellect, emotions and intuition, and by learning to use your power with grace and generosity, you will not only have far more creative resources, but you will produce better outcomes. Like a chef, whose culinary knowledge knows which herb is needed to enhance a dish, you will know which part of you is needed to enhance a situation because you have knowledge of your instrument. Otherwise, if you have no experience of who in you is needed at different times, how can you fulfill your needs?

As a well-rounded life actor, you can set your basic character traits by naturally performing from the Performance Style in which you excel. Yet, you do not get stuck there. To make positive performance changes, you understand the Five PSs and a full range of character options to enjoy fluent use of your whole instrument. In challenging circumstances, you are able to completely change your routine way of acting. That is the definitive skill of the QCA.

By having command of the mental, physical, emotional, dynamic and spiritual, you are better equipped to meet all kinds of situations. In many ways, the LPPractices are like having a higher education in self-awareness and the practical skill to execute the necessary performance needs. With committed rehearsal time, you will be able to live up to the greater potential within you. That doesn't mean you will excel in every Performance Style, but that you will no longer feel so fragmented. You will have filled in the missing links of self-knowledge and learned how to use yourself in more useful ways.

II. The Director

It's hard to see ourselves in action, making it hard to direct and play our own leading role simultaneously. In directing a play or film, the director sees the action as it is being played out and can call "Cut", stopping the scene if the performance he/she sees is not satisfactory.

In our daily performance, however, we are the actors, so we don't always see our own actions in a scene until we play a rerun* on our mindstage. If we can't access our own director to redirect our action in the moment, then we usually walk away from a bad life performance feeling bad.

As a QCA though, our inner director can see the action as it is happening and simultaneously perform the scene. Because self-awareness is directing, we can make personal on-the-spot changes when we see that a scene is not working. Some people might feel they can do this naturally but maintaining sincere motivation without ulterior intentions is what is at issue here.

The ESA allows us to see ourselves in action. It gives us the inner stability to make accurate changes without a lot of thought themes masking our vision. Having this ability, we can interact with others in more perceptive ways. Because we can self-correct our own actions, we can also see the motivations and intentions of others and know how to best interact with them. You must be patient, learning to be your own director is a new role for us and takes conscientious practice.

III. THE WORLD PLAYER

Having the know-how of the well-rounded life actor and the keen eye of your director is what allows us to be a World Player. We can aptly interact in our own world as well as the world at large. In addition to our family household, we easily relate to our coworkers and bosses, our social circles, schoolmates, our neighborhood communities, spiritual congregations and political organizations.

The World Player realizes the need to perform well in all areas of life. If you aspire to global influence, your focus may become the world stage. Yet to be a successful World Player of this magnitude with staying power, you must have good character traits in order to maintain people's respect. Whether you're a player only in your own domain or on the global stage, being able to recognize the Performance Style, roles and emotional character of others, helps you interact in constructive ways. Some of us get stumped when we are faced with someone whose Performance Style is different from our own. For these reasons, being able to identify all 5 Performance Styles in others is invaluable – especially if theirs is not your primary style.

Not everyone aspires to be a player with global power. In fact, a World Player can be a follower as well as a leader. You know the follower within you and when to follow. And likewise, you know the leader within you and when to lead. As a World Player, you have little ego investment in whether you play the lead or an extra.

Regardless of your role, you perform with confidence. You are sure-footed, clear speaking, open hearted and present minded. The accomplishment of these three roles power the success of the QCArtist in us all.

SCENE 4   TODAY'S URGENT NEED TO BE A QUICK CHANGE ARTIST

He was indeed the glass wherein the noble
youth did dress themselves.

~ Henry IV

L et me encourage you to embrace the QCA as a new role model for a healthy and prosperous future. Today we must be able to cross-perform because life demands our participation on the vast cross-cultural world stage. To do that, we need multi-business skills, magnetizing skills on social media, and the aptitude and ease to live crossover lifestyles. Flourishing technology and ever-changing global interactions require that we learn to be Quick Change Artists (QCA) in the most inspiring and productive ways.

There are certain roles we play in life where it is important to be predictable, to be credible and consistent. In business, it is good character to assume responsibility and let people know they can count on you. Yet today, it is equally important to be spontaneous, to change quickly when the situation or facts change. It is also good to be sharp and adaptable when a new player comes on the scene or when someone you know acts out of character.

With The Practices, you will gain a large perspective of human abilities and inabilities. You will be able to interact with most people without losing your own mental stability. You will also be able to sense the hidden troubles in certain people and situations and know when to help, or to walk away.

As a Quick Change Artist, if need be, you can set your principal character in each Performance Style, yet develop a fuller range of emotions, so you will be able to make spontaneous character changes as needed. Don't limit your talents by type-casting yourself. As a QCA, you need options for quick change-ability if you find tragic characters taking control. Here is a practice to develop such options:

Practice – Developing Quick Change-Ability Options
Go to your ESAwareness.
- State your tragic character traits in each Performance Style.
- Allow your tragic characters to express their grievances.

- What is your tragic character's message to your entire cast of characters?
- Is the message negatively affecting your comic character who wants to make progress?
- If so, go to the ESA – clear and soften.
- If your mind-trolling character persists, use the "Cut!" practice and make a scene change.
- If it is still disturbing your mindstage, call out your Director to redirect your troubled character.
- Quickly make a new character choice from your comic side and perform it.

Concurrently…
- **Rehearse** new character choices that are useful to your life's progress.
  Examples: calm, assertive, productive, kind, loving, etc.
- **Begin** to use these character traits with people in your daily routines.

The Transition Practice lets you recognize who in you is performing well and who needs to transition into a more valuable player. Remind yourself that all your characters – comic or tragic – are transient and have no real solidity unless you continually rehearse and solidify them. This practice develops flexible self-command over your inner cast of characters – a must for the QCA.

SCENE 5 THE PERFORMANCE STYLE VALUES OF THE QCA

The art itself is nature.
~ The Winter's Tale

Each Performance Style has its own set of values and if we are clear about them, then we know who we are at heart. Though one or two may be your primary PSs, you will find other PS values are yours as well. In that way, you can see how you utilize all five PSs values from the comic viewpoint. So, check off the ones you claim as your own, and put an asterisk by the ones you would like to work on.

MENTAL PS

- Acknowledge others for their ideas and viewpoints.
- Recognize when I am wrong and self-correct, or humbly stand-corrected.
- Assess others by their standards and not by my own.
- Stay curious and open to new insights.
- Honor people's time – be as punctual as possible.
- Be considerate of another's mindstate – don't add to their worries with thoughtless neglect or negativity.
- Your own MPS Values?

EMOTIONAL PS

- Appreciate both sides of our human character. Gain self-love.
- To avoid hurting others, seek understanding.
- Do not hide my faults from myself; hiding them makes me a liar.
- Watch how my feelings are affecting others.
- Have empathy for what others are going through without taking it on as my own.
- Love without expecting return.
- Your own EPS Values?

Physical PS

- Be accountable for my own actions.
- Take responsibility for the quality of my work.
- Be disciplined and dependable in duty.
- Avoid aggression, act from my bravery and helpfulness.
- Exercise agility – be ready for action as needed.
- Do the healthy thing – notice rewards or consequences.
- Your own PPS Values?

Dynamic PS

- Show respect to others and others will return the respect.
- Be ethical – demonstrate human decency to all people.
- Maintain integrity – a truthful code of honor.
- Use my voice to empower others, create win-win closures.
- Do not display my power, use it quietly and anonymously where I see it is needed.
- Speak of the good in others. Do not amplify the bad, as it does not speak well of me. Maintain a noble heart.
- Your own DPS Values?

Spiritual PS

- Have faith in myself.
- Don't focus on my fears as that makes me susceptible to danger.
- Inspire the highest view of humanity.
- Know gratitude and compassion. Spread life's goodness.
- Ground in the service of others, especially when I'm weak. It will make me strong.
- See the big picture and work for a peaceable future.
- Sense and intuit the reality of a moment.
- Your own SPS Values?

Playing Your Values

What's aught but as 'tis valued?

~ Troilus and Cressida

Some of these values may seem unattainable or even absurd because we may not consistently think to practice our highest ideals. We usually go with what we feel, which isn't always best. Often, we act out of hurt and fear – the very basis of tragedy. Those two emotional characters cause us enormous unhappiness and confusion. Watch how quickly hurt can turn love into hatred and how fear can turn self-defense into violence.

Through lessons learned the hard way, the QCA well knows how these tragic feelings constrict our freedom to live as we would like. So, we challenge ourselves to act from love and joy, the basis of our comic side. We rehearse being open and content; free to act in honest ways so that we remain conscious of our values.

The QCArtist has integrated the 5 Performance Styles into daily life and knows how to apply any of the values as scenes change. If we can't connect these values to our everyday interactions with others we lose our integrity. And, it is those esteemed ideals we hold in our heart/mind that give us reason for acting and being in the world. If you harden those values into self-importance, they become rigid rules you depend on to support your self-image. Therefore, sustaining the ESAwareness on our mindstage is crucial.

Whether it is a family, business, or social setting we enter, knowing the Performance Style you are using helps maintain a connection with the people and issues that arise in daily scenarios. However, do not use them to separate yourself from those whose values seem lesser or different from your own. That makes it a personal bias that only causes greater separation. Our values exist to help us bridge the gaps between us.

SCENE 6 THE PLAYERS AND SETS ON OUR REVOLVING STAGE OF LIFE

How many ages hence
Shall this our lofty scene be acted over
In states unborn and accents yet unknown.

~ *Julius Caesar*

Though internally we live on the Empty Stage of Our Mind, externally we perform on the Revolving Stage of Life. We leave our house in the morning and go to work. After work, we socialize with friends at the local bar or restaurant, or we go shopping, or attend a special event. But wherever we go, eventually we circle back home.

As we encounter the changing scenarios on our personal revolving stage, our ESAwareness is the stable thru-line* that enables us to link our character values to our actions. If we have not stabilized our mind, the revolving stage will make us dizzy and all spun out trying to establish and secure our chosen reality. So, let's look at the players and settings and how we can best hold the ESA as we revolve on the stage of everyday life.

FAMILY AND THE HOME SETTING

In the best possible world, family is there to protect and nurture us. Family is our bloodline, our roots. The players are parents, children, grandparents, aunts and uncles, cousins, nieces and nephews, or any group of people we choose. No matter what, our family setting is a place of trust and support. It's why we call it home.

Family values today are not always as described above. Some of us are distant toward our family, some of us are at odds with certain family members, or out and out detest our family, often destroying trust and support. And sadly, some of us have no family at all.

The QCA seeks to create good family relations in spite of any negative feelings we might have of each other. There is a way – but we have to be willing to dip deep down into our hearts and find a common ground.

Physically, we are there for each other no matter what. Emotionally, we offer support. Mentally, we think things through together. Dynamically, we empower each other, and Spiritually, if we tune in, we can sense each other's needs without having to ask. The values are that of loyalty and steadfastness.

Romantic Loves and Life Partners – the Bedroom Setting

In the best possible world, when you go to bed at night, your life partner is there to love, comfort, and befriend you. If that bond is not there, insecurity is there. Sex is not just an expression of passion or an on-again, off-again attraction, but more beautifully, good sex expresses the love bond between you.

In today's distractive world, it is easy to be aroused by attractions to others. For some who have not found self-love or self-acceptance, arousal can become a desperate lifestyle. Or sometimes we find ourselves in a relationship that isn't right, or was once good but as we have changed, that romantic bond changed. If you have taken vows with someone, *for better, for worse,* consider whether the promises can be revitalized. If irreconcilable or too toxic, then try to soften the hurt of separation with mutual compassion.

For the QCA, life can be superb with the right partner. Mentally, we listen to each other's desires. Physically, we are committed to the long run. Though we may feel other attractions, we always bring that titillation back to our partner. Emotionally, our love communicates empathy and intimacy. Dynamically, we find ways to voice our love and repower our attraction to each other. And Spiritually, we are connected to each other's highest purpose, which is the common ground for maintaining a loving connection. The values are that of faithfulness and communication.

Our Business Associates – the Office or Field Setting

In the best possible world, our work environment has an ambiance of creative streaming.* The players are our bosses, associates, colleagues, clients, or classmates and patients. Our interactions are respectful of each other's talents and physical abilities. We build our business and our products or services based on integrity.

Here is where we can bring out the noble character in ourselves and our company. If we follow our values, the money will follow. Affluence is a value that reaches out with self-assurance and generosity.

In our 21st century work-a-day world these character values are rare. In many businesses, employees say there is an atmosphere of cynicism or blind acceptance of our CEOs and world leaders. Through greedy self-favoring, prejudice, gossip, brash upstaging and character assassination, we create an environment of negativity and defeat. Whether we are in an office, work from home, or do field work, holding to our character values is difficult because those in power do not necessarily provide a sense of safety.

By contrast, as a QCA, we perform our values without fanfare when interacting with people in our work environment. Confident in our own power, we enable and encourage our colleagues to do their best. If others display bad character, without reacting, we use the clarity of the ESAwareness to mirror their behavior. Patience and courage is our motto.

Mentally, we listen and engage in productive dialogue. Physically, we are available to those who need our help. Aware of a colleague's shortcomings, we understand their intimidation and want to put them at ease. Emotionally, we level the playing field by not acting superior, which develops respectful relations. Dynamically, we encourage and invest in each other's talents, and Spiritually, we develop a sense of unified team spirit that is contagious. The workplace values are that of ethics, generosity and confidence.

OUR FRIENDS – THE SOCIAL SCENE

In the best possible world, our friends provide more than just a social outing. Really good friends are like family to us. A true friend is a confidant – someone we trust and feel comfortable in discussing our deepest fears, our biggest dreams and greatest joys. Our friends root for our success and offer creative ideas to boost us forward. They happily share our woes and do what they can to encourage us when we are down. Friends go to concerts, movies, parties, lectures and all kinds of events with us – even if they don't want to. Why? Because that's what friends do.

On the other hand, many of us suffer the noxious effects of "Frenemies," who are phony friends. These kinds of friends can't be trusted with personal information – they will tell your secrets and make fun of you behind your back. They talk badly about you, intent on discrediting your value in the eyes of others. Why? Because that's what self-hating, unfulfilled frenemies do.

The friendship of a QCArtist is tried and true. We care about our friends. Mentally, we engage in positive, creative thinking with each other. Physically, we go places together, share meals, work and play sports and games. We help our friends heal when they are ill or in need. Emotionally, we can have fun and also get deeply serious; we give and take, laugh and cry together. Dynamically, we sing each other's praises and don't play power games. And Spiritually, we lift each other's spirits when our world is falling apart. The values of friendship are that of trust, affection and openheartedness.

RELIGIOUS/SPIRITUAL COMMUNITY – A SCENE OF WORSHIP

In the best possible world, our religious/spiritual community offers a scene of peace and joy. We share our divine views and aspirations. It is a place of comfort for us – a place where we can release our woes into celestial space. Whatever our beliefs, our spiritual community is there to help us balance the divine experience with our earthly concerns. We do it by gathering together in prayer and devotion to a greater power, taking the edge off our own self-importance. We share in joyful events and celebrate the greater good. There is an atmosphere of deep affection for the human spirit.

Though this is the reason most of us might join a spiritual community, our human foibles are at play even in our so-called spiritual endeavors. As human beings, we try to gain a more enlightened approach to life, yet we are still caught up in our personal comic and tragic performance habits. We may be subject to the Physical PS's sexual desires, the DPS's desires for power, and the EPS's need to be liked and loved. These self-demands result in spiritual phoniness. We walk into a place of worship and "act spiritual," softening our behavior and feigning niceties at each other.

We insult, abuse and harbor secret cravings – then ask, "The Lord" to forgive and help us when it is really our own ignorance that we must forgive and self-correct. If our spiritual friends do not know how to creatively support us in achieving self-awareness, then we reinforce artificial attitudes toward them and become disillusioned about our spiritual path and clergy. It is usually not the path that is lacking but our own inability to stay focused on its truth.

The QCArtist is observant and accepting of our earthly conditions. In that, we are focused on our ultimate desire to find inner composure. We are aware that peace originates and radiates from within and that we won't find it anywhere else. We know that our path, if properly understood, relieves our ignorance and provides a setting for deeper self-awareness. We interact with our spiritual leaders and community to explore and learn from one another.

Mentally, we engage in learning and exploring spiritual ideals with each other. Physically, we work together in turning our resistances and prejudices into helping others. Emotionally, we strive for emotional balance that gives way to spiritual equanimity. Dynamically, we use our voice to elevate personal and global ideals and refrain from negative discussions. And Spiritually, we meditate, pray together, and act on our spiritual values. Even if we have different paths and don't understand each other's view, we are respectful of our differences. The spiritual community values are that of an uplifting nature.

Personal Wellbeing – A Scene of Health & Fitness

In the best possible world, our health is cared for – not in the hospital but in self-care. We do regular checkups, attend some type of physical attunement or fitness exercise, and eat healthy, energizing foods. In general, we not only tend to our physical body, but our mental and emotional life as well. We love our life and want to live to our fullest potential. As a protective measure, we quickly acknowledge when a part of us is harmfully starting to act out. In such cases, we "allow" that part of us to express what the impending ailment or annoyance is about.

Health exists in each Performance Style, but most of us tend to our physical health only when a body part breaks down. We seem unaware of the interconnection and interdependency linking all parts of our human instrument. Unaware, we neglect mental and emotional health because we may not know how to handle them. Our tendency is to relieve our mental tension and emotional unhappiness with excesses and conduct we know is self-destructive in the long run.

The QCA knows that by taking care of our overall health, the healthy energy we possess, radiates out to others. Our goal is to give others as much as we can. We know that our health is important to maintaining a clear view, resilient functionality, and good spirit.

Mentally, we take brain breaks and practice the ESA as often as possible. We watch our thoughts and self-correct if our thinking is aggravating how we feel and act. Physically, we are in tune with the foods our body needs on a changing daily basis. We exercise to stay strong and vital. Emotionally, we are aware of how our feelings are affecting our health and will change characters, if necessary, to improve our wellbeing. We are also aware how keeping company with toxic people can affect our health and counter-act it with character choice. Dynamically, we maintain command of ourselves and our energy. Spiritually, we know that being in the ESA is complete and total inner well-being. Our minds are free of thoughts, attitudes and behaviors that conjure affliction. Spiritual health is the QCArtist's way of life.

THE SOCIETAL STAGE – THE PUBLIC SCENE

In the best possible world, when entering the public stage of civic duties, political groups, social organizations and such, we interact with tolerant and informed interaction. We are able to debate, not simply set on winning or changing people's viewpoint, but with an interest in understanding each other's differences. We want to learn about values in other cultures in order to avoid any unnecessary affronts. Because we are respectful of each other, we can speak freely without fear of retribution.

In today's world, however, the above is hardly the case on most public stages, particularly the political stage. There is a growing global atmosphere of anger, resentment and hatred stemming from widespread hurt and fear. We have become hypersensitive to our cultural, political, racial, religious and societal preferences and differences. As a result, we have developed an intolerance to listening or caring about each other. There is no safe place on the World Stage anymore.

Using a social media platform, ordinary people, celebrities and so-called dignitaries alike, sling obscenities at anyone who counters their view. In our live public debates, our interactions are not focused on common interests but on character assassinating the opponent, or worse. All this, being performed on the societal stage only adds to the public storehouse of hurt, anger, and fear.

And too, we've lost our sense of humor; for what used to be entertaining satire has turned into offensive displays of hatred. Sadly, we still have the emotionality of cave people, however, our weapon is no longer a club, but social media accounts and a nuclear button. The uglier we play out our aggressions on the world stage, the uglier our lives become.

The QCArtist can foresee the future of this path and is vowed to perform our daily activities in the light of self-awareness. We vow to help heal the hurts, listen to the fears and act from love in spite of surrounding ugliness. The QCA is aware of the need for hope and happiness if we are to create a safe and sane world.

Mentally, we think of the effect we will have on others before acting on the societal stage. Physically, we take responsibility for our overall performance. Emotionally, we engage with others with empathy and sincere affection. Dynamically, we can advise and guide the diverse needs of different populations on the societal stage. Spiritually, we serve as an altruistic inspiration to the global community.

Being a QCArtist, we maintain a joyful heart, yet know the road ahead can be bumpy. However, if each of us sees the value of stabilizing our mind and changing the tragic scenes on our own revolving stage, the darkness on our global stage can revolve with sanity. You see, it truly takes a societal effort to create an age of light.

THE QCA AS A WHOLE PERSON

Because we feel irritated one moment and sad the next, by the end of the day we may have mindlessly played out our entire cast of characters. One of the main purposes in doing Character Study is to bring our fragmented parts into a sense of wholeness. Becoming a QCA, the need to splinter off into separate characters who are unaware of each other is unnecessary. We know how to identify each character and work with them gainfully. We now have a harmonious, multifunctional cast of characters to draw on who are lively and relevant to the world we want to create, both personally and internationally.

As a QCA, you are aware that your on-going worries, fears, obsessions, aggressions and most of your obstacles in life are created by insular self-concern and maintained by constant replay. The way you walk, talk, think, feel and act is habit and you now know how to rehearse the parts of you that can counter act any tragic traits. Your motivation as an artist brings beauty and well-being to others and yourself.

You have learned to fill in the underdeveloped parts of yourself. You are like a prism, beautifully whole, while aware of your many facets. Given the wholeness and awareness you experience by living on the empty stage, you no longer need to make character choices as your direction is obvious. You may come to a crossroad in which the way is not clear, however, you have learned to stay open to spatial signs and with patience the right path will become clear. Too, there are always those times in life when others don't get you, disagree with you, or act in hurtful ways. Though painful, your compassion shines through. You get them.

And there may be times when you want to refer back to The Practices to help you clarify something. But as an actor learns his lines and throws away the script, you have learned the practices and integrated them into your life. You are complete as a Quick Change Artist.

SCENE 7 THE FINALE

Our revels now are ended. These our actors, As I foretold you, were all spirits and Are melted into air, into thin air.

~ The Tempest

All things come to an end. Yet, by living on The Empty Stage of the mind, there is the continuum of space in which all things come and go. Within that magical act, as we perform on the Revolving Stage of Life, there is a kind of material recycling that happens. As life actors, we are in essence, *"all spirits and are melted into air."* And though the *"insubstantial pageant"* of each life eventually fades *"into thin air,"* the Revolving Stage circles back with new life and new actors who create new stories, new scenes, and a new era.

The attributes of every new era depend on us – our individual choices in how we act and care for ourselves, each other, and our planet. It's that simple. The self-awareness we give to our personal character habits and overall life performance holds the power to advance the times.

We are all very connected in ways that we can't even see or fathom. Once we recognize that correlation and learn to use ourselves in artfelt ways, we can make the kinds of changes we all long for.

With that in mind, if we each make a dedicated effort to perform at our best in this life we have now, we can be sure that as the stage of life revolves through space – someone, somewhere, at some time will have evolved.

EPILOGUE

To show our simple skill, that is the true beginning of our end.
~ A Midsummer Night's Dream

I created Life Performance Practices because I needed a way to clarify my confusions and improve my own life. I wanted a practical daily process with a spiritual framework that helped me successfully interact in ways that were useful and gratifying. I'm still learning. In teaching this process through the years, many people asked me to put it into a book. I resisted, claiming that LPP is a changing, experiential process that can't be nailed down in words.

However, now approaching the end of my life, I decided to give it a go. My new reasoning was that we all needed a cohesive overview of LPPractices to inspire us to complete the process. I felt a book could help us see where we can go as individuals if we understood our human instrument and had a daily performance practice that could provide us with a sense of wholeness.

Even though I had taught this process for years, putting it on paper was a new challenge for me. Now, after four years of writing in pretty much retreat mode and enduring much impatient teasing from friends and colleagues, I have finally completed the book. In doing so, I managed to organize my thoughts about the process and further appreciate why I developed The Practices in the first place.

As I wrote, I learned so much more than I could ever have imagined. Truthfully, most of the time, I felt I was spontaneously downloading information from the vast array of unidentified scholars, artists, technicians, teachers and people in every walk of life who had gone before me. And most gratefully, I received my inspiration from the ancient, universal wisdom of my enlightened teachers.

In spite of this help, it took a lot of time to organize these downloaded insights and put them into a new theatrical language and creative context that anybody could comprehend. It was brain wracking. Because of that, I developed the practice of taking short ESA Brain Breaks. I also worked the many practices with willing participants and on myself, eliminating my chronic back pain with the *Allowing* process.

There were times, when sinking deeply into presence, I observed the elimination of all dis-ease. Those moments made me realize that our worries, anxieties, fixed fears, and repressed hurts instigate most of our chronic ills. I learned that a steady mind gives you infinite patience with others because you understand their challenges. We can then develop deep compassion for our troubled, fragmented self and gain wholeness.

With all that, please know I do not claim to be "a completed whole" in these practices. I am, like all of us, only a student of life, working with my own comic and tragic character traits. Happily, now with the help of my patient, generous and ingenious editor and publisher, Rick Benzel, the basic foundation of LPP is documented in this book and we can all practice it.

I leave you with my favorite wake-up cue for whenever I feel myself slipping into my habitual *Olivia Oblivia* character, I say…**Don't let your mindstage go dark. Keep a spotlight on your Awareness.**

Continuing Your LPP Education

If you're thinking, *"This is a bit much – too much self-awareness for me, thank you very much."* Well, you're not alone. I get it. We aren't accustomed to constantly observing our self and see it as hard work. It's much easier to space out, go numb, have an awareness blackout and indulge our unhappiness. Because of this, we can't possibly know the benefits of Living on the Empty Stage until we try it. Though I along with everyone else haven't accomplished it, I've had a few tiny glimpses to know it's worth it.

Once read, the book can be used as a Lodestar, something to turn to whenever needed. However, as you have done with most things you've learned in life like math and language, etc., it is most useful when learned as a complete process to integrate into your daily life, making it so natural that you yourself become the lodestar for others.

The Practices are designed for both solo use and ensemble work. First learn the ESA, which you can do on your own along with its various derivative practices in this book. If further interested, you can sign up for a solo session with me, or a Life Performance Lab and learn the LPP basics taught by me or a qualified Life Performance Director.

For information:
www.LifePerformancePractices.com
info@LifePerformancePractices.com

APPENDICES

SUGGESTIONS FOR LOGGING YOUR PRACTICE

After you have done a particular LPPractice in the book, log your experience using the following categories to see when and what Performance Styles and Character Traits are actually changing. I recommend you start a notebook using these and other categories of your own. Regular logging helps you see and measure your progress. You may or may not use every logging category for every practice.

Ideas – Log any new thoughts and insights
Example: 1) I realize that I need to talk to my boss about that perk 2) I had this great idea for a new business

Feelings – Log any feelings and emotional reactions during interactions
Example: 1) I felt really stupid doing that exercise 2) Once I started talking, I loved standing in the spotlight

Body Sensations – Log body reactions
Example: 1) The palms of my hands got sweaty 2) I had this weird feeling in my stomach

Sensory Perceptions – Identify what you are sensing

Example: 1) I sensed something was off when I walked into the room. 2) I'm not sure about his story, smells a little fishy to me.

Where's the Power? – Who holds the power?

Example: 1) I felt really intimidated in his presence 2) I had a real power surge

Self-observations – Identify what you are noticing about yourself

Example: 1) After all these weeks, I realized I had stopped tapping my foot 2) Somehow, I'm not quite so critical of my coworkers. Do I like them better? Or do I like myself better?

Self-Correct Suggestions – Identify what you are changing

Example: 1) Rehearse and think of myself as happier – explore ways to get there. 2) Stop talking down to people

Observations & Suggestions from Others – Identify what others tell you

Example: 1) John said my silent strength in the class scenario was very supportive of his dialogue. 2) Mary suggested I put "a little more oomph" into our interactions. 3) I heard Jerry tell Daisy he thought I was not very spontaneous...how do I feel about that?

GLOSSARY OF LPP TERMS

A CHARACTER — A person, or a role in a play or film.

A CUE — A sign, an indication to take action, or not. A life actor gets cues from the situation at hand.

A PART — Can refer to a particular Performance Style, or role and character you are playing

A PART OF ME — *Refers to emotional characters: Example: One part of me wants to...and another part of me doesn't.*

A ROLE — A role is what we do in life; it is job, task-oriented. Ex: mother, doctor, artist, mechanic, teacher, etc.

ART — The production of something beautiful or thought-provoking.

ARTFELT — The personal expression of beautiful feelings.

AUDITIONING — Life is a constant audition. Interviewing, trying out new situations, new people & jobs without fear of rejection or the hope of acceptance. Just try-out and see what happens.

AWARENESS BLACKOUT — Lack of self-awareness, your mindstage has gone dark.

BLACK BOX THEATRE — A small theatre with black walls, ceiling, and floor. Analogous to being inside your head, pre-occupied with your own thoughts, your inner lighting (how you color things) and special effects (your elaborations) Being self-absorbed.

BRAIN BABBLE

Too many characters on your stage at once. It is total confusion – a clarity crisis. Multiplicity of mind.

BRAIN BREAK

Recognizing your busy brain babble and willfully relaxing it. Going to the ESA.

CHANGE-ABILITY

The ability to make quick changes in your emotional character and Performance Style when the situation requires it. Developed fluidity & versatility.

CHARACTER

An emotion, attitude or feeling that characterizes who you are – how you play to your role.

CHARACTER CHOICE

Instinctively evaluating a situation and making a conscious emotional choice as to what character gives life to a role and will get the best results.

CHARACTER CONFLICT

Comic and tragic character traits at odds within you. Opposing emotions and beliefs that cause hesitation or inactivity. (See *Performance Style Clash*)

CHARACTER REPERTOIRE

The full range of emotions you have developed and can access in any given situation. An expanded repertoire increases your ability to communicate.

CHARACTER RESIDUE

Carrying an emotion unconsciously, unnecessarily or inappropriately from one scene into the next.

CHARACTER SCLEROSIS

Hardening of character. Limiting yourself to set ideas and activities. Acting in fixed, predictable ways.

CHARACTER STUDY

The study and honest assessment of your comic and tragic performance and character traits in each Performance Style. Commitment to redesign what doesn't work.

CHARACTER TRAITS	An emotion that gives character to the roles you play in life. Ex: *He was a very kind father to me. My manager always seems angry.* In LPP, character is synonymous with emotion.
COMEDY (comic)	A joyful, positive way of seeing the world. A light-hearted tone that usually supports a peaceful, productive or favorable outcome.
COMIC CHARACTER TRAITS	Set emotions that you purposely rehearse to have a positive impact on your daily life. Enriched character.
COUNTER-ACTING	Recognizing that an emotion isn't playing well and counter-acting it with another more suitable character choice.
COVER CHARACTER	An insincere or pretentious emotional attitude contrived to cover fear, hurt, or any unwanted feeling.
CREATIVE BLOCK	Character traits that undermine and block your goals. Creative blocks arise when you are acting from the tragic side of your character.
CREATIVE CRITIQUE	Objectively studying your life performance with the help of others, or on your own. Exploring what works, needs work, or complete change.
CREATIVITY	Having the ability to generate something new. Using imagination to develop original ideas.
CREATIVE PRESENCE	Acting from Genuine Presence, yet resourceful and functional with your interactions.
CREATIVE PROCESS	The space between the unformed and the formed. A period of development.

CREATIVE SKILL   Character traits that display your resourcefulness and talents. Creative Skills arise when you are acting from the comic side of your character.

CREATIVE STREAMING   Receiving information and ideas from collaborators and/or the great unknown.

CUT!!!   Stop the brain babble. Go to the Empty Stage!

DEFAULT CHARACTER   The character emotion you automatically use because it is your habit. Your "go-to" character.

DOUBLE FEATURE   This happens when you are trying to focus on something, but another scenario starts running across your mindstage and your attention gets split.

EMOTIONAL OSMOSIS   A gradual, often unconscious process of absorbing another person's mood and taking it on as your own. An exchange of energy and feelings.

EMPTY STAGE AWARENESS (ESA)   A spacious internal environment. A clear state of awareness capable of *seeing what is actual* without bias. It's your personal identity, your change-ability, energy resource, and creative potential.

EMOTIONAL DISCIPLINE   Being aware of an inappropriate emotion and having the discipline to curtail or change it.

EMPATHY   To feel deeply or identify with another's situation. Learning to do this without getting attached.

EMOTIONAL BOOMERANG   The "You hurt me, so I'll hurt you" game. Throwing an emotional boomerang at someone.

EMOTIONAL RANGE   The complete choice of emotions available to us. Learning to recognize and express the complete range of feelings.

EMOTIONAL RESTRAINTS	A limited ability to express feelings.
GENUINE PRESENCE	Being present to what is actual in a given moment. Feeling grounded in your body and aware of your environment. Letting ESAwareness guide you.
INTENTION	Your plan of action – what you do to achieve your desire.
IN THE WINGS	Actors wait in the wings off-stage for their cue to make an entrance. We have inner characters who have been waiting in the wings of our mindstage all our life wanting to make an entrance.
INNER RESEARCH	The study of your own thoughts, emotions, actions and attitudes – sometimes exploring backstory.
I WENT UP	Commonly said when an actor forgets his lines. Losing it. You can't remember why you walked into a room or what you were going to say…your attention flew away.
JUNK THINKING	Mentally running storylines, thoughts and attitudes about nothing important. Brain fillers. Mind smog.
LIFE ACTOR	All who play out a given or chosen role in daily life & are held responsible for personal conduct.
LIVING THE PART	Being truly present to your thoughts, actions and feelings in and of the moment. No pretense.
MARKING IT	Not playing a scene full out. This is a type of rehearsal – not playing it for real. Just going through the motions.

MINDSTAGE	The conceptual platform of our mind from which all things are imagined and seen. All our thoughts, attitudes, and beliefs move on and off our mindstage.
MISCAST	Acting in an unsuitable life role or being cast in the wrong job.
MIS-TAKE	When your first try at something was amiss – Take 1 didn't go well.
MOTIVATION	Your emotional desire for doing something; a reason for acting a certain way.
OBSTACLE CHARACTER	An emotion that is acting out as an obstacle in your life. Stopping your progress, causing creative blocks.
OFF-NIGHT	When an actor doesn't perform at his best. When you're in a funky mood and can't get with it.
PERFORMANCE STYLE CLASH	Two or three PSs conflicting with one another. Can be an inner self-dispute or, with people whose PSs differ from your own.
PERFORMANCE ROUTINES	Specific actions & mannerisms we routinely perform and become identified with. Each Performance Style has both comic and tragic routines – i.e. *He always gets angry at the slightest thing*, or *He always has a smile for everyone*.

PERFORMANCE STYLE (PS)	The 5 PSs are the mental, physical, emotional, dynamic, and spiritual ways of acting in life. Everyone has all five PS to different degrees. Your primary, secondary, etc. displays your way of being in the world. The PSs are the five parts of the Human Instrument. Defines the personality.
PERSONALITY	The overview of your attitudes and disposition in life that form an identifiable way of being and acting.
PLAY IT DOWN	Subduing your performance, lessening animation and expression in order to minimize its importance.
PLAY IT UP	Maximizing your performance or emphasizing a particular action, phrase or word for greater effect.
POV	A point of view. EX: *That's your POV, not mine!*
PRACTICE	A daily, customary procedure. Also, an action or exercise. In LPP, to practice is to rehearse and study.
PROFESSIONAL ACTOR	One whose career is to take on fictitious roles and characters to entertain or educate people. Performing in theatre, film and television.
QUICK CHANGE ARTIST (QCA)	Skilled at changing performance styles, roles or character because you want to meet the needs and elevate the situation.
REHEARSAL	Trying out new ways of doing things. Testing what works and what doesn't work. Practicing what works until it becomes natural.
REPLAY	Replaying a scene in your mind either to review or remember an incident. *(See Scenario Rerun)*

REVOLVING STAGE   A theatrical device for scene changes by which sets change and revolve in front of the audience. We live on the revolving stage of life.

SCENARIO RERUNS   Mentally rerunning recent or past personal scenarios over and over with the desire to relive the pleasure, justify the wrong, or change the situation.

STAGE FRIGHT   Fear of being judged by others, distrust in your own ability to perform. Performance anxiety.

TAKE 2   If you perform a mis-take, without blame or guilt, try improving it a second time with new choices.

THE FIVE TALENTS   Each PS provides us with a specific talent. Mental – the intellect; Physical – the body; Dynamic – the voice; Spiritual – sense perception; Emotional – range of emotional expression. How well and how much you use each determines the degrees of your PS.

THE HUMAN INSTRUMENT   The whole person comprised of five human talents. Our thoughts, mind, body, voice, senses, and emotions are displayed through our 5 Performance Styles.

THE SCRIM   A gauze-like curtain that appears solid when a scene is front lit and is see-through when a scene is back lit. Our Hidden & Obstacle Characters hide behind the scrim of our mindstage.

THRU-LINE   A theme or driving force used from beginning to end in a story. The thru-line of a specific situation or life itself.

TYPECASTING	Getting stuck in a role by typecasting yourself. You play it so well that others can't see you in any other way. Acting from habit and unable to make a change. *(See Character Sclerosis)*
TRAGEDY (tragic)	An antagonistic, sardonic way of seeing the world. A heavy or dark tone that usually brings about suffering, insecurity or an unfavorable outcome.
TRAGIC CHARACTER TRAITS	Set emotions that you constantly rehearse and have a negative impact on your daily life. Sullied character.
UPSTAGING	Out and out Take-Over. Taking the spotlight away from another person/actor. Stealing the attention Also known as *scene stealing*.
WHO'S HERE?	Character check-in. When you are confused as to who in you is acting, ask, "Who's here?" What emotion(s) are you playing?

ACKNOWLEDGMENTS

Everyone in my life, whether an ongoing relation or a brief encounter, must be acknowledged here. Whether a positive or negative experience for either of us, all have been my teachers, and to them I am grateful.

To the two people who helped me with direct contributions in the editing, creative design and production of this book, I owe my deepest thanks. First, an eternal thanks to my longtime friend, editor, and publisher, Rick Benzel, for his expertise, editorial insights, generous hours of editing work, a very detailed eye, and for putting up with me during the years of this book's development and publishing. He deserves a purple heart for, in Shakespeare's words, suffering "*the slings and arrows*" of an outrageous author. Without Rick's help, this book would not be as well organized and clear as I think you have found it. And to Ciara Staggs for her generous friendship, and keen artistic and technical skills in manifesting my visions for the cover and copious marketing assistance, I bow in grateful acknowledgment.

In addition, I want to thank my sister and brother-in-law, Harriet and Stuart Meyer, who were so kind to me when I began writing this book at their house in Dallas, Texas. I also want to thank my dear friends who have always given me emotional, mental and physical support: Karen Arthur, Jorjana and Roger Kellaway, Natalie Gaynes, Ronnie Rubin and Marty Piter, Marilyn and Paul Mortensen, Ron Williams, Mindi Lindsey, Avis Ives, Tom Boldrey, Dorre Ray, Ani Rioh, Jane Villarreal, Susan Goldberg, and my many heart friends who lent an attentive ear during my creative process.

With artfelt thanks to all,
Sondra

ABOUT THE AUTHOR

As a young actor, Sondra saw a need for the life actor to receive the same kind of training for life performance as the professional actor receives for theatrical performance. Seeing similar dilemmas and rewards that occur for both the professional actor and all of us who perform in daily life, she created Life Performance Practices. She has taught LPP in corporations like Walt Disney Imagineering, Hughes Aircraft, as well as at UCLA Extension School, in hospitals and clinics, and many organizations in the private sector.

Sondra has studied several world religions, particularly Tibetan Buddhism. In her youth, she was a professional actor in New York City and Los Angeles, but in her early thirties, she found her real passion was in using the art of acting to help everyone better their life.

As the creator of Life Performance Practices, she has seen how her process helps people see how the way they act in life affects the outcome of situations. She has been called "uncanny" in her ability to see people's hidden and obstacle character traits and help them self-correct to achieve their goals. When you work with her, she directs you to discover the parts of yourself that can break through long-held resistances causing creative blocks and even illness. In the personal advancement you achieve working with LPP, you open to a clear and honest self-assessment to arrive at Genuine Presence and versatility in all you do.

To quicken and enhance your own Life Performance Practices, email Sondra at info@LifePerformancePractices.com, or visit her website at www.LifePerformancePractices.com for more information on classes or becoming a Director to teach the LPP process to others.

Made in the USA
San Bernardino, CA
02 February 2019